Prentice Hall

Biology

California Standards
Review Book

Upper Saddle River, New Jersey
Boston, Massachusetts

ISBN 0-13-203616-9

2 3 4 5 6 7 8 9 10   11 10 09 08 07

Contents

California Biology/Life Sciences
Content Standards

Cell Biology

Grade 7

1. **All living organisms are composed of cells, from just one to many trillions, whose details usually are visible only through a microscope. As a basis for understanding this concept:**

    7 1.c. *Students know* the nucleus is the repository for genetic information in plant and animal cells.

    7 1.d. *Students know* that mitochondria liberate energy for the work that cells do and that chloroplasts capture sunlight energy for photosynthesis.

    7 1.e. *Students know* cells divide to increase their numbers through a process of mitosis, which results in two daughter cells with identical sets of chromosomes.

Grade 8

6. **Principles of chemistry underlie the functioning of biological systems. As a basis for understanding this concept:**

    8 6.b. *Students know* that living organisms are made of molecules consisting largely of carbon, hydrogen, nitrogen, oxygen, phosphorus, and sulfur.

    8 6.c. *Students know* that living organisms have many different kinds of molecules, including small ones, such as water and salt, and very large ones, such as carbohydrates, fats, proteins, and DNA.

Biology/Life Sciences

1. **The fundamental life processes of plants and animals depend on a variety of chemical reactions that occur in specialized areas of the organism's cells. As a basis for understanding this concept:**

    BI 1.a. *Students know* cells are enclosed within semipermeable membranes that regulate their interaction with their surroundings.

    BI 1.b. *Students know* enzymes are proteins that catalyze biochemical reactions without altering the reaction equilibrium and the activities of enzymes depend on the temperature, ionic conditions, and the pH of the surroundings.

    BI 1.c. *Students know* how prokaryotic cells, eukaryotic cells (including those from plants and animals), and viruses differ in complexity and general structure.

    BI 1. d. *Students know* the central dogma of molecular biology outlines the flow of information from transcription of ribonucleic acid (RNA) in the nucleus to translation of proteins on ribosomes in the cytoplasm.

BI 1.e. *Students know* the role of the endoplasmic reticulum and Golgi apparatus in the secretion of proteins.

BI 1.f. *Students know* usable energy is captured from sunlight by chloroplasts and is stored through the synthesis of sugar from carbon dioxide.

BI 1.g. *Students know* the role of the mitochondria in making stored chemical-bond energy available to cells by completing the breakdown of glucose to carbon dioxide.

BI 1.h. *Students know* most macromolecules (polysaccharides, nucleic acids, proteins, lipids) in cells and organisms are synthesized from a small collection of simple precursors.

***BI 1.i.** *Students know* how chemiosmotic gradients in the mitochondria and chloroplast store energy for ATP production.

***BI 1.j.** *Students know* how eukaryotic cells are given shape and internal organization by a cytoskeleton or cell wall or both.

Genetics

Grade 7

2. **A typical cell of any organism contains genetic instructions that specify its traits. Those traits may be modified by environmental influences. As a basis for understanding this concept:**

    7 2.a. *Students know* the differences between the life cycles and reproduction methods of sexual and asexual organisms.

    7 2.c. *Students know* an inherited trait can be determined by one or more genes.

    7 2.d. *Students know* plant and animal cells contain many thousands of different genes and typically have two copies of every gene. The two copies (or alleles) of the gene may or may not be identical, and one may be dominant in determining the phenotype while the other is recessive.

    7 2.e. *Students know* DNA (deoxyribonucleic acid) is the genetic material of living organisms and is located in the chromosomes of each cell.

Biology/Life Sciences

2. **Mutation and sexual reproduction lead to genetic variation in a population. As a basis for understanding this concept:**

    BI 2.a. *Students know* meiosis is an early step in sexual reproduction in which the pairs of chromosomes separate and segregate randomly during cell division to produce gametes containing one chromosome of each type.

    BI 2.b. *Students know* only certain cells in a multicellular organism undergo meiosis.

    BI 2.c. *Students know* how random chromosome segregation explains the probability that a particular allele will be in a gamete.

BI 2.d. *Students know* new combinations of alleles may be generated in a zygote through the fusion of male and female gametes (fertilization).

BI 2.e. *Students know* why approximately half of an individual's DNA sequence comes from each parent.

BI 2.f. *Students know* the role of chromosomes in determining an individual's sex.

BI 2.g. *Students know* how to predict possible combinations of alleles in a zygote from the genetic makeup of the parents.

3. **A multicellular organism develops from a single zygote, and its phenotype depends on its genotype, which is established at fertilization. As a basis for understanding this concept:**

   BI 3.a. *Students know* how to predict the probable outcome of phenotypes in a genetic cross from the genotypes of the parents and mode of inheritance (autosomal or X-linked, dominant or recessive).

   BI 3.b. *Students know* the genetic basis for Mendel's laws of segregation and independent assortment.

   ***BI 3.c.** *Students know* how to predict the probable mode of inheritance from a pedigree diagram showing phenotypes.

   ***BI 3.d.** *Students know* how to use data on frequency of recombination at meiosis to estimate genetic distances between loci and to interpret genetic maps of chromosomes.

4. **Genes are a set of instructions encoded in the DNA sequence of each organism that specify the sequence of amino acids in proteins characteristic of that organism. As a basis for understanding this concept:**

   BI 4.a. *Students know* the general pathway by which ribosomes synthesize proteins, using tRNA to translate genetic information in mRNA.

   BI 4.b. *Students know* how to apply the genetic coding rules to predict the sequence of amino acids from a sequence of codons in RNA

   BI 4.c. *Students know* how mutations in the DNA sequence of a gene may or may not affect the expression of the gene or the sequence of amino acids in the encoded protein.

   BI 4.d. *Students know* specialization of cells in multicellular organisms is usually due to different patterns of gene expression rather than to differences of the genes themselves.

   BI 4.e. *Students know* proteins can differ from one another in the number and sequence of amino acids.

   ***BI 4.f.** *Students know* why proteins having different amino acid sequences typically have different shapes and chemical properties.

5. **The genetic composition of cells can be altered by incorporation of exogenous DNA into the cells. As a basis for understanding this concept:**

BI 5.a. *Students know* the general structures and functions of DNA, RNA, and protein.

BI 5.b. *Students know* how to apply base-pairing rules to explain precise copying of DNA during semiconservative replication and transcription of information from DNA into mRNA.

BI 5.c. *Students know* how genetic engineering (biotechnology) is used to produce novel biomedical and agricultural products.

***BI 5.d.** *Students know* how basic DNA technology (restriction digestion by endonucleases, gel electrophoresis, ligation, and transformation) is used to construct recombinant DNA molecules.

***BI 5.e.** *Students know* how exogenous DNA can be inserted into bacterial cells to alter their genetic makeup and support expression of new protein products.

Ecology

Grade 6

5. **Organisms in ecosystems exchange energy and nutrients among themselves and with the environment. As a basis for understanding this concept:**

6 5.b. *Students know* matter is transferred over time from one organism to others in the food web and between organisms and the physical environment.

6 5.c. *Students know* populations of organisms can be categorized by the functions they serve in an ecosystem.

6 5.e. *Students know* the number and types of organisms and ecosystem can support depends on the resources available and on abiotic factors, such as quantities of light and water, a range of temperatures, and soil composition.

Biology/Life Sciences

6. **Stability in an ecosystem is a balance between competing effects. As a basis for understanding this concept:**

BI 6.a. *Students know* biodiversity is the sum total of different kinds of organisms and is affected by alterations of habitats.

BI 6.b. *Students know* how to analyze changes in an ecosystem resulting from changes in climate, human activity, introduction of nonnative species, or changes in population size.

BI 6.c. *Students know* how fluctuations in population size in an ecosystem are determined by the relative rates of birth, immigration, emigration, and death.

BI 6.d. *Students know* how water, carbon, and nitrogen cycle between abiotic resources and organic matter in the ecosystem and how oxygen cycles through photosynthesis and respiration.

BI 6.e. *Students know* a vital part of an ecosystem is the stability of its producers and decomposers.

BI 6.f. *Students know* at each link in a food web some energy is stored in newly made structures but much energy is dissipated into the environment as heat. This dissipation may be represented in an energy pyramid.

***BI 6.g.** *Students know* how to distinguish between the accommodation of an individual organism to its environment and the gradual adaptation of a lineage of organisms through genetic change.

Evolution

Grade 7

3. **Biological evolution accounts for the diversity of species developed through gradual processes over many generations. As a basis for understanding this concept:**

   7 3.a. *Students know* both genetic variation and environmental factors are causes of evolution and diversity of organisms.

   7 3.b. *Students know* the reasoning used by Charles Darwin in reaching his conclusion that natural selection is the mechanisms of evolution.

   7 3.c. *Students know* how independent lines of evidence from geology, fossils, and comparative anatomy provide the bases for the theory of evolution.

Biology/Life Sciences

7. **The frequency of an allele in a gene pool of a population depends on many factors and may be stable or unstable over time. As a basis for understanding this concept:**

   BI 7.a. *Students know* why natural selection acts on the phenotype rather than the genotype of an organism.

   BI 7.b. *Students know* why alleles that are lethal in a homozygous individual may be carried in a heterozygote and thus maintained in a gene pool.

   BI 7.c. *Students know* new mutations are constantly being generated in a gene pool.

   BI 7.d. *Students know* variation within a species increases the likelihood that at least some members of a species will survive under changed environmental conditions.

   ***BI 7.e.** *Students know* the conditions for Hardy-Weinberg equilibrium in a population and why these conditions are not likely to appear in nature.

   ***BI 7.f.** *Students know* how to solve the Hardy-Weinberg equation to predict the frequency of genotypes in a population, given the frequency of phenotypes.

8. **Evolution is the result of genetic changes that occur in constantly changing environments. As a basis for understanding this concept:**

BI 8.a. *Students know* how natural selection determines the differential survival of groups of organisms.

BI 8.b. *Students know* a great diversity of species increases the chance that at least some organisms survive major changes in the environment.

BI 8.c. *Students know* the effects of genetic drift on the diversity of organisms in a population.

BI 8.d. *Students know* reproductive or geographic isolation affects speciation.

BI 8.e. *Students know* how to analyze fossil evidence with regard to biological diversity, episodic speciation, and mass extinction.

*BI 8.f. *Students know* how to use comparative embryology, DNA or protein sequence comparisons, and other independent sources of data to create a branching diagram (cladogram) that shows probable evolutionary relationships.

*BI 8.g. *Students know* how several independent molecular clocks, calibrated against each other and combined with evidence from the fossil record, can help to estimate how long ago various groups or organisms diverged evolutionarily from one other.

Physiology

Grade 7

5. **The anatomy and physiology of plants and animals illustrate the complementary nature of structure and function. As a basis for understanding this concept:**

7 5.a. *Students know* plants and animals have levels of organization for structure and function, including cells, tissues, organs, organ systems, and the whole organism.

7 5.c. *Students know* how bones and muscles work together to provide a structural framework for movement.

6. **Physical principles underlie biological structures and functions. As a basis for understanding this concept:**

7 6.j. *Students know* that contractions of the heart generate blood pressure and that heart valves prevent backflow of blood in the circulatory system.

Biology/Life Sciences

9. As a result of the coordinated structures and functions of organ systems, the internal environment of the human body remains relatively stable (homeostatic) despite changes in the outside environment. As a basis for understanding this concept:

BI 9.a. *Students know* how the complementary activity of major body systems provides cells with oxygen and nutrients and removes toxic waste products such as carbon dioxide.

BI 9.b. *Students know* how the nervous system mediates communication between different parts of the body and the body's interactions with the environment.

BI 9.c. *Students know* how feedback loops in the nervous and endocrine systems regulate conditions in the body.

BI 9.d. *Students know* the functions of the nervous system and the role of neurons in transmitting electrochemical impulses.

BI 9.e. *Students know* the roles of sensory neurons, interneurons, and motor neurons in sensation, thought, and response.

***BI 9.f.** *Students know* the individual functions and sites of secretion of digestive enzymes (amylases, proteases, nucleases, lipases), stomach acid, and bile salts.

***BI 9.g.** *Students know* the homeostatic role of the kidneys in the removal of nitrogenous wastes and the role of the liver in blood detoxification and glucose balance.

***BI 9.h.** *Students know* the cellular and molecular basis of muscle contraction, including the roles of actin, myosin, Ca^{+2}, and ATP.

***BI 9.i.** *Students know* how hormones (including digestive, reproductive, osmoregulatory) provide internal feedback mechanisms for homeostasis at the cellular level and in whole organisms.

10. Organisms have a variety of mechanisms to combat disease. As a basis for understanding the human immune response:

BI 10.a. *Students know* the role of the skin in providing nonspecific defenses against infection.

BI 10.b. *Students know* the role of antibodies in the body's response to infection.

BI 10.c. *Students know* how vaccination protects an individual from infectious diseases.

BI 10.d. *Students know* there are important differences between bacteria and viruses with respect to their requirements for growth and replication, the body's primary defenses against bacterial and viral infections, and effective treatments of these infections.

BI 10.e. *Students know* why an individual with a compromised immune system (for example, a person with AIDS) may be unable to fight off and survive infections by microorganisms that are usually benign.

***BI 10.f.** *Students know* the roles of phagocytes, B-lymphocytes, and T-lymphocytes in the immune system.

Investigation and Experimentation

Scientific progress is made by asking meaningful questions and conducting careful investigations. As a basis for understanding this concept and addressing the content in the other strands, students should develop their own questions and perform investigations. Students will:

Grade 6

6 7.c. Construct appropriate graphs from data and develop qualitative statements about the relationships between variables.

6 7.e. Recognize whether evidence is consistent with a proposed explanation.

Grade 7

7 7.c. Communicate the logical connection among hypotheses, science concepts, tests conducted, data collected, and conclusions drawn from the scientific evidence.

Grade 8

8 9.b. Evaluate the accuracy and reproducibility of data.

8 9.c. Distinguish between variable and controlled parameters in a test.

Biology/Life Sciences

***BIIE 1.a.** Select and use appropriate technology (such as computer-linked probes, spreadsheets, and graphing calculators) to perform tests, collect data, analyze relationships, and display data.

***BIIE 1.b.** Identify and communicate sources of unavoidable experimental error.

BIIE 1.c. Identify possible reasons for inconsistent results, such as sources of error or uncontrolled conditions.

***BIIE 1.d.** Formulate explanations using logic and evidence.

***BIIE 1.e.** Solve scientific problems by using quadratic equations and simple trigonometric, exponential, and logarithmic functions.

BIIE 1.f. Distinguish between hypothesis and theory as scientific terms.

***BIIE 1.g.** Recognize the usefulness and limitations of models and theories as scientific representations of reality.

***BIIE 1.h.** Read and interpret topographic and geologic maps.

BIIE 1.i. Analyze the locations, sequences, or time intervals that are characteristic of natural phenomena (e.g., relative ages of rocks, locations of planets over time, and succession of species in an ecosystem).

BIIE 1.j. Recognize the issue of statistical variability and the need for controlled tests.

***BIIE 1.k.** Recognize the cumulative nature of scientific evidence.

***BIIE 1.l.** Analyze situations and solve problems that require combining and applying concepts from more than one area of science.

***BIIE 1.m.** Investigate a science-based societal issue by researching the literature, analyzing data, and communicating the findings. Examples of issues include irradiation of food, cloning of animals by somatic cell nuclear transfer, choice of energy sources, and land and water use decisions in California.

***BIIE 1.n.** Know that when an observation does not agree with an accepted scientific theory, the observation is sometimes mistaken or fraudulent (e.g., the Piltdown Man fossil or unidentified flying objects) and that the theory is sometimes wrong (e.g., the Ptolemaic model of the movement of the Sun, Moon, and planets).

Standards identified with an asterisk (*) are not tested on the California Standards Test. However, they are important to the comprehension of the strand and all students should have the opportunity to learn them.

Biology/Life Sciences Standards: Cell Biology

8 6.b. *Students know* that living organisms are made of molecules consisting largely of carbon, hydrogen, nitrogen, oxygen, phosphorus, and sulfur.

8 6.c. *Students know* that living organisms have many different kinds of molecules, including small ones, such as water and salt, and very large ones, such as carbohydrates, fats, proteins, and DNA.

BI 1.h. *Students know* most macromolecules (polysaccharides, nucleic acids, proteins, lipids) in cells and organisms are synthesized from a small collection of simple precursors.

Like other forms of matter, living organisms are made up of elements. Elements are substances that cannot be broken down into simpler substances. Each element consists entirely of one type of atom. Examples of elements are carbon (C), hydrogen (H), and oxygen (O). Compounds are combinations of particular elements in definite proportions. The smallest units of compounds are molecules.

Small Molecules in Living Organisms Water is one of the most common compounds found in living organisms. Individual water molecules are small. Each water molecule contains two atoms of hydrogen and one atom of oxygen. Another common compound in living things is the salt sodium chloride. Sodium chloride molecules are also small, containing just one atom of sodium and one atom of chlorine.

Organic Compounds Compounds that make up organisms are called organic compounds. There are four major types of organic compounds: nucleic acids (such as DNA), proteins, lipids (fats), and carbohydrates. Nucleic acids carry genetic information. Proteins are required for growth and repair. Lipids are needed for membranes. Along with carbohydrates, lipids also provide energy.

Organic compounds consist largely of six elements: carbon, hydrogen, nitrogen, oxygen, phosphorus, and sulfur. Lipids and carbohydrates contain carbon, hydrogen, and oxygen. In addition to these three elements, nucleic acids contain nitrogen and phosphorus, and proteins contain nitrogen and sulfur.

Macromolecules The molecules of organic compounds generally are so large that they are called macromolecules, or "giant molecules." Most macromolecules are made from thousands of smaller molecules, called monomers. The monomers are joined together, like links in a chain, to form much larger molecules. Chains of monomers are called polymers. The process in which monomers join together to form polymers is known as polymerization.

Biology/Life Sciences Standards: Cell Biology

Proteins are polymers consisting of monomers called amino acids. The monomers that make up nucleic acids are known as nucleotides. As shown in Figure 1–1, carbohydrates, such as starch, are polymers made up of monomers of glucose or other sugar molecules. Single sugar molecules are known as monosaccharides. Polymers of monosaccharides are called polysaccharides.

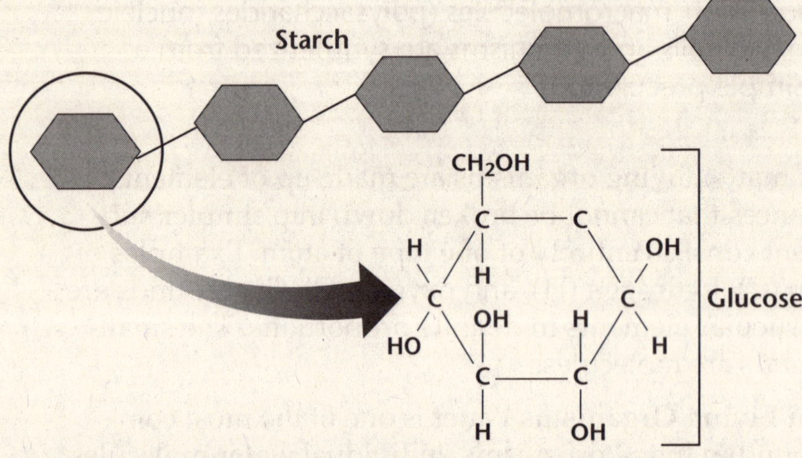

Figure 1–1 Starch molecule This starch molecule is a carbohydrate made up of many molecules of glucose, a simple sugar.

Review Questions

1 Which is a small molecule found in living organisms?

  A salt

  B protein

  C starch

  D DNA

2 Types of organic compounds include

  A lipids.

  B nucleic acids.

  C carbohydrates.

  D all of the above

3 Which six elements are found in organic compounds?

  A carbon, hydrogen, nitrogen, oxygen, phosphorus, sulfur

  B carbon, phosphorus, sodium, nitrogen, hydrogen, sulfur

  C nitrogen, carbon, sodium, hydrogen, oxygen, chlorine

  D sulfur, chlorine, carbon, hydrogen, oxygen, nitrogen

Biology/Life Sciences Standards: Cell Biology

4 Most macromolecules are made up of thousands of smaller molecules called

A proteins.

B polymers.

C monomers.

D polysaccharides.

5 An example of a monosaccharide is

A DNA.

B starch.

C lipid.

D glucose.

Biology/Life Sciences Standards: Cell Biology

BI 1.b. *Students know* enzymes are proteins that catalyze biochemical reactions without altering the reaction equilibrium and the activities of enzymes depend on the temperature, ionic conditions, and the pH of the surroundings.

Everything that happens in living organisms depends on chemical reactions. A chemical reaction is a process that changes certain chemicals, called reactants, into other chemicals, called products. All chemical reactions need energy to get started. This energy is called the activation energy. The lower the activation energy, the faster a reaction occurs. Some chemical reactions occur very slowly unless they get help from a catalyst. A catalyst is a substance that speeds up a chemical reaction by lowering the activation energy.

Enzymes Enzymes are proteins that act as biological catalysts. They speed up chemical reactions that take place in organisms. Like other catalysts, enzymes act by lowering the activation energy. This is illustrated in Figure 1–2.

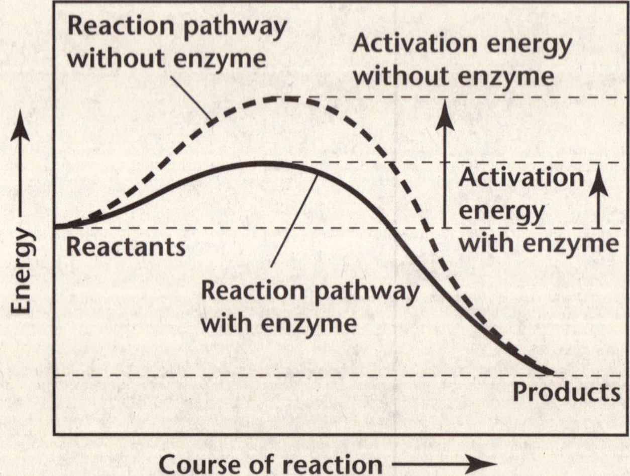

Figure 1–2 Effect of an enzyme In this reaction, only about half as much energy is needed to start the reaction when the enzyme is present.

Most enzymes are very specific. Each enzyme generally catalyzes just one type of chemical reaction. Enzymes typically work by providing a site where the necessary reactants can be brought together to react. This lowers the activation energy and speeds up the reaction. Enzyme molecules are not reactants in the reactions they catalyze, so they are not used up in the reactions. As a result, they can catalyze additional reactions.

Biology/Life Sciences Standards: Cell Biology

Reaction Equilibrium and Enzymes Many chemical reactions can proceed both forward and backward. As products form in the forward direction, some of the products are broken down again in the backward direction. A stable condition eventually occurs in which the forward and backward reactions have the same rate and cancel each other out. This stable condition is called the reaction equilibrium. For a given reaction, the reaction equilibrium occurs when reactants and products reach a certain concentration.

Enzymes speed up reactions, but they do not change the reaction equilibrium. An enzyme increases the rate of both the forward and backward reactions, so the reaction equilibrium is reached faster. However, the concentration of reactants and products at which equilibrium occurs is the same whether or not an enzyme is present.

Enzyme Activity The activity of enzymes can be affected by any variables that influence chemical reactions. These variables include temperature, ionic conditions, and pH.

- Many enzymes work well only within a certain temperature range. For example, enzymes produced by human cells generally work best at temperatures close to normal human body temperature (37°C).
- Most enzymes are affected by ionic conditions. Ions are atoms that have lost or gained electrons so they have a positive or negative electric charge. The concentration of certain ions may speed up or slow down the activity of an enzyme.
- Most enzymes work best when their surroundings have a certain pH, or concentration of hydrogen ions. For example, the enzymes that help digest food in the human stomach work best at low pH values. Substances with low pH values are called acids. The stomach secretes strong acids that allow digestive enzymes to work.

Review Questions

6 Proteins that speed up chemical reactions in organisms are called

  A reactants.

  B products.

  C enzymes.

  D ions.

7 How do enzymes increase the rate of chemical reactions?

  A by secreting strong acids

  B by lowering the activation energy

  C by changing the reaction equilibrium

  D by increasing the concentration of ions

Biology/Life Sciences Standards: Cell Biology

8   **Enzymes typically work by**

A   providing reaction sites.

B   increasing temperature.

C   becoming reactants.

D   lowering pH.

9   **Variables that can affect the activity of enzymes include**

A   temperature.

B   ionic conditions.

C   pH of surroundings.

D   all of the above

10

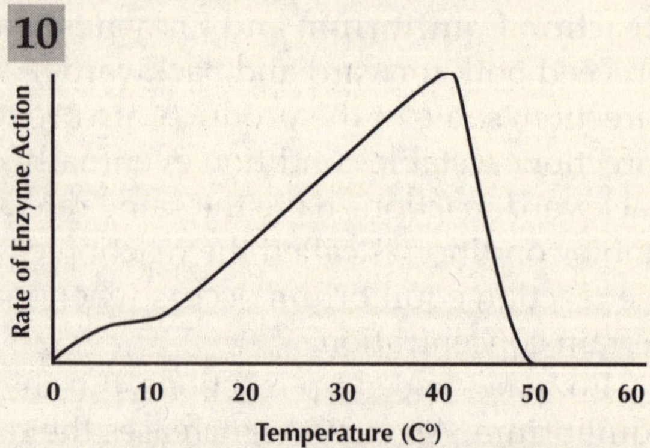

The graph shows the rate of an enzyme's action at different temperatures. From the graph, you can conclude that

A   the rate of enzyme action increases as temperature decreases.

B   the rate of enzyme action decreases as temperature increases.

C   the highest rate of enzyme action occurs at a temperature of about 40°C.

D   the highest rate of enzyme activity occurs at a temperature of about 50°C.

Biology/Life Sciences Standards: Cell Biology

BI 1.c *Students know* how prokaryotic cells, eukaryotic cells (including those from plants and animals), and viruses differ in complexity and general structure.

All living organisms are made of cells that are surrounded by a membrane and contain genetic material. Cells fall into two broad categories, depending on whether their genetic material is contained within a nucleus: prokaryotic cells, which do not have a nucleus, and eukaryotic cells, which do have a nucleus. Viruses are tiny particles containing genetic material and proteins. They are not made up of cells, so they are not considered living things.

Prokaryotic Cells Prokaryotic cells, or cells without a nucleus, are generally very small and simple. They typically have few internal structures. Despite their simplicity, prokaryotic cells carry out all the activities of living things. They grow, reproduce, and respond to the environment. Bacteria are examples of prokaryotic cells.

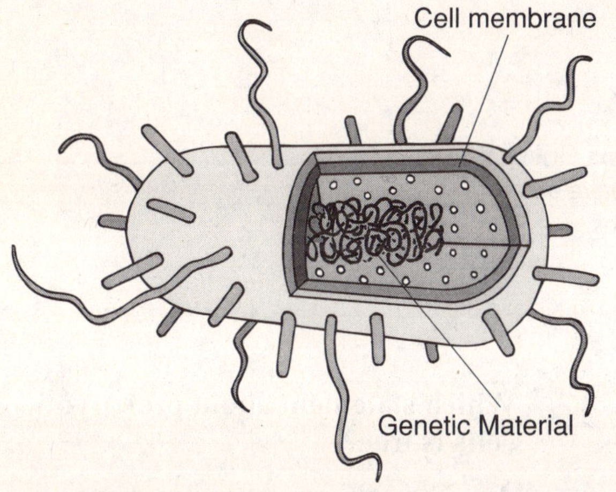

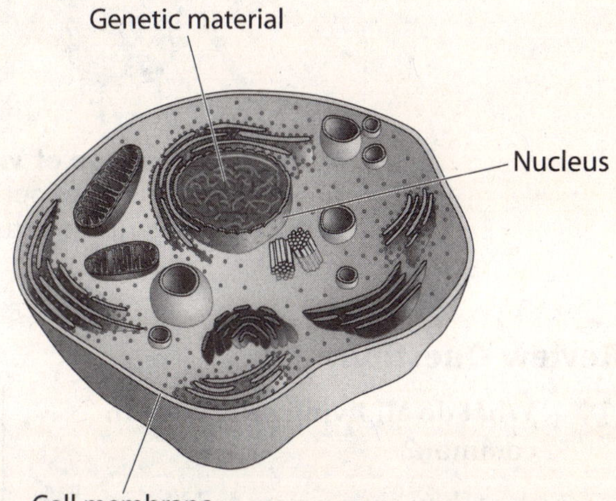

Figure 1–3 Prokaryotic cell Genetic material in this typical prokaryotic cell is not contained within a nucleus. The cell also has few other structures.

Figure 1–4 Eukaryotic cell (animal cell) Eukaryotic cells, such as this animal cell, have genetic material contained within a nucleus. The cell also has many other structures.

Eukaryotic Cells Eukaryotic cells, or cells with a nucleus, are usually larger and more complex than prokaryotic cells. Eukaryotic cells may contain dozens of structures, and many are specialized to perform certain functions. Some eukaryotic cells are single-celled organisms. Other eukaryotic cells are found in large organisms that have many cells. Plants and animals have eukaryotic cells.

Biology/Life Sciences Standards: Cell Biology

Viruses Viruses typically consist of a core of genetic material surrounded by a protein coat. There are many different types of viruses, and they come in a wide variety of sizes and shapes. However, all viruses have one thing in common: they enter living cells and use structures inside the cells to reproduce. Viruses are classified as parasites. They depend entirely upon living cells for their existence and harm the cells in the process.

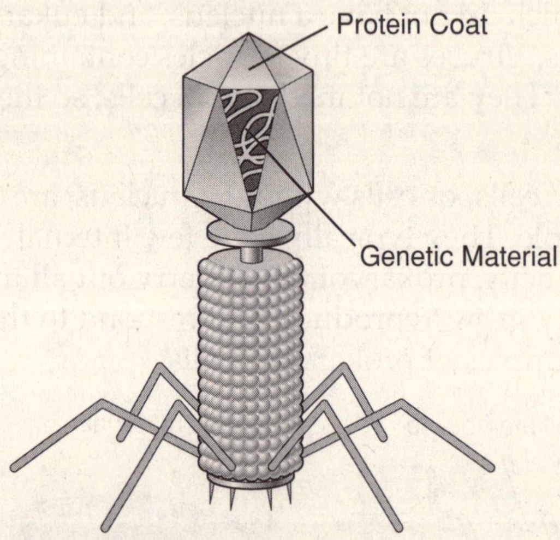

Figure 1–5 One type of virus Unlike a living cell, this virus does not have a cell membrane or internal structures.

Review Questions

11 What do all living cells have in common?

   A They are surrounded by a membrane.

   B They contain a nucleus.

   C They have a protein coat.

   D They contain dozens of structures.

12 Which statement about prokaryotic cells is true?

   A They always have a nucleus.

   B They contain few internal structures.

   C They do not have a cell membrane.

   D They are not considered living things.

Biology/Life Sciences Standards: Cell Biology

13 **Eukaryotic cells are found in**

A   viruses.

B   bacteria.

C   plants and animals.

D   all living organisms.

14 **What is true of all viruses?**

A   They have a nucleus.

B   They have prokaryotic cells.

C   They are living things.

D   They reproduce inside living cells.

15 **Which structure is typically largest and most complex?**

A   prokaryotic cell

B   eukaryotic cell

C   nucleus

D   virus

Biology/Life Sciences Standards: Cell Biology

7 1.c *Students know* the nucleus is the repository for genetic information in plant and animal cells.

Plants and animals, like all living things, are made up of cells. The cells of plants and animals are eukaryotic cells. These are cells that contain a nucleus (plural: nuclei).

Structure of the Nucleus The nucleus of a eukaryotic cell is a relatively large structure. As shown in Figure 1–6, the nucleus is surrounded by membranes referred to as the nuclear envelope. Tiny holes in the nuclear envelope, called nuclear pores, let materials move into and out of the nucleus.

Within the nucleus are molecules of the nucleic acid DNA. Most of the time, DNA molecules are scattered throughout the nucleus in tiny particles called chromatin. When a cell divides, the DNA forms thread-like structures known as chromosomes. Most nuclei also contain a small, dense region called the nucleolus.

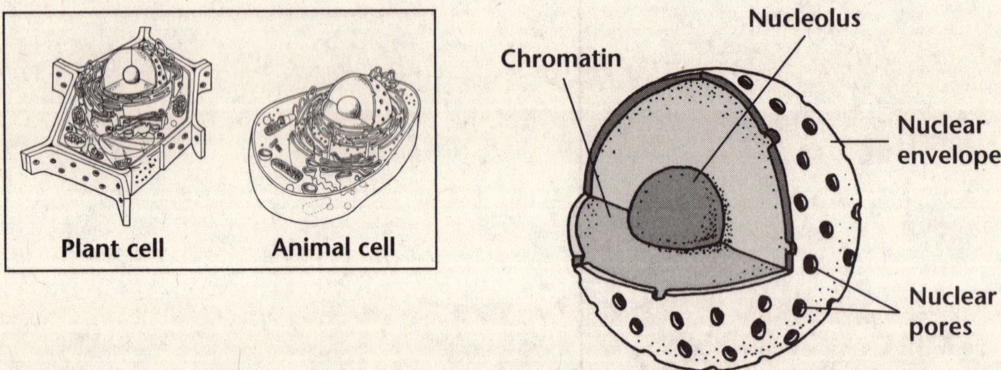

Figure 1–6 Nucleus of a eukaryotic cell Only eukaryotic cells have a nucleus.

Function of the Nucleus The nucleus is the "control center" of the cell. It controls most of the cell's activities and stores genetic information. The genetic information is encoded in the DNA. The DNA instructs the cell how to make proteins and other molecules. Although proteins are made outside the nucleus on structures called ribosomes, the assembly of ribosomes begins in the nucleolus. When cells divide, the genetic information in the DNA is copied and passed on to the new daughter cells that form.

Biology/Life Sciences Standards: Cell Biology

Review Questions

16 The nucleus of a cell is enclosed by the

A nucleolus.

B chromatin.

C ribosomes.

D nuclear envelope.

17

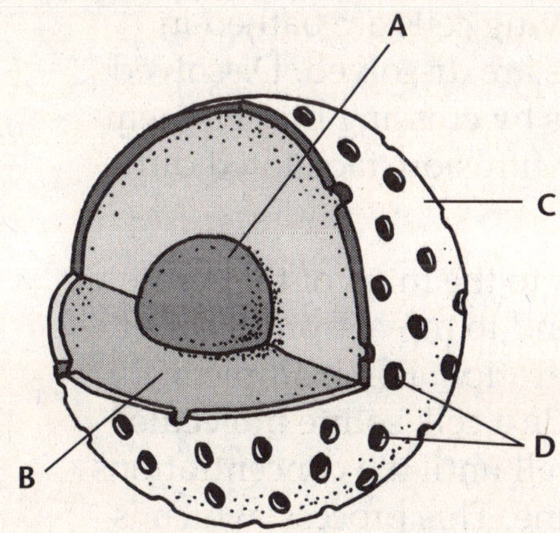

In the drawing of a nucleus, where does the assembly of ribosomes begin?

A A

B B

C C

D D

18 Chromatin consists of

A chromosomes.

B particles of DNA.

C nuclear pores.

D membranes.

19 One function of the nucleus is to

A store genetic information.

B produce energy.

C enclose the cell.

D make proteins.

Biology/Life Sciences Standards: Cell Biology

BI 1.a *Students know* cells are enclosed within semipermeable membranes that regulate their interaction with their surroundings.

Cells are the basic units of structure and function of living things. All living cells are surrounded by a thin, flexible barrier known as the cell membrane. The cell membrane consists of two layers of lipid (fat) molecules and also contains protein molecules.

Functions of the Cell Membrane One function of the cell membrane is to protect and support the cell. Another function is to control the movement of substances into and out of the cell. Living cells are bathed in and contain liquids in which many substances are dissolved. Dissolved substances, or solutes, may enter or leave cells by crossing the cell membrane. This can occur in three different ways: diffusion, facilitated diffusion, or active transport.

Diffusion The concentration of a solute refers to the mass of the solute in a given volume of liquid. Solutes always tend to move from areas of higher concentration to areas of lower concentration. For example, if there is a higher concentration of solute outside a cell, solute molecules will move across the cell membrane into the cell until the concentrations are the same on both sides of the cell membrane. This process, which is shown in Figure 1–7, is called diffusion. It requires no energy.

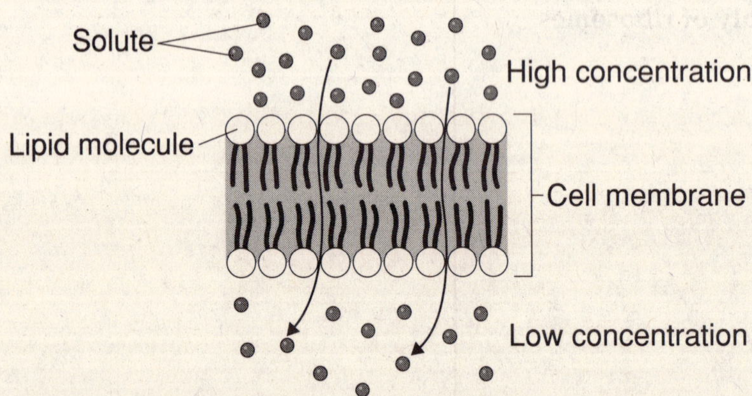

Figure 1–7 Diffusion Solute molecules move through this cell membrane to an area of lower concentration.

Facilitated Diffusion Cell membranes are semipermeable. This means that only certain substances can diffuse across them. Water can easily diffuse across cell membranes, but many substances dissolved in water cannot. Proteins in cell membranes, called carrier proteins, help these substances cross the membranes as needed. This process is called facilitated diffusion. It also requires no energy.

Biology/Life Sciences Standards: Cell Biology

Active Transport Sometimes cells must move solutes from a less concentrated area to a more concentrated area. This is accomplished by active transport, which requires energy. Active transport can occur in different ways. Figure 1–8 shows how small particles may be actively transported across cell membranes by proteins in the membranes that act like pumps. For example, sodium crosses cell membranes in this way. Large particles may be transported across cell membranes by movements of the membranes themselves. For example, a cell membrane may surround a large particle and pull it inside the cell.

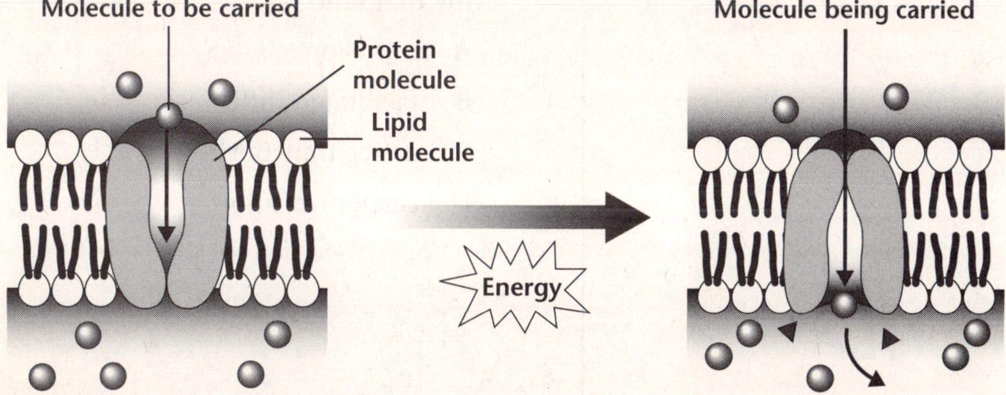

Figure 1–8 Active transport The protein molecule in this cell membrane "pumps" a solute molecule across the membrane to an area of higher concentration.

Review Questions

20 Functions of the cell membrane include

    A protecting cells.

    B supporting cells.

    C controlling what enters and leaves cells.

    D all of the above

21 Diffusion of a solute into a cell occurs when the solute is

    A more concentrated inside the cell.

    B more concentrated outside the cell.

    C semipermeable.

    D pumped across the cell membrane.

Biology/Life Sciences Standards: Cell Biology

22 Which process requires energy?

   A diffusion

   B facilitated diffusion

   C active transport

   D all of the above

23

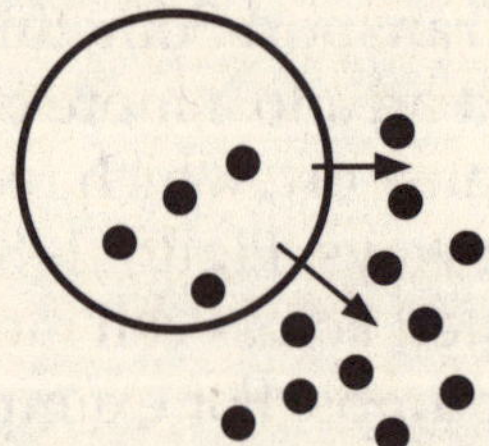

The diagram shows solute particles crossing a cell membrane. What is the name of the process shown in the diagram?

   A diffusion

   B facilitated diffusion

   C active transport

   D carrier transport

Biology/Life Sciences Standards: Cell Biology

***BI 1.j.** *Students know* how eukaryotic cells are given shape and internal organization by a cytoskeleton or cell wall or both.

Eukaryotic cells are cells that contain a nucleus. Like all living cells, eukaryotic cells are surrounded by a cell membrane that protects the cell. Some eukaryotic cells also have a cytoskeleton, cell wall, or both. The cytoskeleton and cell wall give cells support and help them keep their shape. The cytoskeleton also allows the cells to move.

Cytoskeleton The cytoskeleton is a network of threads, or filaments, inside cells. The filaments are made of protein. There are two main types of filaments: microfilaments and microtubules. Both types are shown in Figure 1–9.

- Microfilaments are tiny filaments that spread throughout some eukaryotic cells. They create a tough, flexible framework that supports cells, similar to the way beams support a house. Microfilaments also help cells crawl along surfaces. The position of a cell gradually changes as new microfilaments build up and old microfilaments break down.

- Microtubules are hollow filaments found in many eukaryotic cells. They help cells keep their shape. They also play a role in cell division. Microtubules may project from the cell's surface. The projections can move and can help the cell "swim" through liquids.

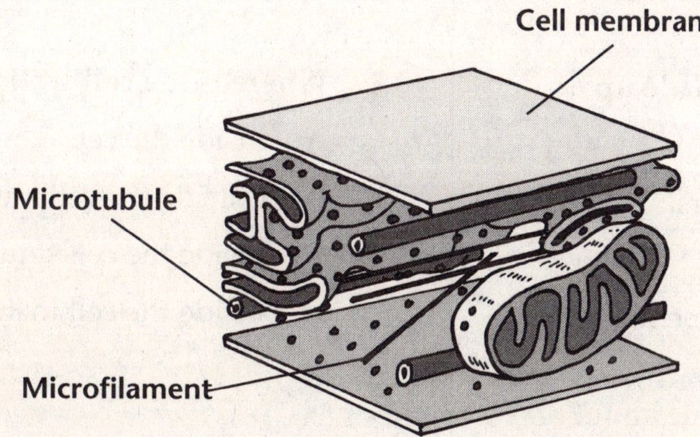

Figure 1–9 Cytoskeleton The cytoskeleton supports the cell and helps it move.

Cell Wall A cell wall surrounds the cells of many organisms, including plants, algae, and fungi. As shown in Figure 1–10, the cell wall lies outside the cell membrane. The main job of the cell wall is to support and protect cells. Most cell walls contain tiny holes that let water, oxygen, carbon dioxide, and certain other substances pass through them.

Biology/Life Sciences Standards: Cell Biology

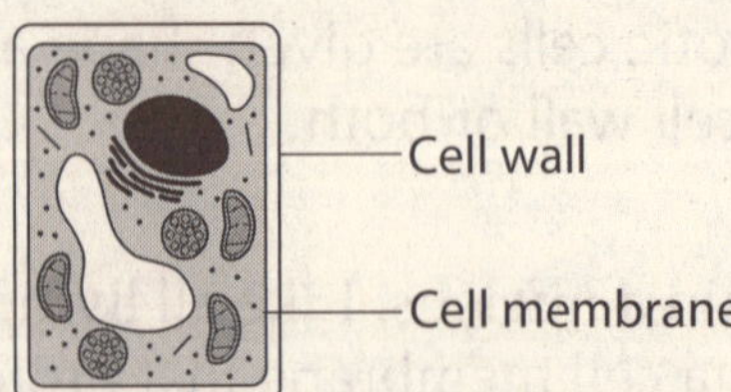

Figure 1–10 Typical plant cell The cell wall of a plant cell encloses the cell membrane and helps the cell keep its shape.

Cell walls are made of fibers of carbohydrate and protein. These substances are produced within the cell and then released at the cell's surface, where they are put together to form the cell wall. Plant cell walls are composed mostly of tough carbohydrate fibers called cellulose.

Review Questions

24 A function of both the cytoskeleton and cell wall is

   A allowing the cell to move.

   B helping the cell keep its shape.

   C controlling what enters the cell.

   D producing microtubules.

25 The cytoskeleton is made up of

   A protein filaments.

   B carbohydrate fibers.

   C cellulose fibers.

   D carbohydrate filaments.

26 Which statement is true about microfilaments?

   A They help cells swim through liquids.

   B They are made of cellulose.

   C They help cells crawl along surfaces.

   D They project from the surface of the cell.

27 Which organisms have cells with cell walls?

   A animals

   B plants

   C all eukaryotes

   D all of the above

28 Where is the cell wall located?

   A inside the cell

   B outside the cell membrane

   C inside the cell's nucleus

   D inside the cell membrane

Biology/Life Sciences Standards: Cell Biology

BI 1.d. *Students know* the central dogma of molecular biology outlines the flow of information from transcription of ribonucleic acid (RNA) in the nucleus to translation of proteins on ribosomes in the cytoplasm.

Nucleic acids are a type of compound found in organisms. They contain genetic information controlling the production of proteins within cells. Types of nucleic acids include DNA (deoxyribonucleic acid) and RNA (ribonucleic acid).

DNA and RNA DNA makes up chromosomes and stores genetic information. In eukaryotes such as plants and animals, DNA is found only in the nucleus of the cell. RNA helps the cell produce proteins. There are three main types of RNA: messenger RNA (mRNA), ribosomal RNA (rRNA), and transfer RNA (tRNA). Each type of RNA plays a different role in protein production.

Both DNA and RNA molecules contain smaller molecules called bases. There are four different bases in each type of molecule, represented by the letters A, C, G, and T (in DNA) or U (in RNA). Pairs of bases attract each other and hold double-stranded DNA and RNA molecules together. A always pairs with T (or U), and C always pairs with G.

Protein Synthesis The production of proteins is called protein synthesis. It is shown in Figure 1–11. In this process, proteins are formed from small molecules known as amino acids. There are 20 different amino acids. The type and order of amino acids in a protein determine its structure and function. Protein synthesis occurs in two steps: transcription and translation.

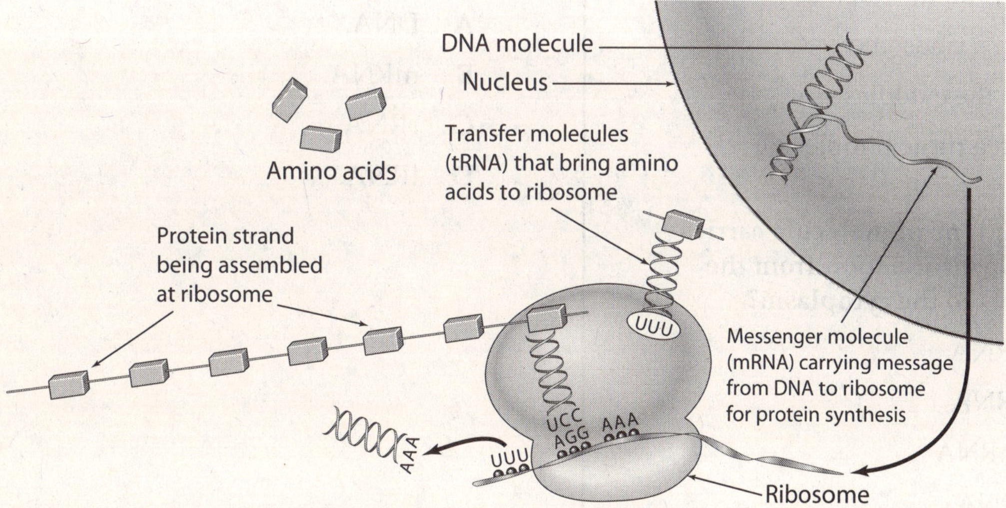

Figure 1–11 Protein synthesis The production of proteins is a two-step process. The first step, called transcription, takes place inside the nucleus. The second step, called translation, takes place outside the nucleus on a ribosome.

Biology/Life Sciences Standards: Cell Biology

Transcription In eukaryotes, transcription takes place inside the nucleus of the cell. During transcription, paired strands of DNA separate, and one strand is copied to form a strand of mRNA. The mRNA leaves the nucleus, carrying the genetic information from the DNA to the cytoplasm.

Translation Translation takes place on ribosomes in the cytoplasm. Ribosomes are small particles consisting mainly of rRNA. During translation, a ribosome uses information in mRNA to produce a protein.

Each group of three bases in mRNA specifies a particular amino acid. For example, UUC specifies the amino acid phenylalanine. As mRNA moves through the ribosome, the amino acids specified by its bases are brought into the ribosome by tRNA. The amino acids are then transferred from tRNA to the growing protein.

Review Questions

29 Genetic information is contained in

   A   DNA.

   B   proteins.

   C   amino acids.

   D   all of the above

30 Where does transcription take place in eukaryotic cells?

   A   within the nucleus

   B   on a ribosome

   C   in the cytoplasm

   D   on a protein molecule

31 Which type of molecule carries genetic information from the nucleus to the cytoplasm?

   A   rRNA

   B   tRNA

   C   mRNA

   D   DNA

32 Each group of three mRNA bases specifies a particular

   A   protein.

   B   amino acid.

   C   ribosome.

   D   gene.

33 Amino acids are brought into a ribosome by

   A   DNA.

   B   mRNA.

   C   rRNA.

   D   tRNA.

Biology/Life Sciences Standards: Cell Biology

BI 1.e. *Students know* the role of the endoplasmic reticulum and Golgi apparatus in the secretion of proteins.

Proteins are important compounds produced by the cells of living organisms. Proteins may be used by the cells in which they are produced or secreted by the cells for use elsewhere in the organism. The secretion of proteins by cells involves two structures: the endoplasmic reticulum and Golgi apparatus.

Endoplasmic Reticulum The endoplasmic reticulum is a cell structure with two parts: rough endoplasmic reticulum and smooth endoplasmic reticulum. The rough endoplasmic reticulum is where proteins for secretion are produced. It is called *rough* because its surface is covered with tiny particles known as ribosomes, as shown in Figure 1–12. Proteins for secretion are assembled on the ribosomes. After being assembled, the proteins are inserted into the rough endoplasmic reticulum.

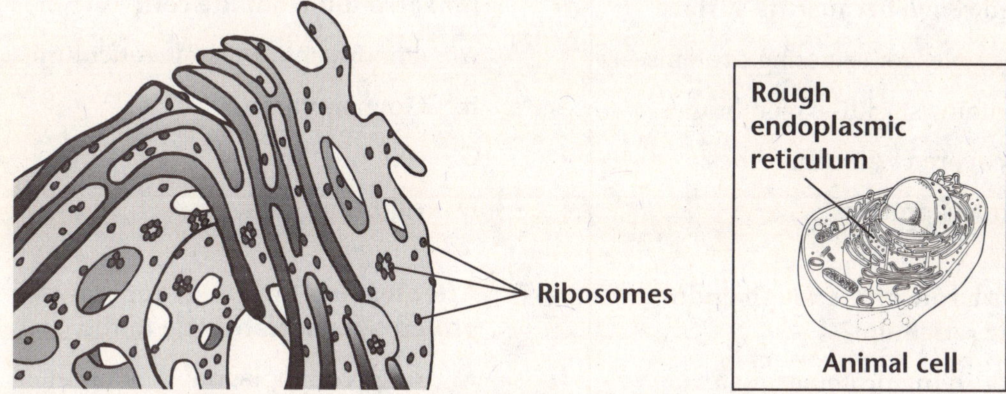

Figure 1–12 Rough endoplasmic reticulum The larger drawing shows the ribosomes that make this part of the endoplasmic reticulum rough. The smaller drawing shows where the endoplasmic reticulum is located in the cell.

Golgi Apparatus From the rough endoplasmic reticulum, proteins for secretion move to the Golgi apparatus. The Golgi apparatus is a cell structure made up of stacklike membranes. This is illustrated in Figure 1–13.

The function of the Golgi apparatus is to prepare proteins for secretion from the cell. It modifies, sorts, and packages the proteins. From the Golgi apparatus, the proteins are transported to the cell membrane and then secreted.

Biology/Life Sciences Standards: Cell Biology

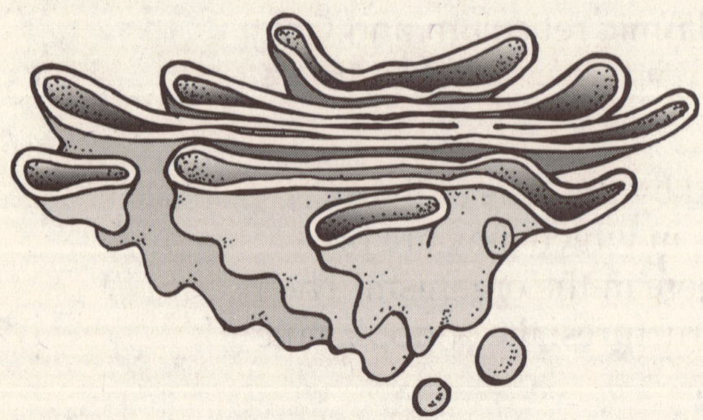

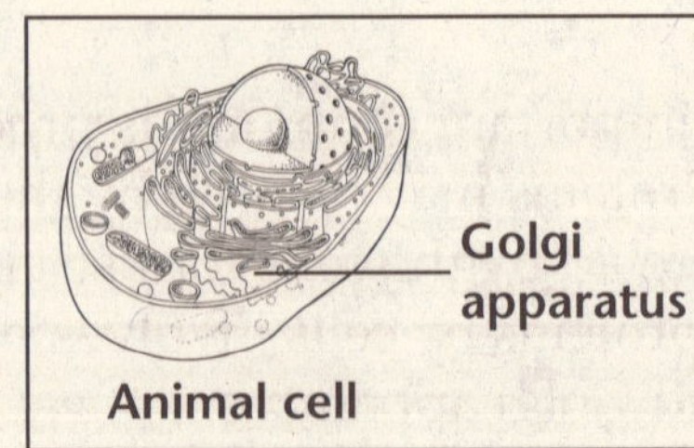

Figure 1–13 Golgi apparatus The larger drawing shows the stacklike membranes that make up the Golgi apparatus. The smaller drawing shows where the Golgi apparatus is located in the cell.

Review Questions

34 **Part of the endoplasmic reticulum is called *rough* because its surface**

    A has holes for secreting proteins.

    B contains stacklike membranes.

    C is covered with ribosomes.

    D attracts proteins.

35 **What is a role of the rough endoplasmic reticulum?**

    A modifying proteins

    B packaging proteins

    C sorting proteins

    D producing proteins

36 **Which structure prepares proteins for secretion from the cell?**

    A smooth endoplasmic reticulum

    B Golgi apparatus

    C cell membrane

    D ribosome

37 **After leaving the Golgi apparatus, proteins for secretion go to the**

    A rough endoplasmic reticulum.

    B smooth endoplasmic reticulum.

    C ribosomes.

    D cell membrane.

Biology/Life Sciences Standards: Cell Biology

7 1.d *Students know* that mitochondria liberate energy for the work that cells do and that chloroplasts capture sunlight energy for photosynthesis.

BI 1.f *Students know* usable energy is captured from sunlight by chloroplasts and is stored through the synthesis of sugar from carbon dioxide.

BI 1.g. *Students know* the role of the mitochondria in making stored chemical-bond energy available to cells by completing the breakdown of glucose to carbon dioxide.

***BI 1.i.** *Students know* how chemiosmotic gradients in the mitochondria and chloroplast store energy for ATP production.

All living things are made up of cells that need energy to function. Most cells obtain energy from either sunlight or food. Cells contain specialized structures that capture or release energy from these sources. The structures are chloroplasts and mitochondria (singular: mitochondrion).

Chloroplasts Chloroplasts are found in the cells of plants and some other organisms. Inside each chloroplast are stacks of membranes, called thykaloid membranes, that contain the green pigment chlorophyll. Chloroplasts capture energy from sunlight and use it to make sugar. This process is called photosynthesis. It is summarized in Figure 1–14.

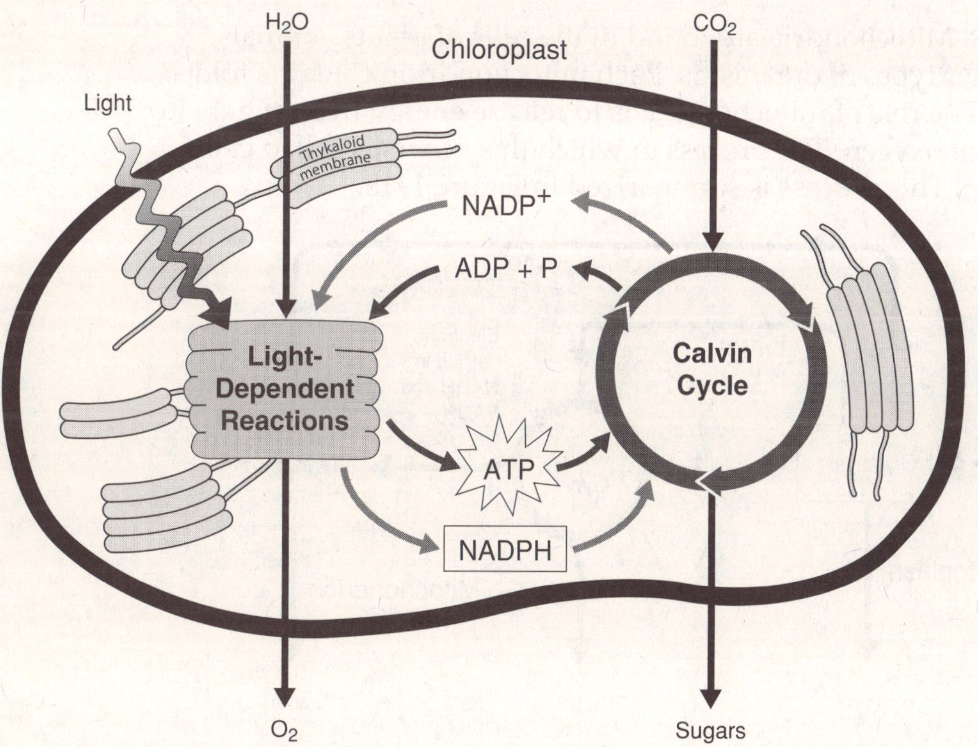

Figure 1–14 Photosynthesis Both stages of photosynthesis—the light-dependent reactions and the Calvin cycle—take place inside a chloroplast.

Biology/Life Sciences Standards: Cell Biology

Photosynthesis can be represented by the following equation:

carbon dioxide + water + energy → sugar + oxygen

The process of photosynthesis occurs in two stages: light-dependent reactions and the Calvin cycle.

- Light-dependent reactions take place in the thykaloid membranes. During this stage, chlorophyll molecules absorb sunlight and release high-energy electrons. The electrons are picked up by molecules of $NADP^+$, forming molecules of the electron-carrying compound NADPH. Some of the energy is also used to form molecules of the high-energy compound ATP from molecules of ADP. ATP stores the energy in a form that is convenient for cells to use. This stage of photosynthesis requires water. It releases oxygen molecules and positively charged hydrogen ions, or protons.

- The Calvin cycle takes place outside the thykaloid membranes. It does not require sunlight. During this stage, the chemical energy stored in NADPH and ATP is used to produce sugar molecules. This stage requires carbon dioxide from the atmosphere, and it releases molecules of $NADP^+$ and ADP.

Mitochondria Mitochondria are found in the cells of plants, animals, and some other types of organisms. Each mitochondrion contains folded membranes. The role of mitochondria is to release energy from sugars in the presence of oxygen. The process in which this occurs is called cellular respiration. This process is summarized in Figure 1–15.

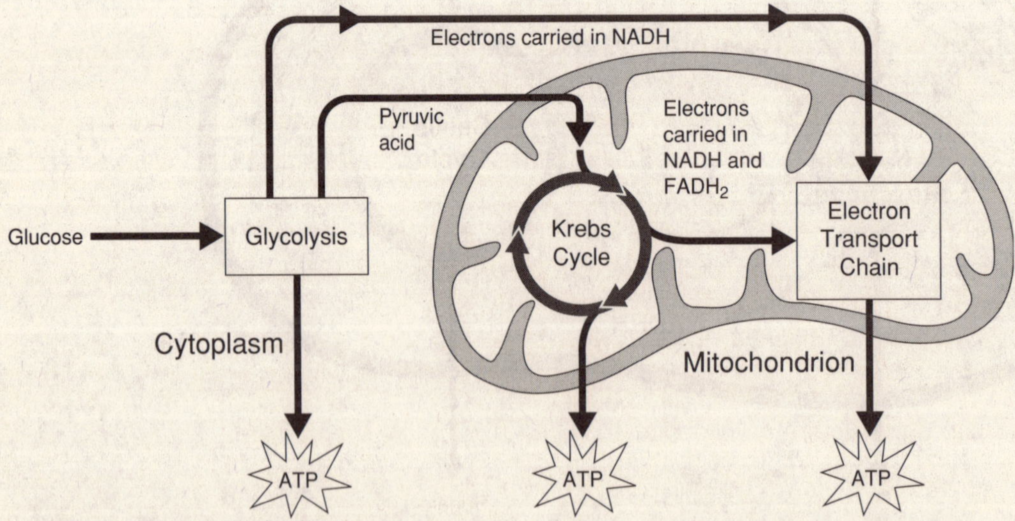

Figure 1–15 Cellular respiration The first stage of cellular respiration, called glycolysis, occurs in the cytoplasm. The other two stages—the Krebs cycle and electron transport—take place inside a mitochondrion.

Biology/Life Sciences Standards: Cell Biology

Cellular respiration can be represented by the following equation:

$$\textbf{oxygen + sugar} \rightarrow \textbf{carbon dioxide + water + energy}$$

The process of cellular respiration takes place in three stages: glycolysis, the Krebs cycle, and electron transport.

- Glycolysis takes place in the cell cytoplasm outside a mitochondrion. During glycolysis, molecules of glucose, a sugar, are broken down to form pyruvic acid. High-energy electrons are also released. The electrons are picked up by molecules of NAD^+, forming NADH, another electron-carrying compound. NADH carries the electrons into the mitochondrion. Some of the energy is also used to form molecules of ATP from ADP.

- The Krebs cycle takes place inside the mitochondrion. During the Krebs cycle, pyruvic acid from glycolysis is broken down into carbon dioxide and more high-energy electrons. Some of these electrons are used to form NADH from NAD^+. The rest of the electrons are picked up by molecules of FAD to form another electron-carrying compound, $FADH_2$. This stage requires oxygen and releases protons.

- Electron transport also takes place inside the mitochondrion. During this stage, electrons carried by NADH and $FADH_2$ provide the energy needed to produce many more molecules of ATP from ADP.

Electron Transport Chain and ATP Production During both cellular respiration and photosynthesis, high-energy electrons flow through the mitochondria and chloroplasts. The electrons are carried by molecules of NADH and $FADH_2$ (in cellular respiration) or NADPH (in photosynthesis). Movement of these molecules is assisted by the electron transport chain, which consists of a series of proteins in the membranes of mitochondria and chloroplasts.

As electrons flow along the electron transport chain, their energy is used to pump positively charged protons across the membranes. As a result, the area inside the membranes becomes positively charged and the area outside the membranes becomes negatively charged. This creates a charge gradient, called a chemiosmotic gradient. When protons are allowed to rush back across the membrane, energy is released. This energy is used for the production of ATP from ADP.

Biology/Life Sciences Standards: Cell Biology

Review Questions

38 Energy from sunlight is captured and used to produce sugars in the process called

A cellular respiration.

B photosynthesis.

C glycolysis.

D electron transport.

39 Which two compounds are needed for photosynthesis?

A water and carbon dioxide

B carbon dioxide and oxygen

C water and oxygen

D sugar and carbon dioxide

40 Light-dependent reactions of photosynthesis take place in the

A chemiosmotic gradient.

B mitochondria.

C thykaloid membranes.

D cytoplasm.

41 What provides energy for the Calvin cycle?

A ATP and NADPH

B ADP

C glucose

D food

42 Which molecules carry electrons during cellular respiration?

A NADPH and ATP

B ATP and ADP

C NADH and FADH$_2$

D ADP and NADPH

43 oxygen + glucose $\rightarrow$ carbon dioxide + water + energy

Which process is represented by this equation?

A photosynthesis

B Calvin cycle

C electron transport

D cellular respiration

44 What is produced during the Krebs cycle?

A carbon dioxide and energy

B glucose and oxygen

C oxygen and carbon dioxide

D glucose and energy

45 What helps electron-carrying molecules move along the membranes of mitochondria and chloroplasts?

A energy stored in ADP

B electron transport chain

C positive hydrogen ions

D chemiosmotic gradient

46 The chemiosmotic gradient is created by

A protons releasing energy.

B protons being pumped across membranes.

C the breakdown of glucose.

D the reverse flow of electrons.

Biology/Life Sciences Standards: Cell Biology

7 1.e *Students know* cells divide to increase their numbers through a process of mitosis, which results in two daughter cells with identical sets of chromosomes.

All living organisms are made up of cells that contain DNA. DNA is the molecule that stores genetic information. In eukaryotic cells, DNA is contained within a nucleus.

Cell Division Most organisms grow by cell division. When a cell divides, it splits into two identical daughter cells. The process of cell division is shown in Figure 1–16.

Before cell division begins, DNA forms structures called chromosomes, and copies are made of each chromosome. After copying, each chromosome has an identical sister chromosome. Pairs of identical sister chromosomes are called chromatids. Cell division begins after chromatids form. It occurs in two stages: mitosis and cytokinesis.

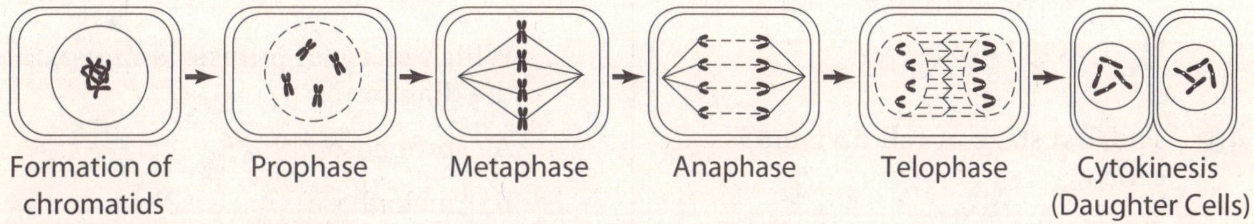

Figure 1–16 Cell division Cell division begins with the formation of chromatids. It proceeds through the four stages of mitosis, and it ends with cytokinesis.

Mitosis Mitosis is the first stage of cell division. In eukaryotic cells, this is the stage in which the nucleus divides. Mitosis occurs in four phases: prophase, metaphase, anaphase, and telophase.

- Prophase: Chromosomes in the nucleus become visible as paired chromatids. Membranes surrounding the nucleus break down.
- Metaphase: Paired chromatids line up across the center of the cell.
- Anaphase: Chromatids separate into individual chromosomes and move apart.
- Telophase: Chromosomes gather at opposite ends of the cell. Nuclear membranes begin to form around each set of chromosomes.

Biology/Life Sciences Standards: Cell Biology

Cytokinesis The second stage of cell division is cytokinesis. During this stage, the cytoplasm of the cell divides, and two new daughter cells form. Cytokinesis differs in plant and animal cells. In most animal cells, the cell membrane is drawn inward until the cytoplasm is pinched into two nearly equal parts. Each part is a daughter cell containing its own nucleus. In plants, a structure known as a cell plate forms across the middle of the dividing cell. The cell plate gradually develops into a cell wall between the two new daughter cells.

Review Questions

47 **When are chromosomes copied?**

    A during prophase

    B following anaphase

    C during cytokinesis

    D before mitosis

48 **The first stage of cell division is called**

    A metaphase.

    B mitosis.

    C anaphase.

    D cytokinesis.

49 **What happens during metaphase?**

    A Membranes surrounding the nucleus break down.

    B Paired chromatids line up across the center of the cell.

    C Chromatids separate into individual chromosomes.

    D Chromosomes become visible as paired chromatids.

50

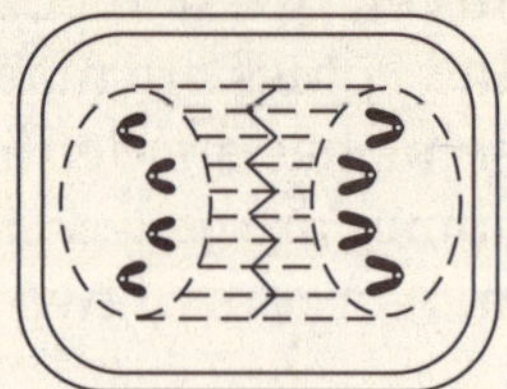

Which phase of mitosis is shown in the diagram?

    A prophase.

    B metaphase.

    C anaphase.

    D telophase.

51 **A cell pinches in half to form two daughter cells during**

    A cytokinesis.

    B anaphase.

    C mitosis.

    D prophase.

Biology/Life Sciences Standards: Genetics

7 2.a. *Students know* the differences between the life cycles and reproduction methods of sexual and asexual organisms.

All organisms reproduce, which means that they produce new organisms of their own kind. Organisms can reproduce by sexual reproduction or asexual reproduction. Some organisms reproduce by both sexual and asexual reproduction, but at different stages in their life cycle. A life cycle includes all the stages an organism goes through from one generation of adults until the next generation reaches adulthood.

Asexual Reproduction In asexual reproduction, a single parent produces offspring that are identical to itself. Most prokaryotes reproduce asexually. Asexual reproduction can occur in various ways, such as fission and budding. In fission, organisms simply copy their genetic material and divide into two new organisms. In budding, adult organisms produce outgrowths that break off and grow into new organisms. Figure 2–1 shows budding in jellyfish.

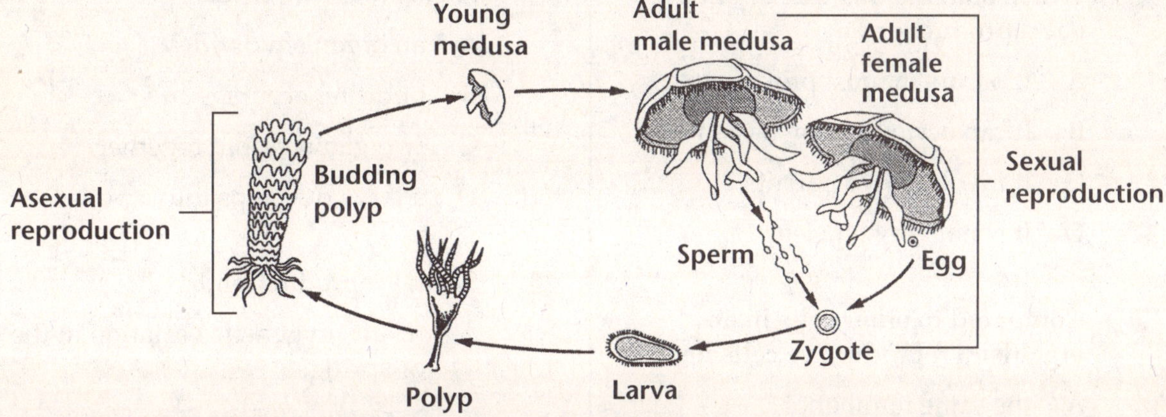

Figure 2–1 Life cycle of jellyfish Jellyfish reproduce both sexually and asexually. In sexual reproduction, a male adult and female adult (both called medusas) produce gametes that join to form a zygote. The zygote develops into a larva, and the larva develops into a polyp. The polyp reproduces asexually by budding off young medusas. The young medusas mature into adult medusas, and the life cycle starts over again.

Asexual reproduction is very efficient. It lets a single parent produce many offspring and take advantage of a favorable environment. However, this type of reproduction results in offspring that are genetically identical. The lack of genetic variation can be a drawback if the environment changes.

Biology/Life Sciences Standards: Genetics

Sexual Reproduction In sexual reproduction, reproductive cells from two different parents join to form the first cell of a new organism. Most eukaryotes reproduce sexually. Sexual reproduction in jellyfish is shown in Figure 2–1.

Reproductive cells are called gametes. Each gamete contains half the normal number of chromosomes found in other cells of the organism. Gametes include sperm, which are produced by males, and eggs, which are produced by females. The joining of a sperm and an egg is known as fertilization. It results in a fertilized egg, or zygote. A zygote contains the normal number of chromosomes for that organism, half from each parent.

Sexual reproduction creates new combinations of chromosomes in each generation. It results in offspring that are not genetically identical. This genetic variation increases the chance that the organisms will be able to adapt if the environment changes.

Review Questions

1 **Which statement is true about asexual reproduction?**

    A It occurs in most prokaryotes.

    B It can occur only by fission.

    C It involves two parents.

    D It is not very efficient.

2 **Compared to other cells in an organism, reproductive cells have**

    A the same number of chromosomes.

    B half as many chromosomes.

    C twice as many chromosomes.

    D no chromosomes.

3 **A zygote forms when**

    A an organism divides.

    B budding occurs.

    C two gametes join together.

    D a larva develops into a polyp.

4 **Sexual reproduction**

    A results in genetic variation in the offspring.

    B is a very efficient means of reproduction.

    C produces genetically identical offspring.

    D occurs in all organisms.

Biology/Life Sciences Standards: Genetics

7 2.c. *Students know* an inherited trait can be determined by one or more genes.

7 2.d. *Students know* plant and animal cells contain many thousands of different genes and typically have two copies of every gene. The two copies (or alleles) of the gene may or may not be identical, and one may be dominant in determining the phenotype while the other is recessive.

Every living thing has a set of characteristics inherited from its parent or parents. A specific characteristic that varies from one individual to another is called a trait. Examples of human traits include eye color and blood type. The particular form of a trait that an individual has is the individual's phenotype. For example, your phenotype for eye color is the color that your eyes appear.

Traits and Genes Traits are controlled by genes, although the environment can also play a role. Each cell in plants and animals contains many thousands of different genes. Some traits, such as ABO blood type, are controlled by just one gene. Other traits, including eye color, are controlled by more than one gene. Traits controlled by more than one gene are called polygenic traits. Polygenic traits often show a wide range of phenotypes. For example, human eye color includes many different shades of brown, blue, green, and gray. Human skin and hair color are also polygenic traits.

A gene for a trait may occur in two or more contrasting forms that produce different forms of the trait. For example, earlobe attachment in humans is controlled by one gene that occurs in two contrasting forms. One form produces attached earlobes, and the other form produces earlobes that are not attached (see Figure 2–2). The contrasting forms of a gene are referred to as alleles.

Figure 2–2 Earlobe attachment Whether earlobes are attached or not attached depends on which alleles are inherited.

Dominance Each individual has two genes for every trait. In organisms that reproduce sexually, the individual receives one gene for each trait from each parent. The two genes may be the same allele or different alleles. If an individual inherits two different alleles, one allele may be dominant. The dominant allele always determines the phenotype.

Biology/Life Sciences Standards: Genetics

The trait plant height is an example of dominance. In pea plants, height is controlled by a single gene with two alleles. One allele results in a plant that is tall, and the other allele results in a plant that is short. The allele for tallness is dominant. As shown in the table, a plant that inherits at least one allele for tallness will be tall. A plant will be short only if it does not inherit the tallness allele.

Height in Pea Plants

Phenotype (Height)	Alleles (T, tallness; t, shortness)
Tall	TT or Tt
Short	tt

Review Questions

5 An example of a human trait that is controlled by one gene is

A eye color.

B skin color.

C hair color.

D earlobe attachment.

6 Any trait that is controlled by more than one gene is called

A dominant.

B recessive.

C phenotypic.

D polygenic.

7 Which term refers to contrasting forms of the same gene?

A traits

B phenotypes

C alleles

D polygenes

8

Phenotype (Blood type)	Alleles (I^A, I^B, i)
A	$I^A I^A$ or $I^A i$
B	$I^B I^B$ or $I^B i$
AB	$I^A I^B$
O	ii

The table shows phenotypes and alleles of the ABO blood type trait. Which allele is recessive?

A I^A

B I^B

C i

D none of the above

Biology/Life Sciences Standards: Genetics

BI 2.a. *Students know* meiosis is an early step in sexual reproduction in which the pairs of chromosomes separate and segregate randomly during cell division to produce gametes containing one chromosome of each type.

BI 2.b. *Students know* only certain cells in a multicellular organism undergo meiosis.

In sexual reproduction, a sperm cell from an adult male and an egg cell from an adult female unite to form a fertilized egg, or zygote. The zygote then develops into an adult organism. Sperm cells and egg cells are called gametes. Gametes are haploid cells produced by the process of meiosis.

Haploid and Diploid Cells Haploid cells have just one chromosome of each type. They have half the number of chromosomes as other cells in the body. Normal body cells are diploid cells. They have two chromosomes of each type, one inherited from the father and one inherited from the mother. Two chromosomes of the same type are called homologous chromosomes.

Meiosis Meiosis is a type of cell division that produces gametes. During meiosis, a diploid cell divides twice, resulting in four haploid cells. Only certain cells undergo meiosis and produce gametes. These cells are called spermatogonia in males and oogonia in females. They are diploid cells, located in the reproductive organs.

Meiosis occurs in two stages: meiosis I and meiosis II. The stages are shown in Figure 2–3. Prior to meiosis I, each chromosome is copied. This is called chromosome replication.

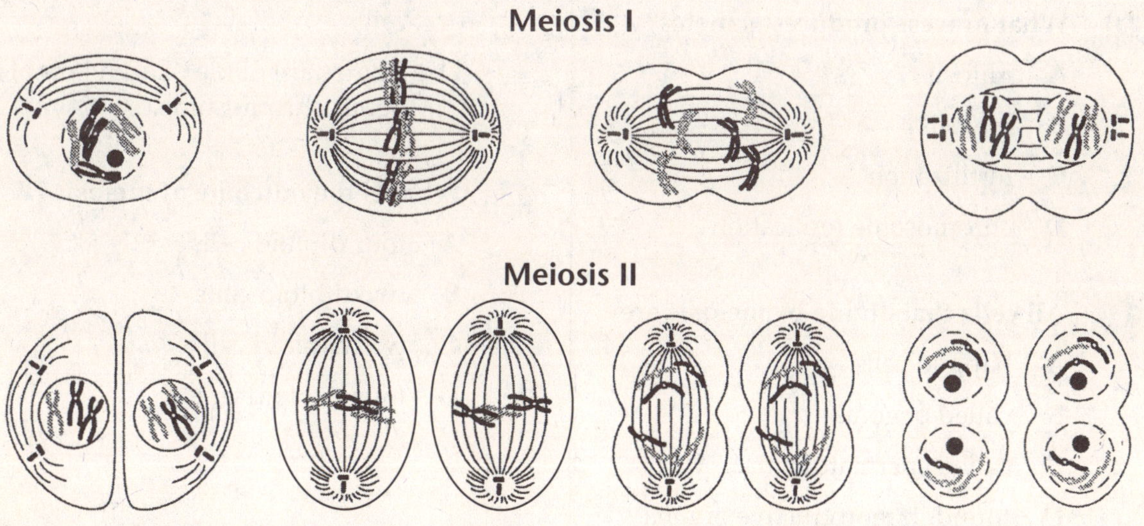

Meiosis I

Meiosis II

Figure 2–3 Meiosis This two-stage cell division results in four haploid cells.

Biology/Life Sciences Standards: Genetics

Meiosis I During meiosis I, the cell divides in a way that is similar to mitosis. However, in meiosis I, homologous chromosomes line up in pairs across the center of the cell, rather than lining up individually, as they do in mitosis. The homologous chromosomes separate and go to opposite ends of the cell, forming two haploid daughter cells. Each daughter cell has just one chromosome of each type. The chromosomes segregate, or separate, randomly. Therefore, each daughter cell has a random mix of the chromosomes that originally came from the father and mother.

Meiosis II During meiosis II, the two haploid daughter cells divide. This time, the chromosomes are not copied before cell division begins. As a result, meiosis II produces four haploid daughter cells. In males, the four haploid daughter cells are sperm cells. In many female organisms, including humans, one of the four haploid daughter cells is bigger than the other three. The large cell is the egg. The other cells, called polar bodies, are not involved in reproduction.

Review Questions

9 **Haploid cells are cells that have**

   A one chromosome of each type.

   B two chromosomes of each type.

   C pairs of homologous chromosomes.

   D two sets of chromosomes.

10 **What process produces gametes?**

   A mitosis

   B meiosis

   C fertilization

   D chromosome replication

11 **All cells that divide by meiosis are**

   A haploid cells.

   B called oogonia.

   C called spermatogonia.

   D found in reproductive organs.

12 **Which event occurs during meiosis I?**

   A Homologous chromosomes line up in pairs in the dividing cell.

   B Homologous chromosomes go to the same gamete.

   C Homologous chromosomes go to the same end of the dividing cell.

   D Copies are made of each homologous chromosome.

13 **What is the outcome of meiosis II?**

   A four diploid cells

   B two diploid cells

   C two haploid cells

   D four haploid cells

Biology/Life Sciences Standards: Genetics

BI 2.c. *Students know* how random chromosome segregation explains the probability that a particular allele will be in a gamete.

BI 3.b. *Students know* the genetic basis for Mendel's laws of segregation and independent assortment.

The inheritance of biological traits is determined by genes, which are located on chromosomes. Each individual has two copies of each type of chromosome. Two chromosomes of the same type are called homologous chromosomes. With two chromosomes of each type, each individual has two copies of each gene. Genes may exist in two or more forms called alleles.

Segregation Gametes are the reproductive cells of sexually reproducing organisms. When gametes form during the process of meiosis, homologous chromosomes separate, or segregate, from one another. The segregation of homologous chromosomes during meiosis results in gametes that contain just one chromosome of each type. Therefore, each gamete contains only one copy of each gene. This is shown in Figure 2–4. In this example, the parent has two different alleles for the gene in question. The alleles are represented by the letters T and t. Each gamete has either T or t, but not both.

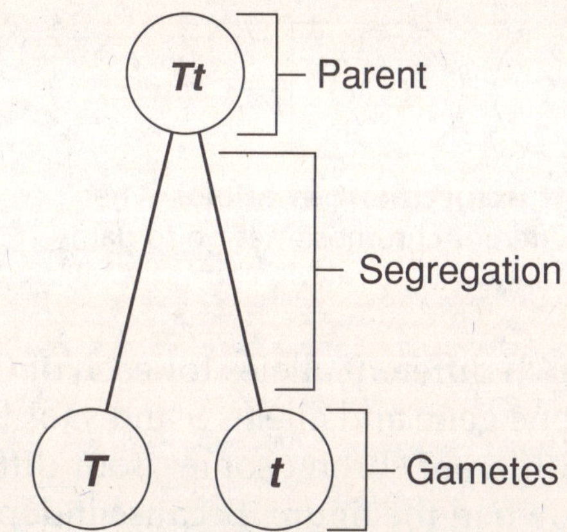

Figure 2–4 Segregation of alleles When gametes form, alleles on homologous chromosomes separate and go to different gametes.

Which of two alleles ends up in a given gamete can be predicted by the laws of probability. The probability of an event is the likelihood that the event will occur. For example, when you flip a coin, the probability of the coin landing heads up (or tails up) is 50 percent. The two outcomes are equally likely because flipping a coin is a random event.

Biology/Life Sciences Standards: Genetics

The segregation of alleles into gametes is similar to flipping a coin. It is a random event, and each allele has a 50 percent chance of being in a given gamete. In Figure 2–4, the probability of T being in a given gamete is 50 percent. The probability of t being in a given gamete is also 50 percent.

Independent Assortment Genes for different traits can segregate independently during the formation of gametes. In other words, the segregation of one pair of alleles does not affect the segregation of another pair of alleles. This is called independent assortment. It is illustrated in Figure 2–5. Independent assortment occurs only when pairs of alleles are located on different (nonhomologous) chromosomes.

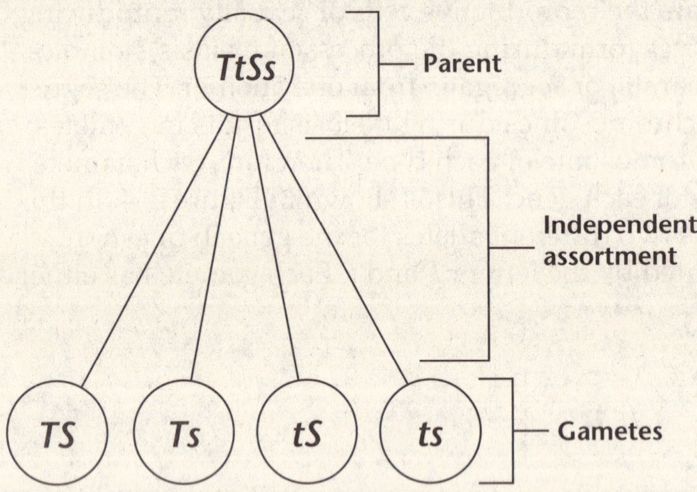

Figure 2–5 Independent assortment of alleles When gametes form, alleles on different chromosomes go to gametes independently of one another.

The parent in Figure 2–5 has two different alleles for each of two different genes—alleles T and t for one gene and alleles S and s for the other gene. If the genes are located on different chromosomes, four different types of gametes can form, as shown in the figure. Because independent assortment occurs randomly, each type of gamete has an equal chance of being produced. Therefore, any given gamete has a one in four, or 25 percent, chance of being produced. Independent assortment helps account for the many genetic variations observed in most organisms.

Biology/Life Sciences Standards: Genetics

Review Questions

14 The segregation of homologous chromosomes during meiosis results in gametes that contain

A two copies of each gene.

B one copy of each gene.

C two homologous genes.

D more genes than the parent.

15 If a parent has two alleles, *R* and *r*, for a gene, what is the chance that a given gamete produced by the parent will have the *R* allele?

A 100 percent

B 50 percent

C 25 percent

D 0 percent

16 During meiosis, the separation of one pair of alleles does not affect the separation of other pairs of alleles because of

A genetic variation.

B homologous chromosomes.

C independent assortment.

D random segregation.

Biology/Life Sciences Standards: Genetics

Bl 2.d. *Students know* new combinations of alleles may be generated in a zygote through the fusion of male and female gametes (fertilization).

Bl 2.g. *Students know* how to predict possible combinations of alleles in a zygote from the genetic makeup of the parents.

During sexual reproduction, male and female gametes join together, or fuse, in the process of fertilization. Fertilization results in a single cell, called a zygote, which develops into a new organism. The possible genetic makeup of a zygote depends on the genetic makeup of the parents.

Gametes and Alleles Gametes are cells produced by the process of meiosis. They are haploid cells, which means they have just one copy of each chromosome, instead of the two copies found in other cells of the organism. Therefore, gametes have just one of copy of each gene.

Many genes have two or more forms, called alleles (represented here by T and t). Individuals can have two of the same allele (TT or tt) or two different alleles (Tt). The combination of alleles in an individual determines which alleles are present in the gametes produced by that individual. For example, an individual with two different alleles (Tt) produces some gametes that have one allele (T) and some that have the other allele (t).

Zygotes and Allele Combinations When two gametes fuse during fertilization, the resulting zygote has two copies of each gene. For example, if a gamete with the T allele unites with a gamete with the t allele, the zygote will have one T allele and one t allele.

If you know the alleles in two parents, you can predict all the possible combinations of alleles in their offspring. Consider two parents that each have one T allele and one t allele. A cross between these two parents can be represented by $Tt \times Tt$. The possible allele combinations in zygotes produced by this type of cross can be determined with a diagram known as a Punnett square, like the one shown here.

Punnett Square for *Tt* × *Tt* Cross

	T	*t*
T	TT	Tt
T	Tt	tt

Biology/Life Sciences Standards: Genetics

The first row and first column of the Punnett square show the alleles in possible gametes produced by each type of parent. The remaining rows and columns show combinations of alleles that would occur if the gametes fused and formed zygotes. For this cross (*Tt* × *Tt*), the Punnett square shows that the zygotes can have three possible combinations of alleles: *TT*, *Tt*, or *tt*. Two of the combinations of alleles in the zygotes (*TT* and *tt*) are different from the combination of alleles in the parents (*Tt*).

Of the four zygotes in the Punnett square, one has the *TT* combination of alleles, one has the *tt* combination, and two have the *Tt* combination. These proportions represent the chance that each type of zygote would be produced in a *Tt* × *Tt* cross. For example, there is a two in four, or 50 percent, chance that a *Tt* zygote would be produced in this type of cross.

Review Questions

17 What kind of gametes can be produced by an individual with the *tt* combination of alleles.

   A   only *T*

   B   *T* and *t*

   C   only *t*

   D   *T* or *t*

18 Which allele combination is produced by the fusion of gametes from a parent with *TT* alleles and a parent with *tt* alleles?

   A   only *TT*

   B   only *tt*

   C   only *Tt*

   D   *TT* or *tt*

Use the Punnett square to answer Questions 19 and 20.

19 **Punnett Square for *TT* × *Tt* Cross**

	T	*T*
T		
t		

How many different combinations of alleles could there be in zygotes produced in this cross?

   A   one

   B   two

   C   three

   D   four

20 What is the chance of this cross producing a zygote that has two different alleles?

   A   0 percent

   B   25 percent

   C   50 percent

   D   100 percent

Biology/Life Sciences Standards: Genetics

BI 2.e. *Students know* why approximately half of an individual's DNA sequence comes from each parent.

BI 2.f. *Students know* the role of chromosomes in determining an individual's sex.

In sexually reproducing organisms, new individuals form when male and female gametes unite. Gametes are haploid cells produced by meiosis. Haploid cells contain just one copy of each type of chromosome. Chromosomes are DNA molecules that contain many smaller molecules, called bases. The sequence of bases in DNA molecules forms the genetic code, which controls the activities of cells.

Inheritance of Chromosomes When two gametes fuse during sexual reproduction, the cell that forms is called a zygote. It will develop into a new individual. Because the zygote forms from the union of two haploid cells, it is a diploid cell. A diploid cell contains two copies of each type of chromosome. Half of the chromosomes in the zygote come from the female gamete. The other half come from the male gamete. Therefore, half of the DNA sequence in the zygote comes from each parent.

Sex Chromosomes In many sexually reproducing organisms, an individual's sex is determined by chromosomes called sex chromosomes. In humans, the sex chromosomes are called the X chromosome and Y chromosome. Normally, females have two X chromosomes (XX), and males have one X chromosome and one Y chromosome (XY).

A mother has only X chromosomes, so all of her gametes have an X chromosome. A father has both X and Y chromosomes, so half of his gametes have an X chromosome and half have a Y chromosome. Because the mother's gametes contain only X chromosomes, it is the father's gametes that determine the sex of offspring.

As shown in the Punnett square, if an offspring inherits an X chromosome from the father, the offspring will be female (XX). If the offspring inherits a Y chromosome from the father, the offspring will be male (XY). There is a 50 percent chance of a male producing gametes of each type, so there is about a 50 percent chance of an offspring being male and about a 50 percent chance of an offspring being female.

Biology/Life Sciences Standards: Genetics

Inheritance of Sex Chromosomes

	X	**Y**
X	XX	XY
X	XX	XY

The X chromosome is large and has many genes that control important cell activities in males as well as females. For example, the X chromosome has genes needed for normal blood clotting. The Y chromosome is much smaller and contains only a few genes. These genes are needed to produce male sexual development. Only one X chromosome is needed for normal cell activity. In females, one of the two X chromosomes is randomly switched off. It becomes a dense region, called a Barr body, in the nucleus of each cell. In males, there is only one X chromosome, so it must be active. Therefore, cells in males do not contain Barr bodies.

Review Questions

21 In sexually reproducing organisms, half of the DNA sequence in an individual comes from each parent because each parent contributes a

  A diploid gamete.

  B haploid zygote.

  C Y chromosome.

  D haploid gamete.

22 What type of sex chromosomes are found in gametes produced by females?

  A only Y chromosomes

  B both X and Y chromosomes

  C only X chromosomes

  D either X or Y chromosomes

23 What is the chance that any given zygote will be male?

  A 25 percent

  B 50 percent

  C 75 percent

  D 100 percent

24 Which statement about sex chromosomes is true?

  A Only one X chromosome is needed for normal cell activity.

  B The X chromosome is small and has few genes.

  C The Y chromosome has genes that are important for both males and females.

  D A switched off Y chromosome becomes a Barr body.

Biology/Life Sciences Standards: Genetics

BI 3.a. *Students know* how to predict the probable outcome of phenotypes in a genetic cross from the genotypes of the parents and mode of inheritance (autosomal or X-linked, dominant or recessive).

***BI 3.c.** *Students know* how to predict the probable mode of inheritance from a pedigree diagram showing phenotypes.

The genetic makeup of an individual is not always obvious from the individual's traits. However, an individual's genetic makeup for a particular trait often can be inferred from the parents' genetic makeup and the mode of inheritance of the trait. The mode of inheritance of a trait refers to whether the trait is controlled by a gene with dominance and whether the gene is on the X chromosome.

Genotype, Phenotype, and Dominance An individual's genetic makeup is his or her genotype. For each gene, the genotype refers to the two alleles present in an individual. The two alleles may be the same or different. For a gene with two alleles, *A* and *a*, there are three possible genotypes: *AA*, *aa*, or *Aa*.

The phenotype of an individual is the individual's physical traits. The phenotype is determined by the genotype, often with influence from the environment. Without dominance, each genotype produces a different phenotype. When one allele is dominant, however, some genotypes produce the same phenotype. For example, if *A* is dominant, *AA* and *Aa* genotypes will produce the same phenotype. Only the *aa* genotype will produce a different phenotype.

Predicting Phenotypes Knowing the genotypes of two parents and which, if any, alleles are dominant lets you predict phenotypes in their offspring. Consider the example of two *Aa* parents. Genotypes of their possible offspring are shown in the Punnett square. If *A* is dominant, three of four offspring (*AA*, *Aa*, *Aa*) would have the dominant phenotype, and only one offspring (*aa*) would have the recessive phenotype.

Punnett Square for *Aa* × *Aa* Cross

	A	*a*
A	AA	Aa
a	Aa	aa

Biology/Life Sciences Standards: Genetics

Sex Chromosomes and Autosomes The X and Y chromosomes are called sex chromosomes, because they determine the sex of the individual. The rest of the chromosomes are called autosomes. Traits controlled by genes on autosomes are called autosomal traits. Inheritance of a dominant autosomal trait is show in the pedigree in Figure 2–6. The trait appears in both males and females and shows up in every generation. Dwarfism is an example of a human dominant autosomal trait. An example of a recessive autosomal trait is cystic fibrosis.

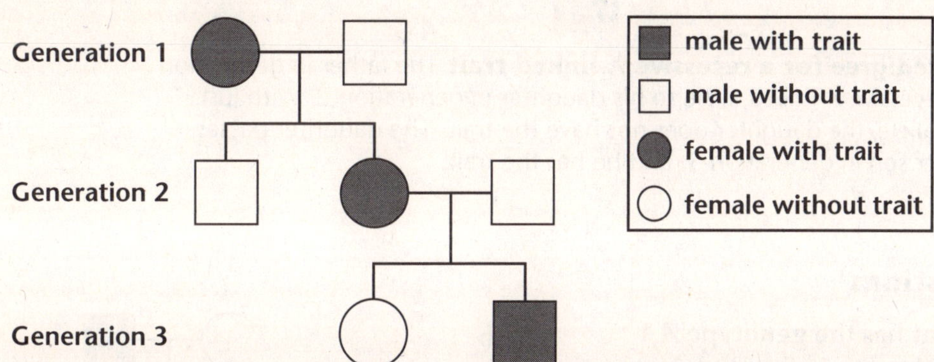

Figure 2–6 Pedigree for a dominant autosomal trait The mother in generation 1 passes the dominant autosomal allele to her daughter in generation 2. The daughter passes the allele to her son in generation 3. Each individual that inherits the allele has the trait because it is dominant.

Traits controlled by genes on the X chromosome are called X-linked traits. (Very few traits are controlled by genes on the Y chromosome.) As shown in Figure 2–7, a recessive X-linked trait appears mainly in males and seems to skip generations. It appears mainly in males because, with only one X chromosome, males need just one recessive allele to have an X-linked trait. The trait seems to skip generations because males pass their X-chromosome only to their daughters, who do not usually have the trait. The daughters then pass their X chromosome to their sons, and the sons have the trait. An example of an X-linked recessive trait is color blindness.

Biology/Life Sciences Standards: Genetics

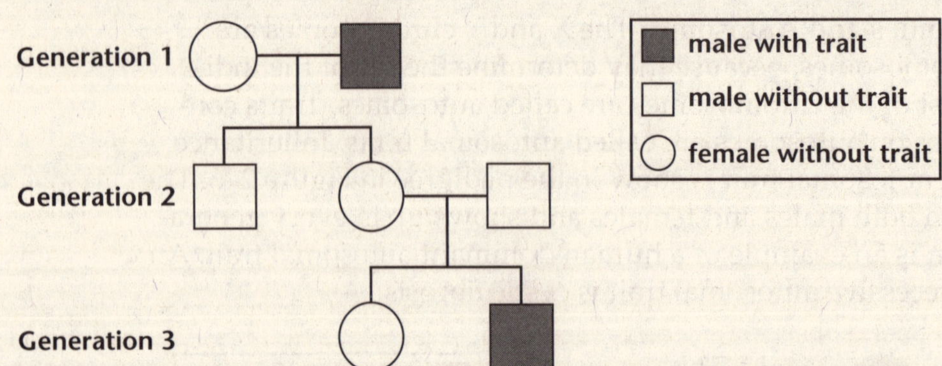

Figure 2–7 Pedigree for a recessive X-linked trait The father in generation 1 passes the recessive X-linked allele to his daughter in generation 2. With just one recessive allele, the daughter does not have the trait. The daughter passes the allele to her son in generation 3, and he has the trait.

Review Questions

25 If a parent has the genotype *AA* and *A* is the dominant allele, what percent of this parent's offspring would have the same phenotype as the parent?

A 0 percent

B 25 percent

C 50 percent

D 100 percent

26

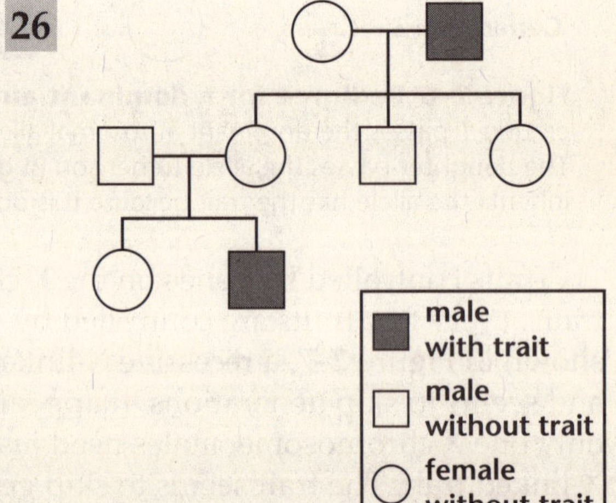

The pedigree shows inheritance of a trait in three generations of a family. Based on the pedigree, what is the most likely mode of inheritance of the trait?

A X-linked recessive

B X-linked dominant

C Y-linked dominant

D autosomal dominant

Biology/Life Sciences Standards: Genetics

***BI 3.d.** *Students know* how to use data on frequency of recombination at meiosis to estimate genetic distances between loci and to interpret genetic maps of chromosomes.

Each individual has two copies of each type of chromosome. Two chromosomes of the same type are known as homologous chromosomes. The position of a gene on a chromosome is called its locus (plural: loci). Homologous chromosomes have the same loci. However, they may have different alleles—or forms of the same gene—at some or all of their loci. During meiosis, homologous chromosomes separate and go to different gametes. The two alleles at each locus on homologous chromosomes also separate and go to different gametes.

Linkage Genes on the same chromosome are called linked genes. Because they are on the same chromosome, alleles for linked genes usually go to the same gametes. This is why specific forms of some traits are usually inherited together. For example, in fruit flies, reddish-orange eye color and miniature wings are usually inherited together. Alleles for these forms of the traits are on the same chromosome.

Crossing Over and Recombination Homologous chromosomes pair up during the first part of meiosis. When they do, crossing-over may occur. Crossing-over is an exchange of parts between homologous chromosomes. It results in new combinations of alleles on each chromosome. Figure 2–8 shows how alleles can be recombined in this way. Crossing-over and recombination explain why traits controlled by alleles on the same chromosome are not always inherited together.

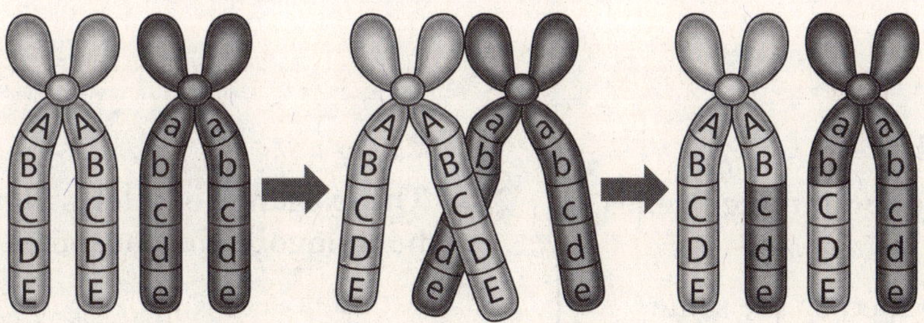

Figure 2–8 Crossing-over and recombination The exchange of alleles between homologous chromosomes during meiosis produces new genetic combinations.

Genetic Distance and Genetic Maps Alleles at loci that are close together on a chromosome are rarely separated by crossing-over. The farther apart loci are, the greater the chance that crossing-over will occur between them during meiosis. In fact, if loci are very far apart on a chromosome, there is a good chance that they will be separated by crossing-over.

Biology/Life Sciences Standards: Genetics

Scientists study pedigrees to determine how often alleles for linked genes recombine. If the combination of alleles is different in an offspring than in either parent, then recombination has occurred. From data on the frequency of recombination, scientists infer the frequency of crossing-over between the genes. Based on the frequency of crossing-over, they can estimate the distance between the loci of the genes. The more often alleles are recombined, the farther apart the loci are assumed to be.

Genetic distance estimates for many loci can be used to create a genetic map. A genetic map shows the positions of certain genes on one or more chromosomes. A genetic map for the human X chromosome is shown in Figure 2–9. It shows the location of genes where abnormal alleles cause certain X-linked genetic disorders.

X Chromosome

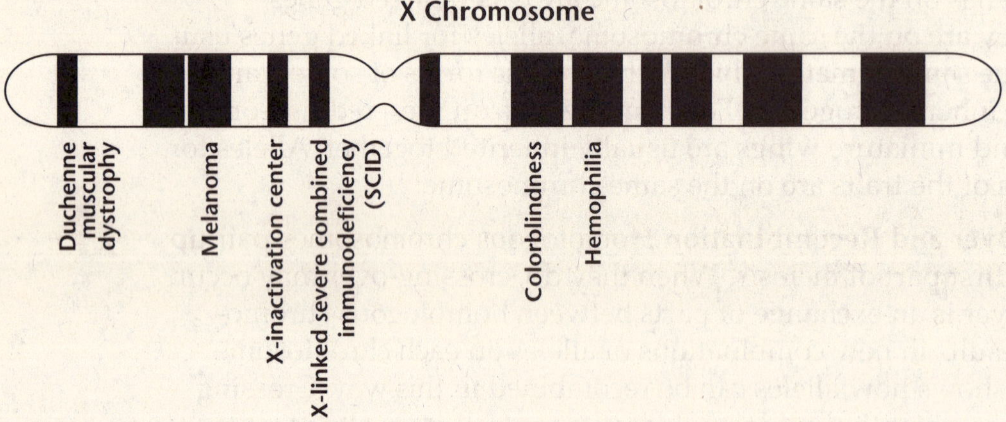

Figure 2–9 Genetic map for the human X-chromosome Distances between these genes on the X chromosome were estimated from the frequency of recombination of their alleles.

Review Questions

27 Which sentence about linked genes is true?

    A They are located on the same chromosome.

    B They always go to different gametes.

    C They control the same traits.

    D They cannot be separated by crossing-over.

28 The exchange of alleles between homologous chromosomes is called

    A meiosis.

    B genetic distance.

    C crossing-over.

    D linkage.

Biology/Life Sciences Standards: Genetics

29

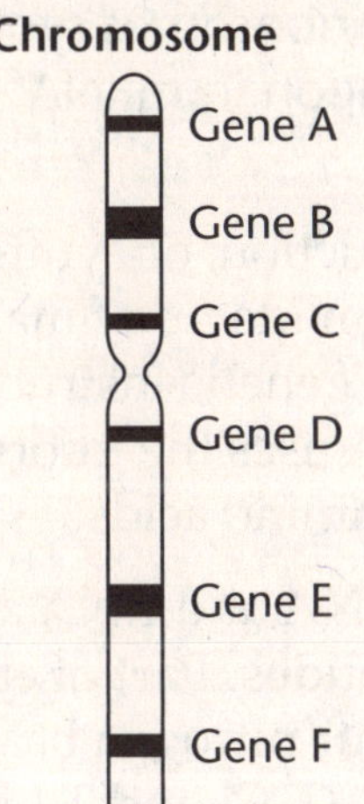

The drawing shows a hypothetical genetic map. Between which two genes would you expect crossing-over and recombination of alleles to occur most often?

A Genes A and B

B Genes C and D

C Genes E and F

D Genes A and F

Biology/Life Sciences Standards: Genetics

Bl 4.a. *Students know* the general pathway by which ribosomes synthesize proteins, using tRNA to translate genetic information in mRNA.

DNA and RNA are nucleic acids involved in the production, or synthesis, of proteins. Proteins are important organic molecules made up of many smaller molecules called amino acids. DNA stores the genetic instructions for the sequence of amino acids in proteins. RNA uses the information to produce proteins with the correct sequence of amino acids.

Nucleic Acids and the Genetic Code Molecules of DNA and RNA are made up of chains of smaller molecules called nucleotides. Part of each nucleotide is a nitrogen-containing base. There are four nitrogen bases in each type of molecule, represented by the letters A, C, G, and T (in DNA) or U (in RNA). Pairs of bases, called complementary bases, form weak bonds. A always bonds with T (or U), and C always bonds with G. Bonds between complementary bases hold together the double strands of DNA molecules. Complementary base pairing is also essential for protein synthesis.

The order of bases in DNA determines the sequence of amino acids in proteins. A sequence of three bases is called a codon. A codon is like a code word. It codes for one of the twenty amino acids that make up proteins. For example, the codon TAC codes for the amino acid methionine.

mRNA and Transcription In eukaryotic organisms, DNA is contained within the cell nucleus. Proteins are synthesized on ribosomes, which are particles in the cytoplasm. Therefore, the genetic code must be copied and carried from the nucleus to the cytoplasm. A type of RNA, called messenger RNA (mRNA), copies, or transcribes, the codons in DNA. The mRNA that forms has a sequence of complementary codons. For example, where DNA has the codon TAC, mRNA would have codon AUG.

tRNA and Translation After transcribing DNA, the mRNA molecule leaves the nucleus and goes to a ribosome. On the ribosome, the sequence of codons in the mRNA molecule is translated into the proper sequence of amino acids in the protein. This process, which is called translation, is shown in Figure 2–10.

Molecules of transfer RNA (tRNA) play a major role in translation. Each tRNA molecule has a single code word, called an anticodon. The tRNA molecule also carries the amino acid specified by its anticodon. As the ribosome moves along the mRNA molecule, tRNA anticodons pair with complementary codons in mRNA. The bonds between the tRNA molecules and the amino acids they carry are broken, and new bonds form between the amino acids of the growing protein.

Biology/Life Sciences Standards: Genetics

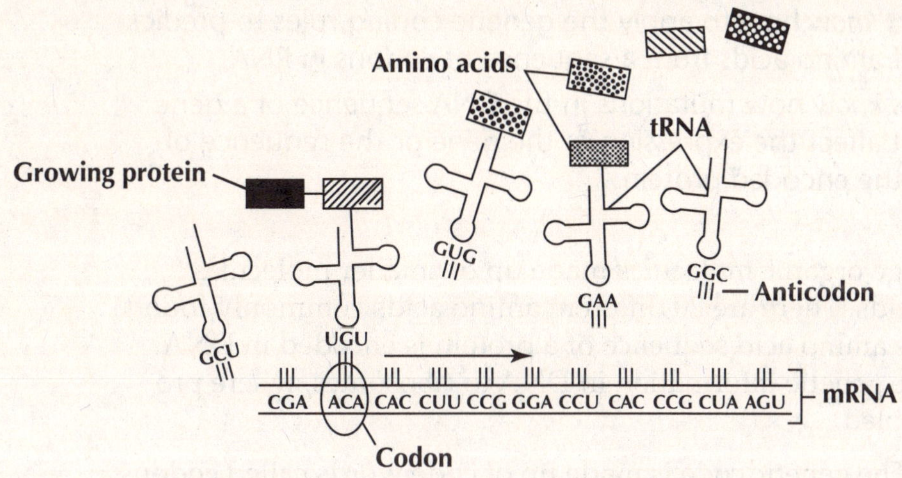

Figure 2–10 Translation A protein molecule is synthesized on a ribosome when tRNA translates the genetic information in mRNA.

Review Questions

30 Genetic information is contained in code words. Each code word consists of three

   A amino acids.

   B nitrogen bases.

   C codons.

   D anticodons.

31 Where is the genetic information in mRNA translated into a sequence of amino acids?

   A in the nucleus

   B inside a DNA molecule

   C on a ribosome

   D in a complementary base

32 Which statement is true about tRNA?

   A It transcribes genetic information in DNA.

   B It translates genetic information in mRNA.

   C It transfers amino acids to the nucleus.

   D It transfers mRNA to a ribosome.

Biology/Life Sciences Standards: Genetics

BI 4.b. *Students know* how to apply the genetic coding rules to predict the sequence of amino acids from a sequence of codons in RNA.

BI 4.c. *Students know* how mutations in the DNA sequence of a gene may or may not affect the expression of the gene or the sequence of amino acids in the encoded protein.

Proteins are large organic molecules made up of smaller molecules called amino acids. There are 20 different amino acids commonly found in proteins. The amino acid sequence of a protein is encoded in DNA. RNA carries the genetic information in DNA to ribosomes, where proteins are assembled.

Genetic Code The genetic code is made up of code words called codons. Each codon has three letters. The letters represent nitrogen-containing bases that found in DNA and RNA molecules. There are a total of four letters: A, C, G, and T (U in RNA). A codon may have letters that are the same or different.

Except for "start" and "stop" codons, each codon in RNA codes for a particular amino acid. A sequence of codons in RNA codes for a sequence of amino acids in a protein. Several amino acids and their RNA codons are shown in the table.

Partial Genetic Code

Amino Acid	RNA Codon(s)
Phenylalanine	UUU or UUC
Tryptophan	UGG
Serine	UCU, UCC, UCA, UCG, AGU, or AGC
Valine	GUU, GUC, GUA, or GUG
Proline	CCU, CCC, CCA, or CCG
Glutamine	CAA or CAG
Threonine	ACU, ACC, ACA, or ACG
Asparagine	AAU or AAC

Mutations and the Genetic Code Sometimes cells make mistakes in copying their own DNA. The mistakes are called mutations. A mutation is a permanent change in the DNA base sequence. RNA copies the mistake, and the mistake may change the encoded protein.

Biology/Life Sciences Standards: Genetics

Some mutations involve changes in just one or a few bases. For example, a mutation might result in an RNA codon changing from CAA, which codes for glutamine, to CCA, which codes for proline. The substitution of the wrong amino acid in the encoded protein might affect the proteins' function.

The deletion or addition of a base is likely to cause an even greater change in the encoded protein. The bases are still read in groups of three, but now those groups are shifted for every codon that follows the deleted or inserted base. This type of mutation is called a frameshift mutation.

Many mutations are neutral. Neutral mutations have little or no effect on the expression of genes or the sequence of amino acids in the encoded proteins. An example of a neutral mutation is a mutation that changes the RNA codon AAA to AAG. Both codons code for the same amino acid, phenylalanine. Therefore, this mutation would have no effect on the encoded protein.

Review Questions

33 **Which sentence is true about the genetic code?**

  A Each codon consists of a sequence of four bases.

  B Each codon codes for just one amino acid.

  C Each amino acid is coded for by just one codon.

  D Some codons code for more than one amino acid.

34 **G-U-U-C-A-A-U-U-U-A-A-U-A-A-C**

Which amino acid sequence would be produced by this RNA base sequence, if the first codon is G-U-U?

  A valine-glutamine-phenylalanine-asparagine-threonine

  B valine-proline-phenylalanine-asparagine-asparagine

  C valine-glutamine-phenylalanine-asparagine-aspargine

  D valine-glutamine-phenylalanine-threonine-asparagine

35 **Which mutation would have no effect on the amino acid sequence of the encoded protein?**

  A UUU → GUU

  B GUU → GUC

  C CAA → AAC

  D UCU → ACU

Biology/Life Sciences Standards: Genetics

BI 4.d. *Students know* specialization of cells in multicellular organisms is usually due to different patterns of gene expression rather than to differences of the genes themselves.

Only a fraction of the genes in a cell are expressed at any given time. An expressed gene is a gene that is transcribed into RNA and translated into a protein. Genes that are not expressed are not transcribed and translated. Organisms have a way to regulate which genes in a cell are expressed.

Regulation of Gene Expression Multicellular organisms have many different types of cells that differ in form and function. All of the cells carry a complete set of genes, but only a tiny fraction of the genes need to be expressed in any given type of cell. For example, a liver cell needs to express the genes that code for liver enzymes, but other types of cells do not need to express these genes.

How do cells "know" which genes to turn on or off? Cells are filled with proteins that bind to DNA and regulate gene expression. The proteins bind to specific sites on the DNA, called regulator sites. The proteins may promote the transcription of certain genes by attracting the enzyme RNA polymerase, which is needed for transcription. Or, the proteins may block access to particular genes so they cannot be transcribed.

Gene expression may also be affected by the environment. For example, the gene in plants that controls production of the green pigment chlorophyll needs sunlight to be expressed. Plants grown in the dark are white instead of green, because their chlorophyll genes are not turned on.

Cell Differentiation Regulation of gene expression is especially important during the early stages of development of a multicellular organism. Each of the specialized cell types found in an adult organism develops from the same fertilized egg cell. This means that cells do not just grow and divide during early development. They also undergo differentiation. During differentiation, cells become specialized in structure and function, like the three different types of human cells shown in Figure 2–11.

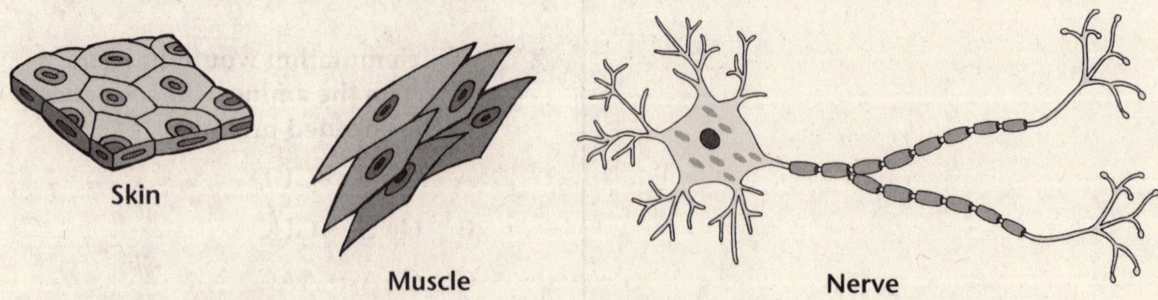

Figure 2–11 Specialized human cells Each of these three cells has the same genes, but the cells differ from one another because of cell differentiation.

Biology/Life Sciences Standards: Genetics

A series of genes, known as hox genes, control the differentiation of cells during the early development of organisms. Hox genes are "master control" genes. A mutation in one of these genes can completely change the organs that develop. For example, mutations affecting the hox genes in a fruit fly can replace the fly's antennae with legs growing out of its head.

Most multicellular organisms, including humans, have very similar clusters of hox genes in their DNA. The function of hox genes in these organisms is about the same as it is in fruit flies: telling the cells of the body how they should differentiate as the body grows. Careful regulation of gene expression in hox genes is needed for normal development.

Review Questions

36 **Which statement is true about all of the cells in a multicellular organism?**

   A They are identical.

   B They have the same genes.

   C They have different genes.

   D They express the same genes.

37 **Proteins in a cell can promote the transcription of certain genes by**

   A binding to DNA and attracting the enzyme needed for transcription.

   B producing the enzyme RNA polymerase.

   C binding to DNA and blocking regulator sites.

   D causing mutations in hox genes.

38 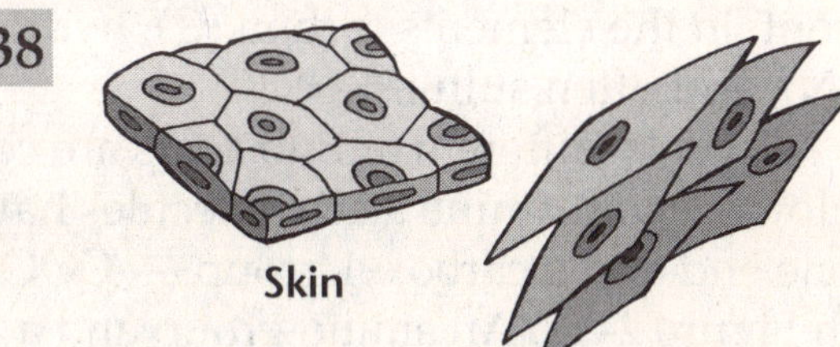

What process explains why these two types of human cells look so different from one another?

   A genetic differentiation

   B cell differentiation

   C cell division

   D cell expression

39 **What controls the differentiation of cells during early development?**

   A regulator proteins

   B RNA polymerase

   C liver enzymes

   D hox genes

Biology/Life Sciences Standards: Genetics

BI 4.e. *Students know* proteins can differ from one another in the number and sequence of amino acids.

***BI 4.f.** *Students know* why proteins having different amino acid sequences typically have different shapes and chemical properties.

Proteins are important molecules in organisms. They are large molecules, made up of many smaller molecules, called amino acids. Proteins can differ from one another in the number and sequence of the amino acids they contain. The number and sequence of amino acids in a protein determines the protein's shape and chemical properties.

Protein Structure Proteins are organic macromolecules consisting of one or more chains of linked amino acids. Amino acids are also called peptides, and chains of amino acids are called polypeptides. Amino acids contain the elements carbon (C), hydrogen (H), oxygen (O), nitrogen (N), and often sulfur (S).

Twenty different amino acids are commonly found in proteins. However, all amino acid molecules have an amino group ($-NH_2$) on one end and a carboxyl group ($-COOH$) on the other end, as shown in Figure 2–12. An amino group and a carboxyl group can form chemical bonds together. This allows any amino acid to be joined to any other amino acid. The part of each amino acid that makes it different is a side chain called an R-group. R-groups vary in their chemical properties. For example, some R-groups are acidic and others are basic. Some R-groups are positively charged and others are negatively charged.

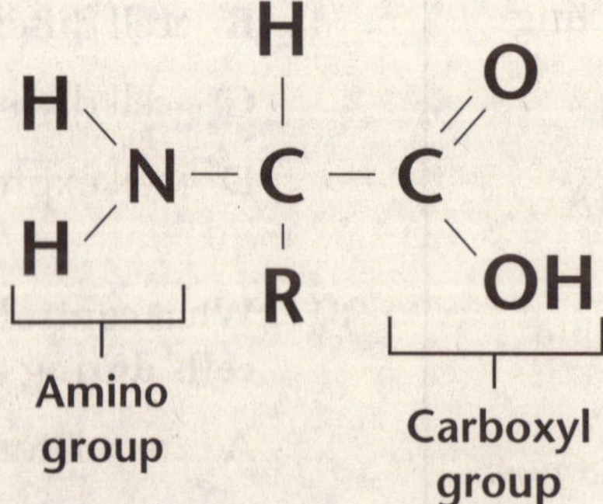

Figure 2–12 General amino acid structure All amino acids have the same general structure.

Biology/Life Sciences Standards: Genetics

Each protein has a specific complex shape, largely determined by the sequence of its amino acids. Amino acids in a polypeptide chain can be twisted or folded, and the polypeptide chain itself is folded. In proteins with more than one polypeptide chain, the chains have a specific arrangement in space. A protein's shape is important because it determines the protein's function.

Form and Function in Proteins Each protein has a specific function in the organism. For example, proteins called enzymes speed up chemical reactions in cells. Enzymes are a good example of how a protein's shape determines its function.

Enzymes speed up reactions by providing a site where the necessary chemicals can be brought together to react. The reaction site needs to have a very specific shape, because the site and the chemicals must fit together like a lock and key. A change in the sequence of amino acids in an enzyme could change the shape of the reaction site. As a result, the enzyme would no longer be able to function.

Review Questions

40 **What is the structure of a protein?**

A an amino group bonded to a carboxyl group

B one or more polypeptides in a complex shape

C a peptide containing one or more elements bonded together

D an R-group bonded to a carboxyl group

41 **Which statement is true about amino acids?**

A A single amino acid is also called a polypeptide.

B Any amino acid can be joined to any other amino acid.

C There are five different amino acids in proteins.

D All amino acids have the same R-group.

42 **The shape of a protein is important because it determines the protein's**

A function.

B amino acid sequence.

C R-groups.

D side chains.

Biology/Life Sciences Standards: Genetics

7 2.e. *Students know* DNA (deoxyribonucleic acid) is the genetic material of living organisms and is located in the chromosomes of each cell.

BI 5.a. *Students know* the general structures and functions of DNA, RNA, and protein.

Nucleic acids are molecules found in living things. They include DNA (deoxyribonucleic acid) and RNA (ribonucleic acid). DNA forms chromosomes and stores genetic information in each cell. DNA is copied and passed on to offspring in gametes. It also "tells" cells how to make proteins. RNA uses the genetic information in DNA to make the proteins.

Proteins Proteins play several vital roles in organisms. Some control the rate of chemical reactions and regulate cell processes. Some are used to form bones and muscles. Others transport substances or help fight disease.

A protein molecule consists of one or more chains of smaller molecules called amino acids. The 20 different amino acids in proteins can be joined together in any order. The sequence of amino acids in a protein determines the protein's shape and function.

DNA DNA consists of two chains of smaller molecules known as nucleotides. The two chains are wrapped around each other in a twisted ladder shape called a double helix. Each DNA nucleotide is made up of a sugar (deoxyribose), a phosphate, and a nitrogen-containing base. There are four nitrogen bases in DNA: adenine (A), cytosine (C), guanine (G), and thymine (T). As shown in Figure 2–13, sugars and phosphates form the backbone of the nucleotide chain, and the bases stick out to the side. Pairs of bases form weak chemical bonds that hold together the two nucleotide chains.

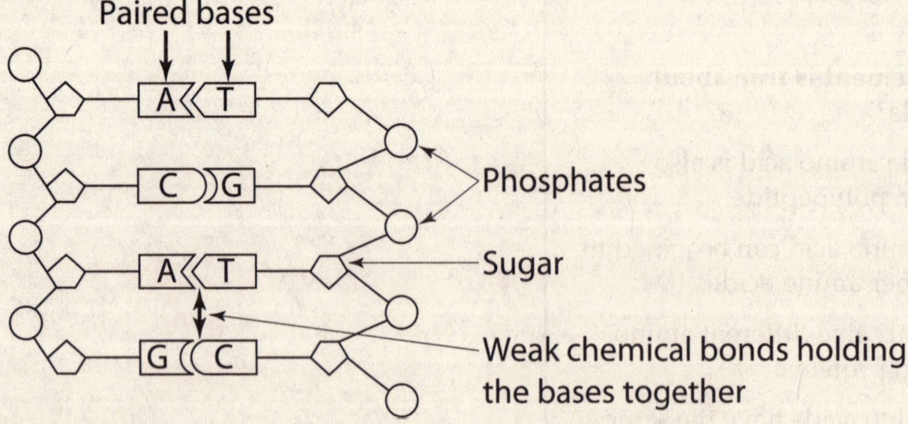

Figure 2–13 Part of a DNA molecule The two sides of a DNA "ladder" are formed by sugars and phosphates. Paired bases form the rungs of the ladder. A always pairs with T, and C always pairs with G.

Biology/Life Sciences Standards: Genetics

The four DNA bases carry genetic information in the form of the genetic code. A sequence of three bases is called a codon. Each codon codes for one amino acid, and a series of codons codes for a particular protein. Therefore, the order of bases in DNA determines a protein's amino acid sequence.

RNA RNA molecules are similar to DNA molecules, except each RNA molecule consists of just one strand of nucleotides instead of two. Also, RNA nucleotides contain the sugar ribose instead of deoxyribose and the base uracil (U), instead of thymine (T).

There are three types of RNA: messenger RNA (mRNA), ribosomal RNA (rRNA), and transfer RNA (tRNA). All three types are needed to make a protein. First, a molecule of mRNA copies that part of a DNA nucleotide chain that codes for a protein. Then, mRNA carries the code to a ribosome, which is a particle consisting mainly of rRNA. Molecules of tRNA bring the correct amino acids to the ribosome to build the protein, based on the code in mRNA.

Review Questions

43 **What are the smaller molecules that join together to make proteins?**

   A nucleotides

   B phosphate groups

   C sugars

   D amino acids

44 **The two chains of a DNA molecule are held together by bonds between**

   A base pairs.

   B sugars and phosphates.

   C amino acids.

   D nucleotides.

45 **What is one way that RNA differs from DNA?**

   A RNA contains thymine instead of uracil.

   B RNA has two nucleotide chains instead of one.

   C RNA contains ribose instead of deoxyribose.

   D RNA forms a double helix instead of a twisted ladder shape.

46 **Which statement describes how DNA, RNA, and proteins are related?**

   A RNA copies DNA and uses the information to make proteins.

   B DNA makes proteins based on the information in RNA.

   C DNA is made up of RNA and proteins.

   D DNA and RNA are two different types of proteins.

Biology/Life Sciences Standards: Genetics

BI 5.b. *Students know* how to apply base-pairing rules to explain precise copying of DNA during semiconservative replication and transcription of information from DNA into mRNA.

DNA stores genetic information in its sequence of nitrogen-containing bases. The base sequence is copied when duplicate molecules of DNA are made prior to cell division. The base sequence is also copied by messenger RNA (mRNA) in the first step of protein production.

Base Pairing Both DNA and RNA contain nitrogen bases. There are four nitrogen bases in each type of molecule, represented by the letters A, C, G, and T (in DNA) or U (in RNA). Pairs of bases form weak chemical bonds together. A always bonds with T (or U in RNA), and C always bonds with G. Bases that form bonds together are called complementary bases. Complementary base pairing holds together the two strands of the double-stranded DNA molecule. It also explains how DNA can be copied precisely.

DNA Replication Before a cell divides, it copies its DNA in a process called DNA replication. The process is shown in Figure 2–14. DNA replication results in two new DNA molecules that are identical to each other and to the original DNA molecule.

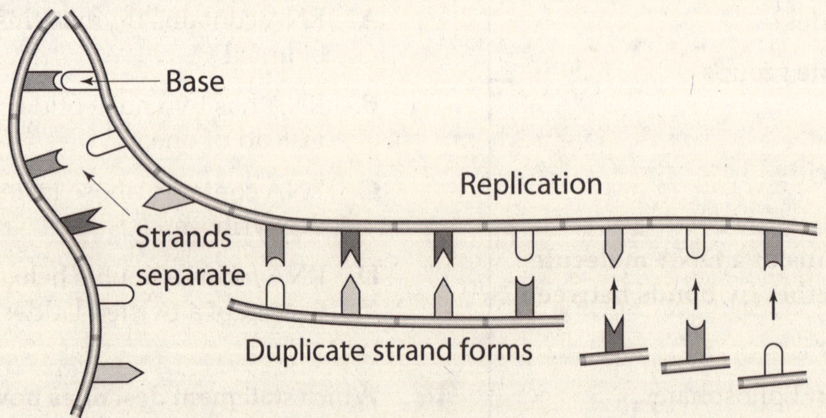

Figure 2–14 DNA replication Two DNA strands separate, and a complementary copy is made of each strand.

During DNA replication, enzymes "unzip" the original DNA molecule by breaking the weak bonds between complementary base pairs. Then, each strand of the original DNA molecule serves as a template, or model, for a new strand with complementary bases. For example, if an original strand had the base sequence ATCGTT, the new strand would have the complementary base sequence TAGCAA. Both strands of the original molecule are replicated at the same time.

Biology/Life Sciences Standards: Genetics

Each of the two new DNA molecules that form during replication consists of one original strand and one new strand. In other words, half of the original DNA molecule is saved, or conserved, in each new DNA molecule. This why DNA replication is described as semiconservative.

DNA Transcription A molecule of mRNA is produced by copying a strand of DNA in a process called transcription. Transcription is similar to DNA replication. During transcription, an enzyme separates the two strands of a DNA molecule, and one strand is used as a template for a single-stranded RNA molecule. The RNA molecule has a base sequence that is complementary to the base sequence of the DNA strand.

Review Questions

47 Which base sequence in DNA is complementary to the base sequence TATCGG?

A   ATAGCC

B   UCUATT

C   GCGUTT

D   ATACAA

48 Which choice describes DNA replication?

A   One strand of DNA is used as a template for one new RNA molecule.

B   Two strands of DNA are used as templates for two new DNA molecules.

C   One strand of RNA is used as a template for one new DNA molecule.

D   Two DNA molecules are copied to produce two new DNA molecules.

49 One way that DNA transcription differs from DNA replication is that transcription

A   uses both strands of DNA as templates.

B   results in one new RNA molecule.

C   does not "unzip" the DNA molecule.

D   results in two new DNA molecules.

Biology/Life Sciences Standards: Genetics

BI 5.c. *Students know* how genetic engineering (biotechnology) is used to produce novel biomedical and agricultural products.

Humans have long produced new types of organisms by letting only those adults with desired traits reproduce. This is called selective breeding. It makes use of naturally occurring genetic variation. Today, scientists can use genetic engineering (biotechnology) to produce new types of organisms. Genetic engineering directly changes DNA, the molecule that carries genetic information and controls the traits of organisms.

Techniques of Genetic Engineering Scientists use a variety of genetic engineering techniques to change DNA. There are techniques to remove DNA from cells, cut DNA into fragments, sort and analyze the fragments, and join together different fragments. DNA that is produced by joining together fragments from different sources is called recombinant DNA.

Many genetic engineering techniques depend on enzymes. Enzymes are proteins that speed up chemical reactions. Most of the enzymes used in genetic engineering either break or form chemical bonds in DNA.

Transgenic Organisms By adding recombinant DNA to the cells of other organisms, scientists can create new types of organisms, called transgenic organisms. Transgenic organisms have the traits that are controlled by the recombinant DNA that was added to their cells. Most transgenic organisms are engineered to produce new proteins, such as enzymes or hormones.

Scientists have created hundreds of useful transgenic organisms. Transgenic crop plants have been created that produce natural insecticides (see Figure 2–15). Other transgenic crop plants can resist viruses or frost. Transgenic fish have been created that grow faster or resist infections.

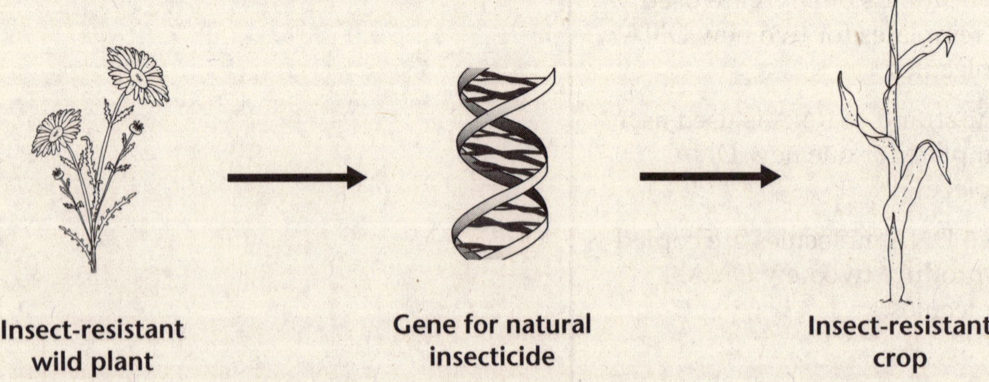

Figure 2–15 Creating an insect-resistant crop plant A wild plant carries a gene for producing a natural insecticide. Scientists remove the gene and transfer it to a crop plant that is not naturally insect resistant. The transgenic crop plant that results can produce the natural insecticide. The new plant remains insect free without the use of artificial insecticides.

Biology/Life Sciences Standards: Genetics

Some of the most useful transgenic organisms are bacteria. Bacteria have been engineered to produce many important biomedical substances. For example, there are transgenic bacteria that produce human vaccines, insulin, and growth hormone, among other substances that help prevent or treat human diseases. Bacteria reproduce very rapidly, enabling a huge supply of these tiny biological "factories."

Gene Therapy Recombinant DNA may soon be used to replace or modify defective genes in humans. Scientists are already testing the use of gene therapy for several serious genetic disorders, including cystic fibrosis and certain types of cancer. This type of therapy would cure the diseases, not just treat the symptoms.

Cloning A clone is a genetically identical copy of a cell or organism. Transgenic bacteria are often cloned to produce millions of identical bacteria that can produce large quantities of a desired protein. Plants and animals have been cloned only recently. Eventually, scientists may be able to clone transgenic crop plants and farm animals or even members of endangered species.

Review Questions

50 Many genetic engineering techniques depend on

A   insulin.

B   defective genes.

C   transgenic cells.

D   enzymes.

51 DNA produced by combining DNA from different sources is called

A   bacterial DNA.

B   recombinant DNA.

C   transgenic DNA.

D   cellular DNA.

52 One reason that bacteria are used to produce human insulin is that bacteria

A   naturally have the insulin gene.

B   reproduce very rapidly.

C   are easy to inject into humans.

D   can cut DNA into fragments.

53 What is cloning?

A   combining DNA fragments from different sources

B   cutting, sorting, and analyzing DNA fragments

C   making genetically identical copies of a cell or organism

D   creating bacteria that contain human DNA

Biology/Life Sciences Standards: Genetics

***BI 5.d.** *Students know* how basic DNA technology (restriction digestion by endonucleases, gel electrophoresis, ligation, and transformation) is used to construct recombinant DNA molecules.

Scientists can use genetic engineering techniques to combine DNA from different sources. The DNA that results is called recombinant DNA. Techniques for constructing recombinant DNA molecules include restriction digestion, gel electrophoresis, ligation, and transformation.

Restriction Digestion One of the first steps in constructing recombinant DNA is cutting an original DNA molecule into smaller fragments. This is called restriction digestion. It is done with a type of enzyme known as a restriction endonuclease. The enzyme cuts DNA at a specific sequence of bases, called a recognition sequence. Different restriction endonucleases recognize different base sequences. For example, the enzyme *Eco*R I recognizes the base sequence CTTAAG. Wherever the enzyme finds this sequence in DNA, it cuts the DNA between the final A and G of the recognition sequence.

Gel Electrophoresis After DNA has been cut into fragments, the fragments can be separated and analyzed by gel electrophoresis. This technique separates DNA fragments on the basis of their length. Gel electrophoresis can be used to locate and identify particular genes or to compare genes from different individuals or organisms.

To separate DNA fragments, the fragments are first poured into wells in a gel (see Figure 2–16). An electric current is then applied to the gel to create a positive end and a negative end. DNA molecules are negatively charged, so the fragments move through the gel toward the positive end. The smaller the fragments, the faster and farther they move.

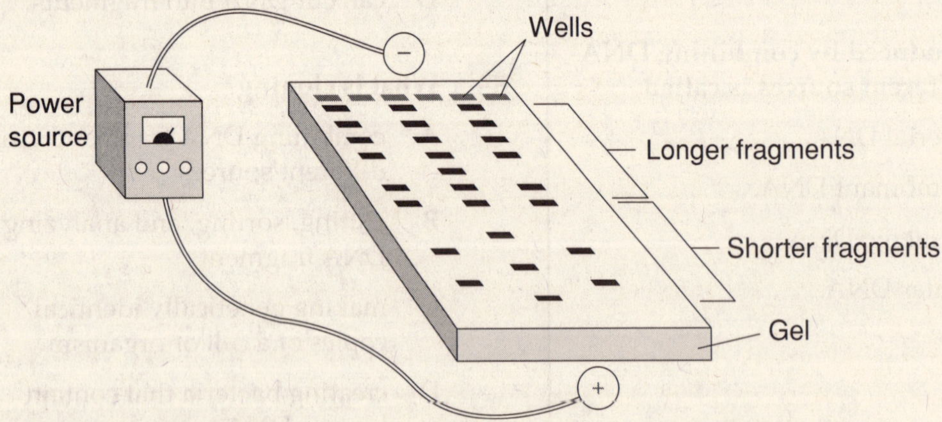

Figure 2–16 Gel electrophoresis Shorter DNA fragments travel farther through the gel than do longer fragments.

Biology/Life Sciences Standards: Genetics

Ligation Recombinant DNA is formed by joining together DNA fragments from different sources. The process of joining together the fragments is called ligation. To join together fragments of double-stranded DNA requires the enzyme DNA ligase. The enzyme creates chemical bonds between the cut ends of both strands of the DNA fragments.

Transformation The cells of living organisms can be changed, or transformed, by adding DNA from outside sources. In transformation, external DNA combines with the original DNA in a cell and becomes part of the cell's genetic makeup. Transformation may be used to add entirely new genes to cells or to replace missing or defective genes.

Review Questions

54 What role do restriction endonucleases play in genetic engineering?

   A They join together DNA fragments.

   B They create new DNA molecules.

   C They transform DNA fragments.

   D They cut DNA into fragments.

55 Gel electrophoresis separates DNA fragments based on their

   A recognition sequence.

   B length.

   C positive charge.

   D chemical bonds.

56

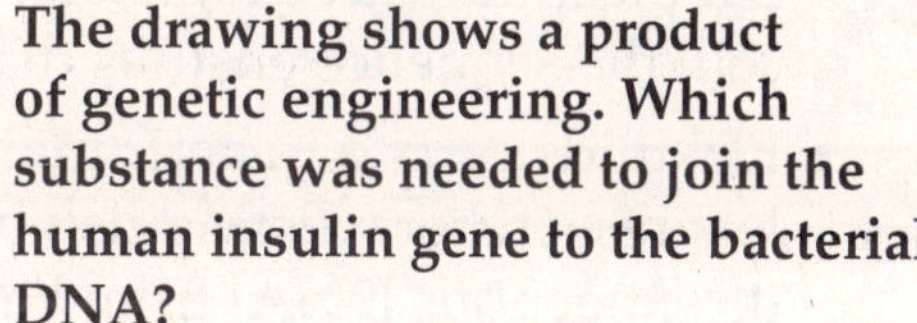

The drawing shows a product of genetic engineering. Which substance was needed to join the human insulin gene to the bacterial DNA?

   A a recognition sequence

   B an enzyme

   C a restriction endonuclease

   D electrophoresis gel

57 Which choice is the best definition of transformation?

   A changing cells by adding new DNA to them

   B cutting DNA molecules at recognition sequences

   C sorting and analyzing DNA fragments

   D creating chemical bonds between DNA strands

Biology/Life Sciences Standards: Genetics

***BI 5.e.** *Students know* how exogenous DNA can be inserted into bacterial cells to alter their genetic makeup and support expression of new protein products.

Many types of bacteria have been genetically engineered to produce useful substances, such as human enzymes and hormones. The bacterial cells are altered, or transformed, with exogenous DNA, which is DNA from an outside source. The exogenous DNA is inserted into a bacterial cell, where it combines with bacterial DNA. The exogenous DNA changes the genetic makeup of the bacterial cell and enables it to make new proteins.

Formation of Recombinant DNA As shown in Figure 2–17, the first step in transforming bacteria with exogenous DNA is forming recombinant DNA. This is done by extracting the exogenous DNA from a cell and joining it to a small, circular DNA molecule, known as a plasmid. Plasmids are found naturally in some bacteria. They are very useful for DNA transfer because they have two essential features:

- Plasmids have a sequence that helps promote plasmid replication. If a plasmid with exogenous DNA manages to get inside a bacterial cell, the sequence ensures that the exogenous DNA will be copied.

- Plasmids carry a genetic marker. A genetic marker is a gene that lets researchers distinguish bacteria that carry the plasmid (with its exogenous DNA) from bacteria that do not carry the plasmid.

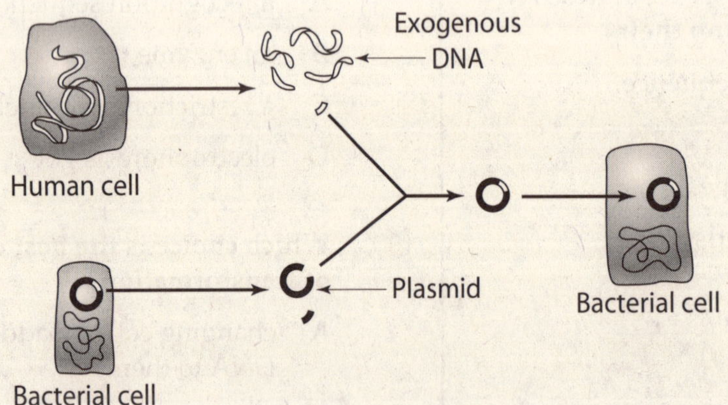

Figure 2–17 Transforming a bacterial cell with human DNA A fragment of human DNA is combined with a plasmid to form recombinant DNA. The recombinant DNA is then transferred to a bacterial cell.

Transfer of Recombinant DNA The second step in transforming bacteria is transferring the recombinant DNA into another bacterial cell. Some types of bacteria naturally pick up DNA from outside the cell.

Biology/Life Sciences Standards: Genetics

In other cases, a virus can be used to carry the recombinant DNA into the bacterial cell. Chemicals or electricity can also be used to insert the DNA. For example, chemicals can be used to make "holes" in a bacterial cell, through which recombinant DNA can enter the cell. Once the recombinant DNA is transferred, it is likely to become part of the genetic makeup of the bacteria.

The bacterial cell with the recombinant DNA replicates over and over. Because bacteria reproduce rapidly, billions of cells carrying the recombinant DNA can be produced in a relatively short period of time. All of the cells carry copies of the exogenous DNA that was transferred to the original bacterial cell with the plasmid. Therefore, all of the cells can produce the protein encoded in the exogenous DNA.

Review Questions

58 **What is one reason that plasmids are used to transform bacterial cells?**

  A They have a sequence that helps promote replication.

  B They do not carry any genetic markers.

  C They cannot be combined with exogenous DNA.

  D They are viruses that can infect bacterial cells.

59 **Which statement is true about the transfer of recombinant DNA to bacteria?**

  A Some types of bacteria naturally pick up DNA from outside the cell.

  B A virus may be able to carry DNA into a bacterial cell.

  C Chemicals or electricity can be used to insert DNA into a bacterial cell.

  D all of the above

60 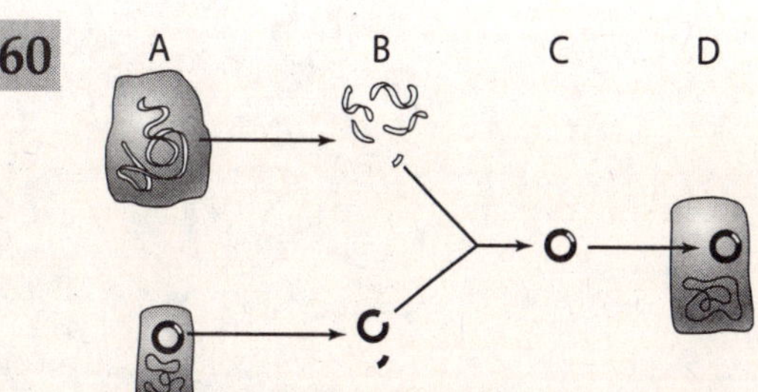

The drawing shows the transformation of a bacterial cell with recombinant DNA. Which letter indicates the formation of the recombinant DNA?

  A A

  B B

  C C

  D D

Biology/Life Sciences Standards: Ecology

6 5.e. *Students know* the number and types of organisms an ecosystem can support depends on the resources available and on abiotic factors, such as quantities of light and water, a range of temperatures, and soil composition.

An ecosystem is a collection of all of the organisms that live in a particular place, together with their nonliving, or physical, environment. The nonliving factors in an ecosystem include temperature, sunlight, soil composition, and water. These factors determine the number and types of types of living things an ecosystem can support.

Abiotic Factors The physical, or nonliving, factors that shape ecosystems are called abiotic factors. Temperature and sunlight are two of the abiotic factors that influence the organisms in an ecosystem. Each living thing has a range of temperatures in which it can survive, so the temperature of the ecosystem determines what kinds of living things are found there. Warmer ecosystems, such as those in tropical rain forests, support more living things than colder ecosystems, such as those in the tundra. The amount of sunlight in an ecosystem directly impacts the number and variety of plants that are able to grow in the ecosystem. In turn, the number and types of plants in an ecosystem determine the number and types of animals that can survive there.

Within any ecosystem, the temperature and amount of sunlight may vary depending on the season. Most ecosystems have less sunlight and lower temperatures in the winter. In deserts, however, the conditions are generally more favorable for living things in the winter. In most other ecosystems, the temperature and amount of sunlight allow the ecosystems to support the most living things in the summer.

Living things need water to survive. The availability of water is an abiotic factor that plays a key role in determining the number of organisms found in an ecosystem. Deserts, where water is scarce, support far fewer living things than tropical rain forests, where water is plentiful. A drought is a long period of time without rain. Droughts can occur in ecosystems that usually have plenty of water. When a drought occurs, the number of organisms in the ecosystem may decline due to lack of water. The types of living things found in the ecosystem may also change, as living things that need less water move into the area.

Soil composition, another abiotic factor, is determined by several factors. Decayed organic material, called humus, and minerals are components of soil that support plant growth. The pH of soil is a measurement of how acidic or alkaline a particular soil is. Together, humus content, minerals, and pH affect the soil composition of an ecosystem. Soil composition is one factor that determines the number and kinds of plants found in an ecosystem.

Biology/Life Sciences Standards: Ecology

Biotic Factors

Abiotic Factors

Figure 3–1 Components of an ecosystem Ecosystems are influenced both by abiotic factors and biotic factors.

Biotic Factors The living factors that shape ecosystems are called biotic factors. In combination with abiotic factors, biotic factors influence the organisms living in an ecosystem. For example, the number and kinds of plants in an ecosystem determine the number and kinds of animals that can survive in that ecosystem. In the Figure 3–1, the animals pictured on the left depend on the plants in the middle picture. The plants depend on the abiotic factors, such as soil and water, shown in the picture on the right.

Review Questions

1

What ecological term includes everything represented in the illustration?

A   ecosystem

B   abiotic factor

C   humus

D   biotic factor

2   What are the major abiotic factors that determine the distribution and types of plant communities?

A   temperature, sunlight, water, soil

B   humidity, location, humans, animals

C   soil type, soil bacteria, soil moisture

D   insects, carbon dioxide, nitrogen

Biology/Life Sciences Standards: Ecology

3 **What are the living factors that shape ecosystems called?**

A organisms

B abiotic factors

C nonliving factors

D biotic factors

4 **Which is *most directly* impacted by the number of plants in an ecosystem?**

A the air temperature in the ecosystem

B the availability of water in the ecosystem

C the climate of the ecosystem

D the number of animals in the ecosystem

Biology/Life Sciences Standards: Ecology

BI 6.a. *Students know* biodiversity is the sum total of different kinds of organisms and is affected by alterations of habitats.

Biodiversity is a measure of the variety of all living things. Ecosystems with a great variety of living things have more biodiversity than ecosystems with fewer kinds of living things. Biodiversity is an important natural resource that can be impacted by many factors.

The Positive Impact of Biodiversity Ecosystems with a high level of biodiversity have many kinds, or species, of living things. These ecosystems are more stable than those with less biodiversity. In a diverse ecosystem, a pest or disease that harms a particular population of living things will have a limited impact. Compare that to the impact a disease or pest could have on a less diverse ecosystem, like the one shown in Figure 3–2. This corn field has very few types of living things. A disease or pest that affects corn plants could destroy the entire ecosystem.

Figure 3–2 Reduced biodiversity This ecosystem has been changed. It now contains only a few species of living things.

Factors That Affect Biodiversity When an ecosystem is changed in any way, the biodiversity of the ecosystem can be diminished. The corn field in Figure 3–2 is an example of how humans negatively impact biodiversity. This corn field was probably once a grassland or forest that supported many different species of living things. Humans have altered this ecosystem; it now supports very few species. Habitat destruction occurs whenever humans alter an area by cutting down forests, destroying grasslands, building homes and roads, or otherwise changing an area that supports populations of living things.

Biology/Life Sciences Standards: Ecology

Human activity can introduce new species into ecosystems. Usually these new species, called invasive or exotic species, have no predators in their new ecosystems. The invasive species can drive out the original species in an area by using up the food supply, acting as predators, or crowding the living spaces in an ecosystem. Invasive species have a negative impact on biodiversity.

Pollution threatens biodiversity in several ways. Pollution in the air, water, and soil can directly harm living things. Some kinds of air pollution also contribute to climate change. The gradual increase in Earth's temperatures, called global warming, may result in altered ecosystems and reduced biodiversity.

Biodiversity is also impacted by natural events. Fires and floods can reduce the biodiversity in an area. An ecosystem changed by a fire or flood may take many years to return to its previous level of biodiversity.

Review Questions

5 Biodiversity is best defined as

A   the number of plants in an area.

B   the total amount of land in an ecosystem.

C   the overall climate in an ecosystem.

D   the variety of the living things in an area.

6 A forest community is made up of thousands of species of organisms and can exist practically unchanged for hundreds of years. This stability is due to the

A   diversity of organisms present.

B   abundance of insects that feed on the plants.

C   changes in the climate of the area.

D   lack of decomposers in the area.

7 Single-crop farming is an example of how humans

A   make an ecosystem more stable.

B   increase biodiversity.

C   reduce biodiversity.

D   change the climate.

8 Introducing new species into an ecosystem, destroying habitats, and polluting the air are all ways in which humans

A   increase natural resources.

B   reduce biodiversity.

C   reduce damage to farmland.

D   limit pests and diseases.

Biology/Life Sciences Standards: Ecology

BI 6.b. *Students know* how to analyze changes in an ecosystem resulting from changes in climate, human activity, introduction of nonnative species, or changes in population size.

Ecosystems can change for many reasons. Some of these changes occur as the result of natural events. Other changes are caused by human activity. Many of the changes that happen in ecosystems occur in predictable ways.

Cycles and Patterns in Ecosystems Many of the abiotic factors in an ecosystem change in seasonal cycles. Temperature, sunlight, and availability of water all vary in predictable ways based on the seasons. For example, most ecosystems are warmest in the summer and coolest in the winter. Many ecosystems have more rain in the spring than they do in the summer. In many ecosystems, the seasonal changes in abiotic factors trigger changes in living things.

Figure 3–3 shows how the size of a rabbit population follows a regular pattern of change associated with the seasons. Notice that the size of the population is smallest in the winter, when the temperature is lowest and food is scarce. The population size increases as the temperature and availability of food increases in the spring. This information can be used to make predictions about the size of the rabbit population at a future time.

Other changes also occur in seasonal cycles. Migration, the periodic movement and return of animals from one place to another, is usually triggered by seasonal changes in ecosystems. Migrations occur when animals leave an ecosystem to avoid cold temperatures or scare food resources. Dormancy, a slowing of an organism's growth and activity, occurs in both plants and animals, and is usually triggered by seasonal changes in an ecosystem.

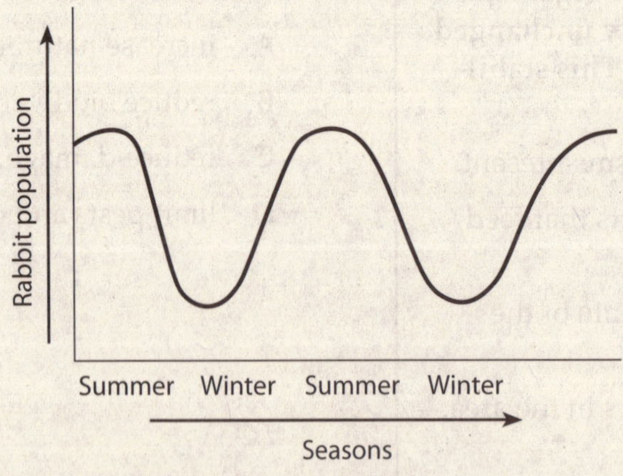

Figure 3–3 Seasonal changes in a population The graph shows a regular pattern of seasonal changes in a rabbit population.

Biology/Life Sciences Standards: Ecology

Other Changes in Ecosystems Some changes in ecosystems, such as forest fires and volcanic eruptions, are not based on natural cycles. The changes caused by these disturbances can be measured and analyzed, but may be difficult to predict. Other changes, such as pollution and habitat destruction, are caused by human activity. Changes in the numbers and types of living things in an ecosystem occur in response to both natural disturbances and human activity.

Succession The series of predictable changes that occurs in a community over time is called ecological succession. Sometimes succession occurs after an abrupt disturbance, such as a volcanic eruption or fire. Succession can also result from slow changes in the physical environment of an ecosystem. Succession that begins in an area with no soil is called primary succession. For example, if a volcanic eruption formed a new island, primary succession would occur.

When primary succession begins, the first species to populate the area, called pioneer species, are able to live without soil. Lichens are a common pioneer species. Lichens, which are combinations of a fungus and a photosynthetic organism, break down rocks, slowly forming new soil. Mosses and grasses are commonly the next species to grow in the ecosystem. After time, conditions are suitable for trees and shrubs to grow. The gradual changes in the plant community cause gradual changes in the populations of animals and other living things in the ecosystem.

Secondary succession is the series of changes that occurs after a disturbance destroys a community without destroying the soil. A forest fire is an example of a change that would be followed by secondary succession. In secondary succession, the ecosystem is gradually restored to its original condition.

How Scientists Study Change Longitudinal analysis is the process of measuring and studying change over a long period of time. Changes in abiotic factors, such as climate, weather, soil composition, pollution, and availability of water, can be measured and studied. Scientists also study changes in the biotic factors in ecosystems, such as the changes in the rabbit population shown in Figure 3–3. The data can be used to draw conclusions about the causes of change and to make predictions about future changes.

Biology/Life Sciences Standards: Ecology

Review Questions

9 What series of predictable changes would occur after a glacier melts, exposing a large area of bare rock?

A primary succession

B seasonal cycles

C secondary succession

D longitudinal analysis

10 What kinds of organisms are found in an area just beginning primary succession?

A those that do not need soil

B those that need very warm temperatures

C those that require no water

D those that do not need any sunlight

Use the graphs to answer Questions 11 and 12.

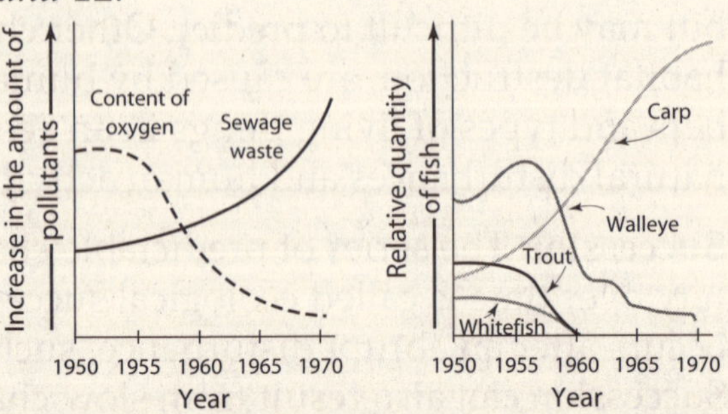

11 What type of change can be studied using the graphs?

A seasonal cycles in an ecosystem

B the impact of human activity on an ecosystem

C a predicable pattern of change based on climate

D how a new species changes an ecosystem

12 Why could the study shown in the graphs correctly be called a longitudinal analysis?

A It includes living and nonliving parts of an ecosystem.

B It includes data from an extended period of time.

C It shows changes that happen in cycles and patterns.

D It gives information about a lake ecosystem.

Biology/Life Sciences Standards: Ecology

BI 6.c. *Students know* how fluctuations in population size in an ecosystem are determined by the relative rates of birth, immigration, emigration, and death.

A population is a group of living things of the same species that live in the same area. To determine if a population's size is increasing, decreasing, or stable, you compare the number of individuals entering the population to the number of individuals leaving the population.

Births and Deaths Births increase the size of a population. The birthrate is a measure of the number of births in a population during a period of time. A population's birthrate can be affected by environmental conditions, such as temperature. Favorable environmental conditions can increase the birthrate; unfavorable conditions can decrease the birthrate. The birthrate is also affected by the availability of resources such as food. If a population has plenty of food, the birthrate typically increases. A lack of food usually causes the birthrate to decrease.

Deaths decrease the size of a population. The death rate is a measure of the number of deaths in a population during a period of time. Populations can experience an increase in death rate as the result of unfavorable environmental conditions, such as drought or pollution, or a lack of resources, such food and water.

Immigration and Emigration Immigration is the movement of individuals into an area. Immigration causes population size to increase. Immigration typically happens in areas where resources such as food and water are plentiful. Immigration is also caused by individuals joining populations to find mates.

Emigration is the movement of individuals out of an area. Emigration causes population size to decrease. A shortage of food, space, water, or other resources in an area can trigger emigration. Emigration also occurs when young animals reach maturity and leave the population into which they were born.

Population Size The equation shown below can be used to determine the overall change in a population's size when all of the births, deaths, immigrations, and emigrations are considered. A population grows if more individuals enter the population (due to birth or immigration) than leave the population (due to death or emigration) in any time period. Conversely, a population's size will decrease if more individuals leave (due to death or emigration) than enter (due to birth or immigration). A population will remain stable in size if the number of individuals entering the population is equal to the numbers that leave.

Change in Population Size = (Births + Immigrations) – (Deaths + Emigrations)

Biology/Life Sciences Standards: Ecology

Review Questions

13 Which of the following could cause a population to decrease in size?

A an increasing birth rate

B a decreasing death rate

C an increase in emigration

D an increase in immigration

14 Which of the following describes an animal emigrating from a population?

A A young animal leaving an area to establish its own territory.

B A drought killing most of the plants in an area.

C A rapid increase in birth rate when resources are plentiful.

D An organism joining a population to search for a mate.

Use the graph to answer Questions 15 and 16.

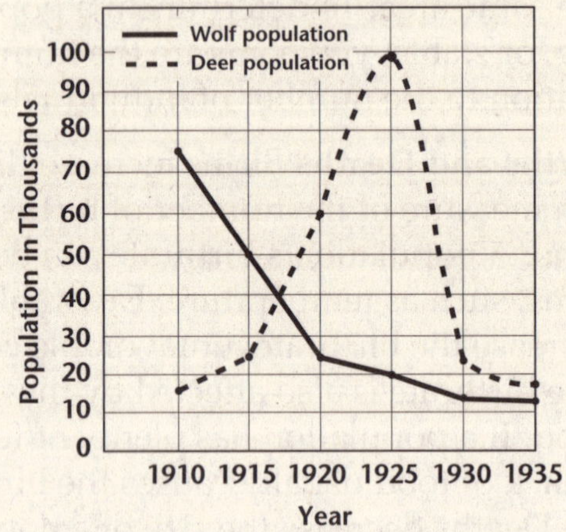

15 During which time period did the number of births and immigrations into the wolf population *most closely* match the number of emigrations and deaths?

A 1910–1915

B 1915–1920

C 1925–1930

D 1930–1935

16 In which population did the total number of births and immigrations exceed the total number of deaths and emigrations?

A the deer population from 1910–1925

B the wolf population from 1910–1920

C the deer population from 1925–1930

D the wolf population from 1920–1930

Biology/Life Sciences Standards: Ecology

BI 6.d. *Students know* how water, carbon, and nitrogen cycle between abiotic resources and organic matter in the ecosystem and how oxygen cycles through photosynthesis and respiration.

Living things need water, carbon, nitrogen, and oxygen to survive. These materials and many other forms of matter cycle between living things and the environment. As these substances move between living things and the environment, they are chemically combined and recombined. The cycles of matter are often called biogeochemical cycles, because they involve biological processes, geological processes, and chemical processes.

Water Cycle Water molecules move in a cycle that includes Earth's bodies of water, Earth's atmosphere, and living things. The sun provides the energy that drives the water cycle. Evaporation is the process by which water changes from a liquid to water vapor, an atmospheric gas. Figure 3–4 shows evaporation from the ocean. Evaporation does not occur only from oceans—any liquid water on Earth's surface can evaporate and become atmospheric gas.

When water vapor in the atmosphere reaches a certain altitude, it cools and condenses, and then returns to Earth in the form of precipitation. Rain is the form of precipitations shown in Figure 3–4; snow, sleet, and hail are also forms of precipitation. If precipitation falls on land, some of the water seeps into the ground and some flows into nearby bodies of water.

Water also moves through living things. Plants take in water through their roots and release water in the process of transpiration, which is evaporation from leaves. Figure 3–4 shows root uptake of liquid water and transpiration of water vapor.

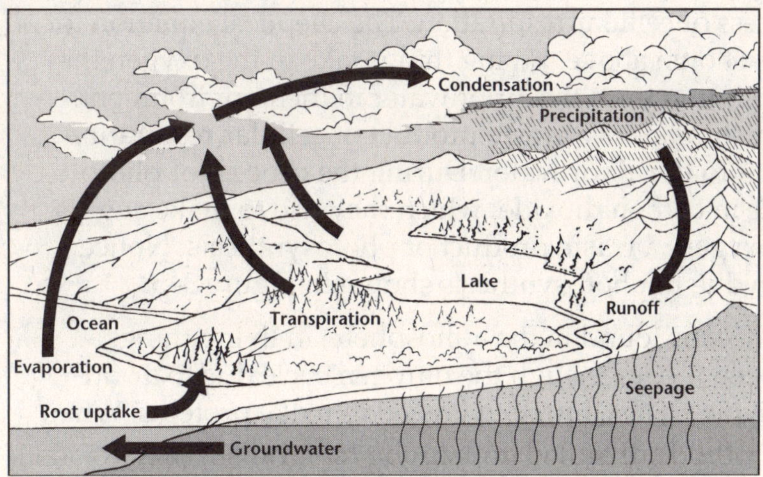

Figure 3–4 The water cycle Water moves continuously through a cycle from Earth's surface to the atmosphere and back.

Biology/Life Sciences Standards: Ecology

Carbon Cycle Carbon is found in all living organisms, in the atmosphere, and in some types of rocks. Several different processes move carbon through its cycle. Photosynthesis and cellular respiration move carbon between living things and the atmosphere. The equations below give an overview of how carbon moves due to photosynthesis and cellular respiration. During photosynthesis, plants take in carbon from the atmosphere in the form of carbon dioxide. The carbon is chemically recombined using energy from sunlight to form sugars. These sugar molecules are broken down in the process of cellular respiration. The energy in the chemical bonds is released, and the carbon again forms carbon dioxide and is released into the atmosphere. Notice the arrows representing the movement of carbon due to photosynthesis and respiration in Figure 3–5.

Photosynthesis

$$6CO_2 + 6H_2O \xrightarrow{\text{light}} C_6H_{12}O_6 + 6O_2$$

Cellular Respiration

$$6O_2 + C_6H_{12}O_6 \longrightarrow 6CO_2 + 6H_2O + \text{Energy}$$

The decomposition of organic matter by living organisms releases carbon dioxide into the atmosphere. Over vast periods of time and under great pressure, some organic matter may be converted into coal and petroleum, or fossil fuels. The formation of fossil fuels stores carbon underground. When fossil fuels are burned, carbon dioxide is released into the atmosphere. Erosion and volcanic activity also release carbon dioxide from Earth to the atmosphere and oceans.

Oxygen Cycle Plants and animals need oxygen to release the energy in food during the process of cellular respiration. The chemical equation for cellular respiration is shown above. Living things take in the oxygen they need for cellular respiration from the air or water in their environment.

Notice that carbon dioxide is a waste product of cellular respiration that is released back into the air or water. During the process of photosynthesis, plants take in carbon dioxide, which they use to make sugars. Plants then release oxygen, a waste product of photosynthesis. Notice the release of oxygen due to photosynthesis shown in Figure 3–5.

Nitrogen Cycle Nitrogen is found in the atmosphere, in living things, and in the soil. Nitrogen moves though the nitrogen cycle due to a variety of processes. In living things, nitrogen is used to make proteins. When a living thing dies, the nitrogen in its body is released by decomposers. Animal wastes also contain nitrogen, which is released during decomposition. Figure 3–5 shows the role of decomposers in the nitrogen cycle.

Biology/Life Sciences Standards: Ecology

Certain bacteria found in the soil convert nitrogen gas to a form that can be used by plants during the process of nitrogen fixation. Other soil bacteria convert nitrates in the soil to nitrogen gas in a process called denitrification.

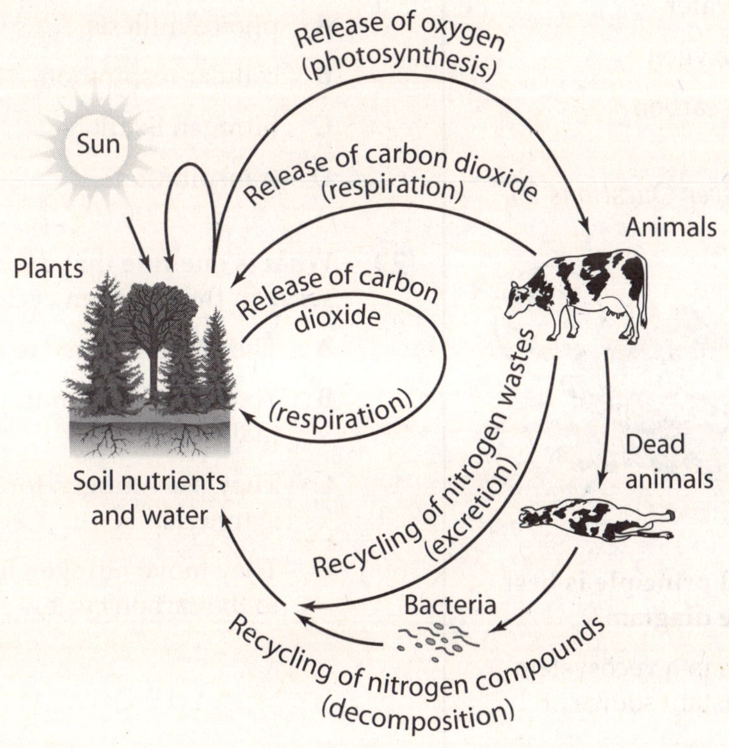

Figure 3–5 Biogeochemical cycles This figure shows some of the processes in the carbon, nitrogen, and oxygen cycles.

Review Questions

17 **Which process in the water cycle moves water from the atmosphere to Earth's surface?**

  A precipitation

  B transpiration

  C fixation

  D evaporation

18 **What is the source of the energy that moves water through the water cycle?**

  A the sun

  B photosynthesis

  C fossil fuel

  D transpiration

Name _______________________________   Class _______________________   Date ___________

Biology/Life Sciences Standards: Ecology

19 Photosynthesis and respiration are important processes in which two cycles of matter?

- A water and nitrogen
- B energy and water
- C carbon and oxygen
- D nitrogen and carbon

Use the diagram to answer Questions 20 and 21.

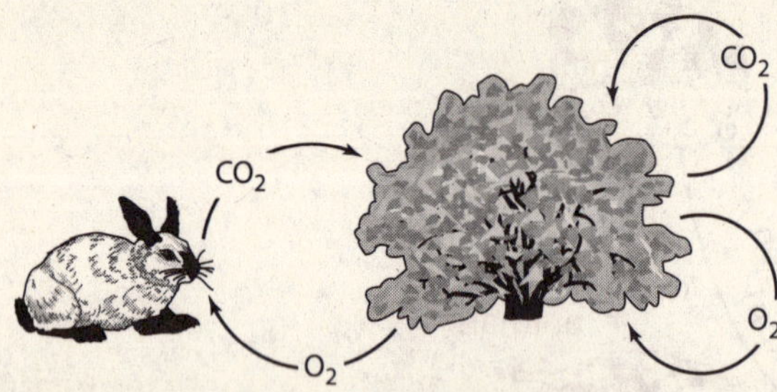

20 Which ecological principle is best illustrated by the diagram?

- A Living things in an ecosystem require a constant source of energy.
- B Living things constantly create new carbon and oxygen.
- C In an ecosystem, the number of producers and consumers is equal.
- D In an ecosystem, material is cycled among the organisms and the environment.

21 The diagram shows both plants and animals releasing carbon dioxide into the atmosphere. This carbon dioxide is the byproduct of what process?

- A photosynthesis
- B cellular respiration
- C nitrogen fixation
- D transpiration

22 What is one role that decomposers serve in the nitrogen cycle?

- A They add nitrogen to animals.
- B They release the nitrogen in animal wastes.
- C They use nitrogen for photosynthesis.
- D They move nitrogen from rocks to the carbon cycle.

Biology/Life Sciences Standards: Ecology

6 5.c. *Students know* populations of organisms can be categorized by the functions they serve in an ecosystem.

BI 6.e. *Students know* a vital part of an ecosystem is the stability of its producers and decomposers.

Every living thing on Earth needs energy to survive. Movement, growth and repair, and all other life processes require energy. One way to describe and categorize organisms is by the way they obtain energy. A stable ecosystem includes organisms that obtain energy in a variety of ways.

Producers Green plants, such as grasses and trees, and photosynthetic microorganisms, such as blue-green algae, are called producers. These organisms carry out photosynthesis, a process that uses light energy from the sun to produce chemical energy. The chemical equation for photosynthesis is shown here. The chemical energy produced during photosynthesis is stored in the chemical bonds of the $C_6H_{12}O_6$ (sugar) molecules produced.

$$6CO_2 + 6H_2O \xrightarrow{\text{light}} C_6H_{12}O_6 + 6O_2$$

Producers, which are also called autotrophs, serve as a source of food for other living things. When a producer is eaten, some of chemical energy stored in the producer's body is transferred to the organism that eats it. All ecosystems depend on producers for a food supply. A stable ecosystem requires stable populations of producers.

Consumers Organisms that rely on other organisms for their energy and food supply are called consumers. Consumers are also called heterotrophs. Examples of consumers include animals, fungi, and many types of microorganisms. Consumers eat other living things to get the energy they need.

Consumers are divided into several different categories. Some consumers, called herbivores, get energy by eating only plants and other producers. Other consumers, called carnivores, eat animals. Consumers called omnivores eat both plants and animals.

Animals are also categorized by how they get food. Predators are animals like owls and cougars that hunt, capture, and eat other animals. Scavengers, such as California condors, find and eat dead animals. Some animals are both predators and scavengers, eating whatever animals they find, either living or dead.

Biology/Life Sciences Standards: Ecology

Decomposers Organisms that get energy by breaking down organic matter, such as dead organisms and wastes, are called decomposers. Fungi and many types of microorganisms are decomposers. All ecosystems need decomposers to recycle organic material. A stable ecosystem requires stable populations of decomposers.

Energy Flow Energy moves from the sun to producers and then to consumers and decomposers. A series of steps in which organisms transfer energy by eating and being eaten is called a food chain. Figure 3–6 shows a typical food chain. A primary consumer, such as the insect in the figure, gets energy by eating producers. The snake is a secondary consumer—an organism that eats primary consumers. Tertiary consumers, such as the owl, eat secondary consumers. The arrows in the figure show the flow of energy from one living thing to another.

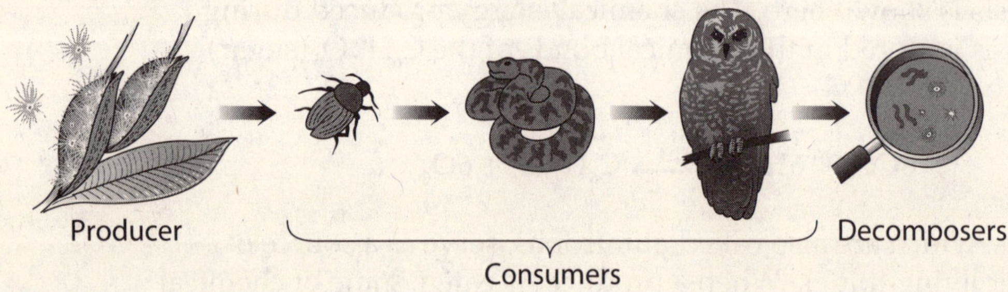

Figure 3–6 Food chain A food chain includes producers, consumers, and decomposers.

Review Questions

23 For a food supply, all ecosystems depend on

A decomposers.

B consumers.

C food chains.

D producers.

24 Which sequence illustrates a generalized food chain in a natural community?

A autotroph → herbivore → carnivore

B autotroph → herbivore → autotroph

C heterotroph → herbivore → carnivore

D consumer → autotroph → carnivore

Biology/Life Sciences Standards: Ecology

Use the diagram to answer Questions 25 and 26.

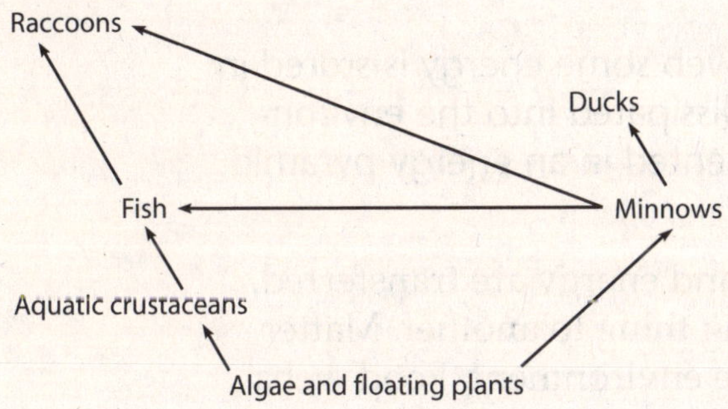

25 **Which group of organisms is *not* represented in the food web diagram?**

A   consumers

B   carnivores

C   producers

D   decomposers

26 **Which organisms in the diagram are tertiary consumers?**

A   fish

B   raccoons

C   ducks

D   aquatic crustaceans

Biology/Life Sciences Standards: Ecology

6 5.b. *Students know* matter is transferred over time from one organism to others in the food web and between organisms and the physical environment.

BI 6.f. *Students know* at each link in a food web some energy is stored in newly made structures but much energy is dissipated into the environment as heat. This dissipation may be represented in an energy pyramid.

When one living thing eats another, matter and energy are transferred. Energy flows in one direction from one living thing to another. Matter moves in cycles though living things and the environment. Food webs are models used to show how matter and energy move between living things. Energy pyramids are models used to show the amount of energy available to different living things in an ecosystem.

Food Webs A food web is a diagram that shows how energy and matter move from one living thing to another. Arrows in a food web show that matter and energy transfer from plants, which are producers, to herbivores, which are first-level consumers. Energy and matter move from the herbivores to carnivores, which are called secondary consumers. Tertiary consumers eat the secondary consumers. Each step in a food web is called a tropic level.

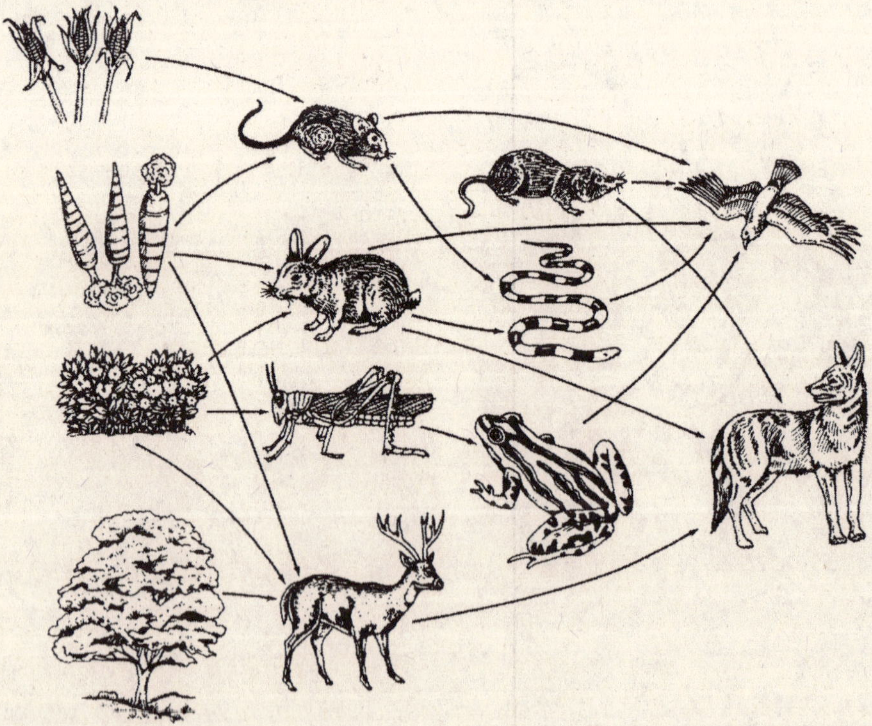

Figure 3–7 Food web This diagram shows how matter and energy move between living things.

Biology/Life Sciences Standards: Ecology

The food web shown in Figure 3–7 shows how matter and energy move between living things that are large enough to see without a microscope. Matter and energy move between microscopic organisms as well. Photosynthetic bacteria and protists are producers in many food webs. These producers are eaten by protozoans, which are heterotrophic protists. In turn, the protozoans are eaten by other small organisms.

Energy Flow The path of energy through an ecosystem is shown in the food web in Figure 3–7. At each tropic level of the food web, much of the energy contained in living things is used for life processes, such as growth and repair. Every living thing constantly releases energy back into the environment in the form of body heat. So, in any food web, the greatest amount of energy is contained in the producers. Some of the energy in the producers is passed to the herbivores. A smaller portion of the energy in the herbivores is passed to the secondary consumers. An even smaller portion of the energy in the secondary consumers is passed on to the tertiary consumers.

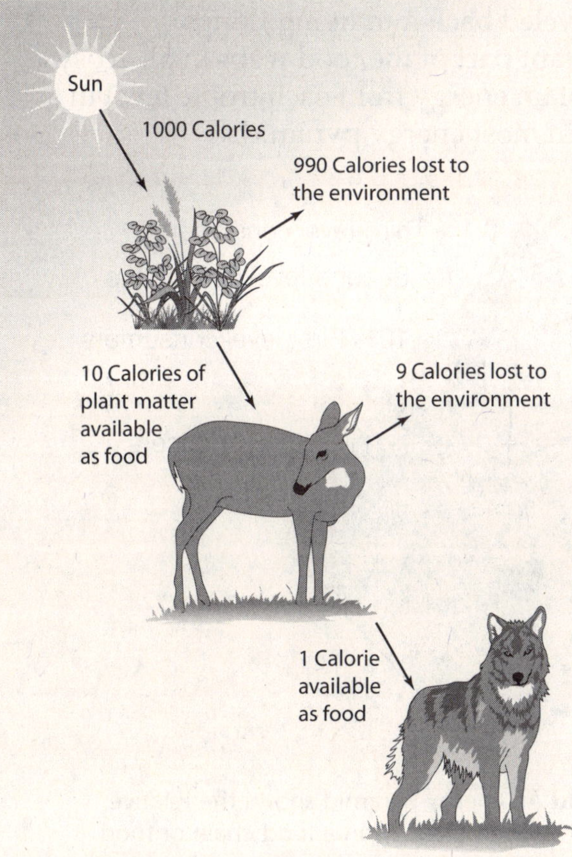

Figure 3–8 Energy flow through an ecosystem As energy is transferred from one organism to another, much of it is lost to the environment.

Biology/Life Sciences Standards: Ecology

Figure 3–8 shows energy transfer in a food chain. Notice that only 10 percent of the energy available within one tropic level is transferred to organisms at the next tropic level. This explains why food chains contain a limited number of living things because at higher tropic levels, less energy is available.

Energy Pyramids The relative amount of energy available at each tropic level in a food chain or food web can be modeled using an energy pyramid, like the one shown in Figure 3–9. Figure 3–9 shows the input of light energy into a food web. Producers use light energy to produce chemical energy, which passes through the food web from one tropic level to the next. Each level of the pyramid represents a higher tropic level in the food web.

Notice the word *HEAT* along the side of the pyramid. This represents the energy that is released into the environment at each tropic level. Although this energy is not destroyed, it is not available to living things at the next tropic level. Unlike matter, which is continually cycled through living things and the environment, energy that is released into the environment cannot be recycled back into living things.

Decomposers are an important part of the food webs in all ecosystems. Because decomposers obtain energy from each tropic level in a food web, they are not shown in most energy pyramids.

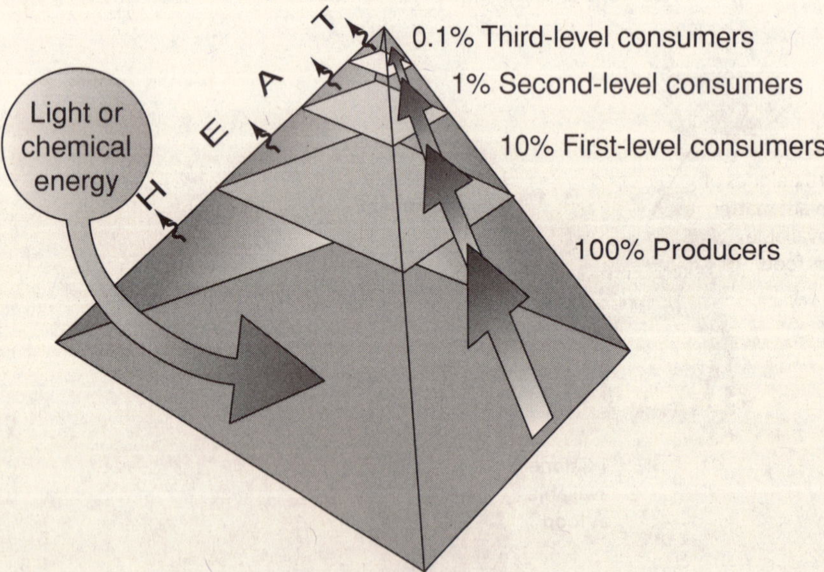

Figure 3–9 Energy pyramid An energy pyramid shows the relative amount of energy available at each tropic level in a food chain or food web.

Biology/Life Sciences Standards: Ecology

Cycles of Matter Recall that matter also moves between organisms and the environment. For example, the process of photosynthesis uses energy from sunlight to chemically recombine carbon dioxide and water to make sugars that living things use for food. When plants or animals carry out cellular respiration, which releases the energy in food, carbon dioxide is released back into the atmosphere. The feeding relationships among organisms are just one part of the cycles of matter in ecosystems.

Review Questions

27 **How are matter and energy transferred from producers to consumers?**

   A through the atmosphere

   B in the water cycle

   C through cellular respiration

   D when one living thing eats another

28 **A hawk that eats a rabbit obtains less energy from the rabbit than the rabbit obtained from the plants it ate. This is because the rabbit**

   A passed most of the energy to its offspring.

   B converted energy from sunlight to chemical energy.

   C used energy for its own life processes.

   D stored the energy in its fat.

Use the diagram to answer Questions 29 and 30.

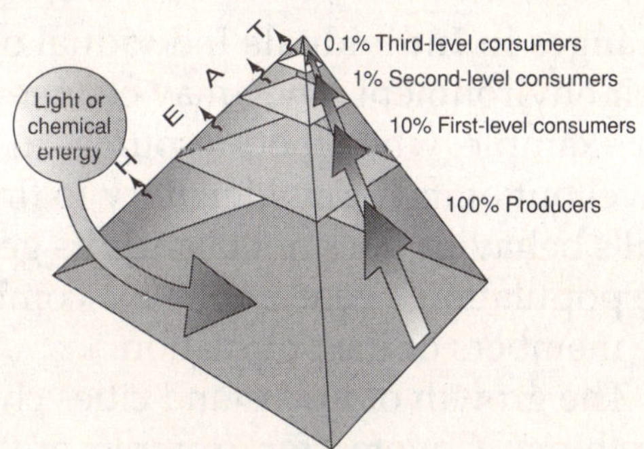

29 **What does the model represent?**

   A how matter cycles in an ecosystem

   B the relative amounts of energy available in an ecosystem

   C how energy is recycled and reused in ecosystems

   D the matter lost at each tropic level

30 **If a fourth-level consumer joined the food web represented by this energy pyramid, what percent of the original energy would be available to that consumer?**

   A 0.01%

   B 0.1%

   C 1.0%

   D 10%

Biology/Life Sciences Standards: Ecology

***BI 6.g.** *Students know* how to distinguish between the accommodation of an individual organism to its environment and the gradual adaptation of a lineage of organisms through genetic change.

Individual organisms may be able to react to, or accommodate, changes in their environment, but they cannot change their genetic make-up to do so. When an environment changes, different individuals within a population may be better suited to the changed environment than others. These individuals will be more likely to reproduce than others. This can lead to a gradual change in the genetic make-up of the population. It is often difficult to distinguish between individual accommodations to environmental change and gradual adaptations within a population.

Changes in Individuals Individual organisms can react to changes in their environment. They may change their behaviors in order to survive. For example, when food resources in an area are scarce, an animal might travel out of its normal territory to find food. This change in the animal's behavior does not change its genetic make-up. Nor does it change the population's gene pool—the combined genetic information of all of the members of the population.

The growth of towns and cities changes the ecosystems of many living things. Coyotes, for example, are a species that have been impacted by habitat loss due to human activity. However, coyotes have successfully learned to find food in areas occupied by humans. Instead of hunting for small prey, many coyotes have learned to find food in trash cans. Despite losing much of their habitat to human development, coyotes are not endangered.

Individuals of other species are far less successful in finding ways to accommodate changes in their environment. The California condor, an endangered species, is one example. Human development has made it difficult for California condors to find the carrion (dead animals) they eat. Unlike coyotes, which have developed an alternate way of finding food, the California condor has become endangered.

Biology/Life Sciences Standards: Ecology

Genetic Change in Populations In all populations some individuals are better able to survive. These individuals are more likely to reproduce than are individuals that are not well suited to the environment. Recall that, during reproduction, genetic information is passed from parents to offspring. If the individuals that are best suited to the environment are more likely to reproduce, their genetic information is more likely to be represented in offspring. Over time, the genetic make-up of the population will change. The traits of the individuals that are better suited to the environment will increase in frequency in the population. In this way, a population of living things can gradually adapt to a long-term change in the environment.

Review Questions

31 An individual plant that grows around an obstacle to get the light it needs is an example of

   A a change in genetics.

   B a change in the genetic make-up of its population.

   C a nongenetic change to adapt to the environment.

   D a change in a species over several generations.

32 Which of the following is an example of an adaptation due to genetic change?

   A a change in the location of a bird's nest due to a forest fire

   B a change in the diet of an individual grasshopper due to a drought

   C a change in the migratory pattern of butterflies due to bad weather

   D a change in the color of a bird species' feathers over 20 generations

Biology/Life Sciences Standards: Ecology

Use the diagram to answer Questions 33 and 34.

First generation

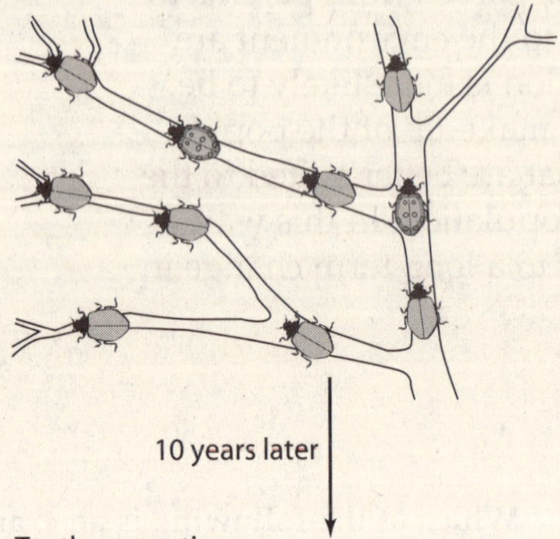

10 years later

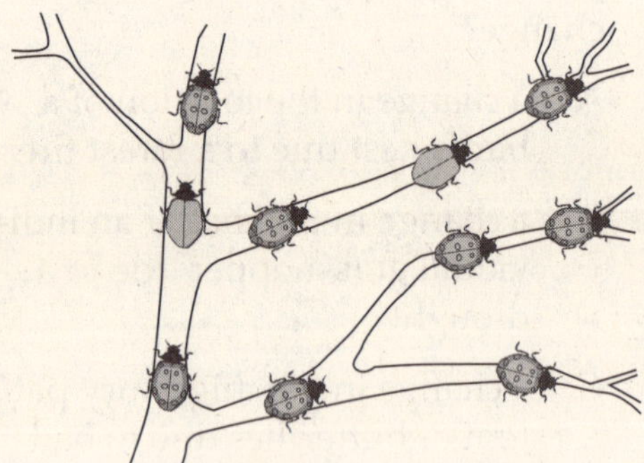

33 **What is the best explanation for the change shown in the picture?**

A Individual insects have made an accommodation to their environment.

B There has been a change in the genetic make-up of this population of insects.

C Some of these insects have changed their behavior over time.

D The genetic make-up of this population has remained the same for 10 generations.

34 **Which is the *most* logical conclusion you could draw when looking at the picture?**

A Spotted insects are more likely than plain insects to survive in this ecosystem.

B Spotted insects have the ability to change their appearance.

C Spotted insects are less likely than plain insects to survive in this ecosystem.

D Spotted insects are likely to become endangered in this ecosystem.

Biology/Life Sciences Standards: Evolution

7 3.b. *Students know* the reasoning used by Charles Darwin in reaching his conclusion that natural selection is the mechanism of evolution.

Charles Darwin was an English scientist who lived in the 1800s. He made a trip around the world observing living things. He also studied the works of other scientists. Darwin's own observations and the ideas of other scientists convinced him that organisms evolve, or change, over time. The same influences also helped Darwin develop a theory about what causes organisms to evolve. Darwin called this theory natural selection.

Darwin's Observations Darwin was impressed with the great variety of plants and animals he observed in many parts of the world. He was especially impressed with the diversity of species on the Galápagos Islands, which lie off the west coast of South America. (A species is a group of similar organisms that can breed and produce fertile offspring.) Darwin saw that there were different species of tortoises and birds on the different islands. He noticed that each species was suited for conditions on its particular island. For example, the islands had different food resources, and birds had different types of beaks that helped them eat the food on their island. Darwin wondered how the different types of beaks and other variations he observed had come about.

Other Influences on Darwin Darwin was influenced by the writings of other scientists, including Jean-Baptiste Lamarck, James Hutton, Charles Lyell, and Thomas Malthus. Darwin was also influenced by the work of plant and animal breeders.

- Jean-Baptiste Lamarck was a French scientist who studied variation in organisms in the early 1800s. He thought that organisms could gain or lose traits during their lifetime and that their offspring could inherit the changes. For example, Lamarck claimed that mice that had their tails cut off would produce offspring without tails. Lamarck's ideas about inheritance were flawed, but his idea that organisms could change over time was an important influence on Darwin.

- James Hutton and Charles Lyell were English geologists who studied Earth's surface in the 1800s. They suggested that Earth was very old and that its surface had changed slowly over a long period of time. These ideas helped Darwin realize that there had been enough time for gradual changes to produce the great variety of organisms he observed.

Biology/Life Sciences Standards: Evolution

- Thomas Malthus was an English economist who lived in the 1700s. He proposed that human populations had the potential to increase faster than the food and other resources they needed to survive. If populations increased too fast, it would lead to competition for scarce resources, and only some individuals would survive. Darwin thought Malthus's ideas applied to most species, not just humans. But he wondered what determined which individuals survived.

- Darwin knew that plant and animal breeders used naturally occurring variation to improve crops and livestock. For example, a racehorse breeder would let only the fastest horses mate and produce offspring. This is how champion racehorses are still bred today. The artificial selection of certain traits by breeders suggested to Darwin how traits might change naturally in wild populations.

Figure 4–1 Artificial selection This champion racehorse was bred for speed.

Natural Selection Darwin's observations and these other influences helped him develop his theory of natural selection. The theory explains how organisms change over time. According to the theory, individual organisms within a species struggle, or compete, for the resources they need to survive and to produce offspring. Individuals with traits best suited for the environment are most likely to survive and reproduce successfully. The traits that help them survive and reproduce are passed on to their offspring. This happens in each generation, causing the species' traits to change gradually over time. Natural selection results in the species as a whole becoming better suited to its environment.

Biology/Life Sciences Standards: Evolution

Review Questions

1 **What is evolution?**

A competition for resources between different species

B changes in traits of species over time

C survival of the fittest members of a population

D struggle for survival among individuals in a species

2 **Darwin's observations on the Galápagos Islands helped him to understand**

A how diversity in organisms is related to the environment.

B why organisms that live on islands have little variation.

C how plant and animal breeders improve livestock.

D why populations grow faster than the resources they depend on.

3 **What idea of Malthus influenced Darwin?**

A There is competition for resources within populations.

B Earth is very old and has changed gradually over time.

C Organisms can pass their traits to their offspring.

D Evolution occurs because of natural selection.

4 **How did knowledge of artificial selection influence Darwin?**

A It supported Lamarck's ideas about inheritance.

B It proved that evolution had occurred in the past.

C It provided evidence that there is a struggle for existence.

D It suggested how traits might change naturally in wild populations.

5 **According to Darwin, what is the process that causes evolution?**

A artificial selection

B inheritance of traits

C natural selection

D change over time

Biology/Life Sciences Standards: Evolution

BI 7.a. *Students know* why natural selection acts on the phenotype rather than the genotype of an organism.

Natural selection occurs when individuals that are better suited for their environment survive and reproduce more successfully than others in the same population. (A population is a group of individuals of the same species that live in the same area.) The traits of these individuals make them more fit and are likely to become more common in the population over time. Traits are controlled by genes, so natural selection also changes the genetic makeup of a population over time. However, natural selection acts on traits, not directly on the genes that control them.

Phenotype and Genotype An individual's traits make up that individual's phenotype. The phenotype depends on the genotype, or the genetic makeup of the individual. For a given trait, the genotype refers to the combination of genes an individual has inherited for that trait. For each gene, an individual inherits two copies of the gene, one copy from each parent.

Genes for most traits occur in two or more contrasting forms, called alleles, that produce different forms of the same trait. For example, a gene with two different alleles produces two different forms of earlobes in humans: attached earlobes and unattached earlobes. The two copies of a gene in an individual may be the same allele or different alleles. If a gene has two alleles (say, A and a), an individual may have one of three possible genotypes (AA, Aa, or aa).

Natural Selection and Dominance Because natural selection acts on traits, it is phenotypes rather than genotypes that are selected. This is an important distinction for traits controlled by dominant alleles. A dominant allele is an allele that is always expressed in the phenotype.

For the same example, assume A is dominant to a. Then, both AA and Aa genotypes will produce the dominant phenotype. Only the aa genotype will produce the recessive phenotype. If the dominant phenotype has greater fitness, then individuals with the AA or Aa genotype will be more fit than individuals with the aa genotype. Both the A allele and the a allele are likely to remain in the population, generation after generation, because of the fitness of the Aa genotype. This is true even if people with the aa genotype never reproduce and pass their a alleles to offspring.

Figure 4–2 shows an example of natural selection in lizards. Over many generaitons, natural selection favored the black phenotype, which became more frequent. If the allele for black color was dominant, many of the black lizards would also have an allele for white or gray color. These alleles would be preserved in the population in the black individuals and their offspring.

Biology/Life Sciences Standards: Evolution

Initial Population	Generation 10	Generation 20	Generation 30
80%	80%	70%	40%
10%	0%	0%	0%
10%	20%	30%	60%

Figure 4–2 Natural selection in a lizard population The initial lizard population had three phenotypes for color: white, gray, and black. Over time, black lizards became more frequent because they had greater fitness in their environment.

Review Questions

6 Natural selection acts directly on

   A phenotypes.

   B alleles.

   C genotypes.

   D genes.

7 Which genotypes produce the same phenotype if allele *A* is dominant?

   A *AA* and *aa*

   B *AA* and *Aa*

   C *Aa* and *aa*

   D all of the above

8

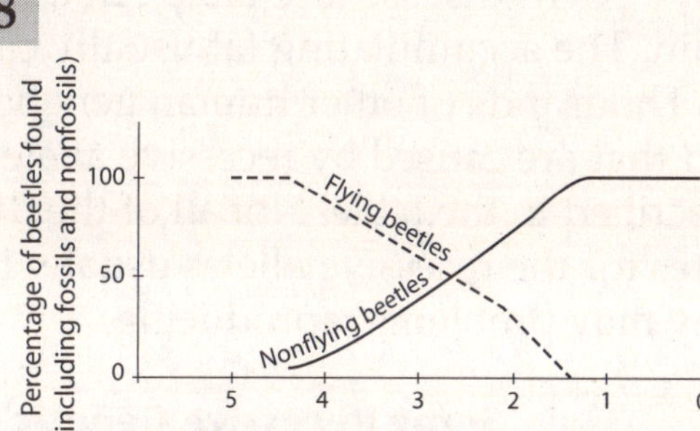

A study of beetles on an isolated island found that none of the beetles currently living on the island can fly. Fossils from the island show it once was populated by flying beetles. The graph shows how the beetles on the island changed. The changes in the graph are probably the result of

   A evolution of predators that ate the wings of beetles.

   B natural selection acting on phenotypes in the beetle population.

   C individuals losing their wings because they did not use them.

   D flying beetles preying on nonflying beetles.

Biology/Life Sciences Standards: Evolution

BI 7.b. *Students know* why alleles that are lethal in a homozygous individual may be carried in a heterozygote and thus maintained in a gene pool.

Alleles, or contrasting forms of the same gene, may be dominant or recessive. Dominant alleles are always expressed in the phenotype, even when just one dominant allele is present in the genotype. Recessive alleles are expressed in the phenotype only when two recessive alleles are present in the genotype. A genotype with two of the same allele is called a homozygote. A genotype with two different alleles is called a heterozygote. At the population level, all the alleles in all the individuals make up the population's gene pool.

Lethal Recessive Alleles Sometimes a mutation, or random change in genetic material, produces a new allele. If the allele causes a fatal disorder, it is said to be lethal. If the lethal allele is recessive, then the disorder occurs only in homozygotes for the recessive allele.

An example of a human disorder caused by a lethal recessive allele is Tay-Sachs disease (see table). In this disorder, fat accumulates in the brain. The accumulating fat usually causes death in early childhood.

Thousands of other human genetic disorders have been identified that are caused by recessive alleles. Some of these disorders are described in the table. Not all of the disorders are lethal, but homozygotes for the recessive alleles usually have reduced fitness. For example, they may problems reproducing.

Some Recessive Genetic Disorders in Humans

Disorder	Major Symptoms
Tay-Sachs disease	Accumulation of fat in brain cells; mental retardation, blindness
Albinism	Lack of pigment in skin, hair, and eyes
Cystic fibrosis	Excess mucus in lungs, digestive tract, and liver; increased susceptibility to infections
Phenylketonuria (PKU)	Accumulation of phenylalanine (an amino acid) in tissues; lack of normal skin pigment; mental retardation
Galactosemia	Accumulation of galactose (a sugar) in tissues; mental retardation; eye and liver damage

Biology/Life Sciences Standards: Evolution

Heterozygote Carriers Homozygotes for lethal recessive alleles usually do not live long enough to reproduce. Therefore, their recessive alleles are removed from the population's gene pool when they die. So how does a lethal recessive allele remain in a population's gene pool? Heterozygotes are the answer.

Because the normal allele is dominant, heterozygotes do not have the disorder. Their one normal allele allows them to survive and reproduce as successfully as individuals with two normal alleles. However, they are carriers of the lethal recessive allele. They are likely to pass the allele to at least some of their offspring. In this way, lethal recessive alleles can remain in a population's gene pool, generation after generation.

Review Questions

9 **An individual who has one allele for Tay-Sachs disease**

    A will have the disease.

    B will be unable to reproduce.

    C will die in early childhood.

    D may pass the allele to his or her offspring.

10 **How is a lethal recessive allele maintained in a gene pool?**

    A Heterozygotes who carry the allele pass it to their offspring.

    B The allele is acted upon by natural selection.

    C Individuals with two recessive alleles pass both of them to their offspring.

    D Natural selection always favors individuals who have two recessive alleles.

Biology/Life Sciences Standards: Evolution

BI 7.c. *Students know* new mutations are constantly being generated in a gene pool.

Mutations are changes in the genetic material. They occur when cells make mistakes copying their own DNA, the molecule that carries genetic information. If mutations occur in reproductive cells (gametes), they may be passed to offspring and become part of the population's gene pool. Mutations are important in evolution as a source of genetic variation.

Types of Mutations Mutations can involve changes in a single gene or an entire chromosome. Mutations that change a single gene are called gene mutations. DNA contains sequences of smaller molecules called bases, which are represented by the letters A, T, C, and G. Gene mutations may involve changes in just one or a few bases in a DNA molecule. Figure 4–3 shows how the base sequence in a strand of DNA can be changed by different types of gene mutations.

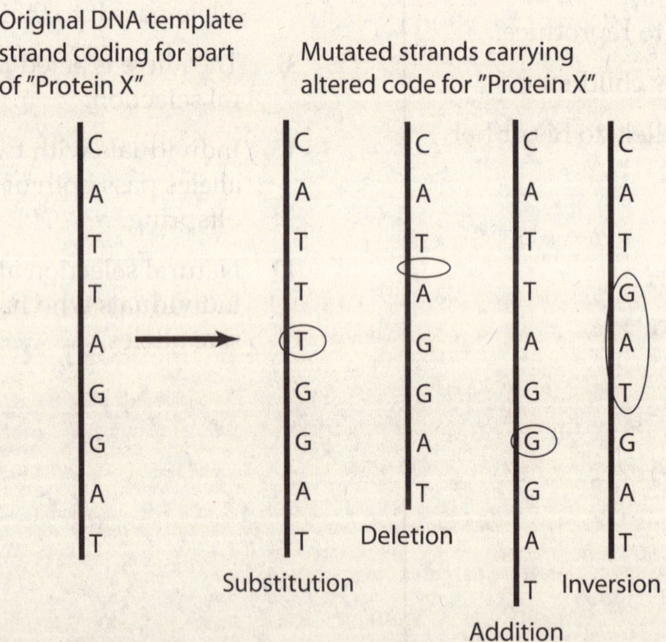

Figure 4–3 Types of gene mutations The DNA strand on the left is part of an original DNA molecule that codes for a hypothetical protein, "Protein X." By comparing the original strand with each of the mutated strands, you can see how the four different types of mutations change DNA.

Mutations that change entire chromosomes are called chromosomal mutations. Chromosomal mutations involve changes in the number or structure of chromosomes. For example, part of a chromosome may break off and reattach to a different chromosome.

Biology/Life Sciences Standards: Evolution

Significance of Mutations Mutations are random events that are constantly occurring. It is estimated that the average person carries at least five new mutations. Mutations are one of the main sources of genetic variation in populations. Without genetic variation, natural selection could not work to improve a population's fitness over time.

If a mutant allele improves fitness, natural selection will increase its frequency. Individuals with the mutant allele will survive and reproduce more successfully than other individuals. As a result, the mutant allele—and the trait it produces—will become more common in the population.

If a mutant allele reduces fitness, natural selection will decrease its frequency. This will happen more quickly if the mutant allele is dominant. A dominant allele produces its trait even in individuals with just one of the alleles. Individuals with the mutant allele will not survive and reproduce as successfully as other individuals, so the mutant allele and its trait will become less common in the population.

Review Questions

11 **Which statement is true about mutations?**

   A Mutations may involve changes in just one base in DNA.

   B Mutations always change entire chromosomes.

   C Mutations occur very rarely.

   D Mutations are caused by natural selection.

12 **What role do mutations play in evolution?**

   A Mutations are one of the main sources of genetic variation in a population.

   B Mutations always produce dominant traits that make populations more fit.

   C Mutations cannot be passed on, so they do not affect a population's gene pool.

   D Mutations are always removed from a gene pool by natural selection.

Biology/Life Sciences Standards: Evolution

7 3.a. *Students know* both genetic variation and environmental factors are causes of evolution and diversity of organisms.

BI 7.d. *Students know* variation within a species increases the likelihood that at least some members of a species will survive under changed environmental conditions.

There is great variation in traits among members of most species. Some of the variation in traits is due to genetic differences among individuals. Some of the variation is due to environmental differences. Variation is needed for natural selection to act on a species and improve its fitness. Variation is also needed for a species to adapt to environmental changes.

Variation Within a Species An example of variation within a butterfly species is shown in Figure 4–4. The trait shown in the figure is controlled by genes. In sexually reproducing organisms—including humans as well as butterflies—the shuffling of genes and chromosomes during the production of gametes (sperm and eggs) results in tremendous genetic variation. Mutations also increase genetic variation by creating new forms of genes.

Many traits are controlled by a combination of genes and environment. Environmental factors such as food supply may contribute significantly to variation in some traits. For example, even without genetic differences, some individuals in a species may be bigger or healthier just because they have a better environment.

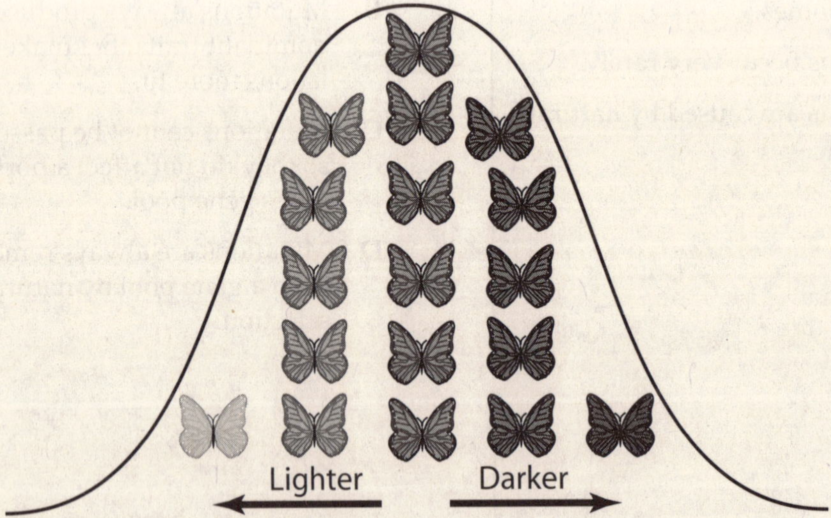

Figure 4–4 Variation in a butterfly species Butterflies in this species vary in color, from very light to very dark, but most are intermediate in color. Natural selection favoring intermediate forms of a trait produces this type of distribution.

Biology/Life Sciences Standards: Evolution

Genetic Diversity and Natural Selection Natural selection can occur only when some individuals in a species have a form of a trait that makes them more suited for their environment than individuals with other forms of the trait. Natural selection takes place when these individuals survive and reproduce more successfully. As a result, alleles for their form of the trait become more frequent over time. In the butterfly species in Figure 4–4, natural selection favors butterflies that are intermediate in color. As a result, alleles for this form of the trait are more frequent in the species as well.

Genetic Diversity and Changing Environments Genetic variation is an advantage to a species that faces a changing environment. The more genetic variation there is in a species, the more likely there will be individuals in the species with traits that suit them for the new environment. These individuals will be favored by natural selection. They will be able to survive and reproduce more successfully in the new environment than individuals with other traits.

An environmental change might make the dark-colored butterflies in Figure 4–4 more fit than the intermediate forms. The dark-colored butterflies would survive and reproduce more successfully in the new environment. As a result, dark-colored butterflies would make up a greater percentage of the species over time. But what would happen if there were no dark-colored butterflies in the species to begin with? Without variation in the trait, the species might not be able to adapt to the new environment. The species might even go extinct.

Review Questions

13 **What contributes to genetic variation in sexually reproducing species?**

    A shuffling of genes and chromosomes during gamete production

    B mutations creating new forms of genes

    C variation in environmental conditions

    D all of the above

14 **Why is variation within a species required for natural selection to occur?**

    A Variation means that some individuals may be better suited to the environment.

    B Variation causes all individuals to be well suited to their environment.

    C Variation eliminates any unfavorable traits.

    D Variation causes all individuals to have the same traits.

Biology/Life Sciences Standards: Evolution

15

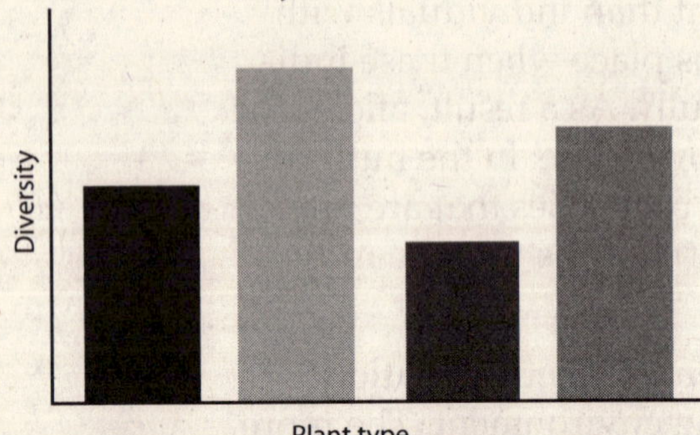

The graph shows the degree of genetic diversity in four species of plants. Which species would have the best chance of surviving an environmental change?

A domestic wheat

B domestic corn

C wild wheat

D wild corn

Biology/Life Sciences Standards: Evolution

***BI 7.e.** *Students know* the conditions for Hardy-Weinberg equilibrium in a population and why these conditions are not likely to appear in nature.

***BI 7.f.** *Students know* how to solve the Hardy-Weinberg equations to predict the frequency of genotypes in a population, given the frequency of phenotypes.

Evolution can be defined as a change in the frequencies, or percentages, of alleles in a population's gene pool over time. The Hardy-Weinberg principle is a model that helps scientists understand how and why allele frequencies change in populations. The principle also may be used to estimate the frequencies of alleles and genotypes in populations.

Hardy-Weinberg Principle To understand how populations evolve, it is useful to know what a population is like that is not evolving. The Hardy-Weinberg principle states that evolution does not take place in a population that meets the following conditions:

- Mating is at random.
- The population is very large.
- No individuals enter or leave the population.
- Mutations do not occur.
- There is no natural selection.

Genetic Equilibrium A population that meets all of these conditions is said to be in genetic equilibrium. A population in genetic equilibrium has constant allele frequencies and constant genotype frequencies. In addition, the genotype frequencies are related to the allele frequencies in a predictable way.

Consider a gene that has two alleles, A and a, in a particular population. Assume the frequency of A in the population's gene pool is represented by p and the frequency of a is represented by q. Because A and a are the only two alleles for this gene in the population, then

$$p + q = 100\%, \text{ or } 1.0.$$

Suppose the population has 20 percent A alleles for this gene. Then $p = 20\%$, or 0.2. Knowing the value of p, you can find the value of q, because $p + q = 1.0$. The value of q must be 1.0 - p, or 0.8. In other words, the population has 80 percent a alleles for this gene.

Biology/Life Sciences Standards: Evolution

When a population is in genetic equilibrium, genotype frequencies can be expressed in terms of the allele frequencies. The table shows how genotype frequencies are related to allele frequencies in an equilibrium population. As long as the population remains in equilibrium, p and q are constant, and the genotype frequencies remain the same as well.

Genotype Frequencies in an Equilibrium Population

Genotype	Frequency	Example ($p = 0.2$, $q = 0.8$)
AA	p^2	$(0.2)^2 = 0.04$ (4%)
Aa	$2\,pq$	$2\,(0.2)(0.8) = 0.32$ (32%)
aa	q^2	$(0.8)^2 = 0.64$ (64%)

Hardy-Weinberg and Natural Populations Hardy-Weinberg conditions are rarely met by populations in nature. Mutations occur in all populations, and natural selection occurs in most populations, at least for some traits. Many populations are too small to meet the condition of very large population size. Very few populations are closed to individuals entering or leaving, and random mating is also rare. As a result, most natural populations are not in genetic equilibrium. In these populations, allele frequencies change and evolution occurs.

Nonetheless, the Hardy-Weinberg principle is helpful to scientists interested in the evolution of natural populations. For example, if a population has a greater frequency of heterozygotes than an equilibrium population would have, this might suggest that heterozygotes are favored by natural selection.

Estimating Allele and Genotype Frequencies Some natural populations occasionally come close to meeting Hardy-Weinberg conditions for some traits. In these cases, it may be assumed that genotypes have about the same frequencies in the natural population as they would in an equilibrium population. Scientists can use this assumption to estimate allele and genotype frequencies in the natural population.

For example, suppose that one percent of a population has a trait controlled by a recessive allele. What percent of the population are heterozygotes that do not have the trait but carry the recessive allele? The following steps can be used to find the answer.

1. **Find q^2** Because the trait is recessive, people who have the trait must have two recessive alleles. If q is the frequency of the recessive allele, the frequency of the recessive genotype is q^2. Therefore,

$$q^2 = 1\%, \text{ or } 0.01.$$

Biology/Life Sciences Standards: Evolution

2. **Calculate q** The frequency, q, of the recessive allele is the square root of q^2, so

$$q = \sqrt{0.01}, \text{ or } 0.1.$$

3. **Calculate p** The frequency, p, of the dominant allele can be calculated once q is known, because $p + q = 1.0$. The value of q is 0.1, so

$$p = 1.0 - 0.1, \text{ or } 0.9.$$

4. **Determine $2\,pq$** The frequency of heterozygotes in the population is assumed to be $2\,pq$. Substituting the values calculated for p and q gives

$$2\,pq = 2\,(0.1)\,(0.9) = .09.$$

Therefore, 9 percent of the population is heterozygotes that carry the recessive allele.

Review Questions

16 **Which is a condition characteristic of a population in genetic equilibrium?**

  A   random mating

  B   mutations

  C   natural selection

  D   movement of individuals into the population

Use the following information to answers Questions 17–19.

For a particular gene, there are two alleles represented by R and r. A certain population is assumed to be in genetic equilibrium for this gene. In this population, 25 percent of individuals have the rr genotype.

17 **What is the frequency of the r allele in this population?**

  A   0.25

  B   0.05

  C   0.75

  D   0.50

Biology/Life Sciences Standards: Evolution

18 What is the frequency of the *R* allele in this population?

A 0.05

B 0.50

C 0.95

D 0.75

19 What percentage of individuals in the population are heterozygotes (*Rr*) for the trait?

A 75%

B 70%

C 50%

D 35%

Biology/Life Sciences Standards: Evolution

BI 8.a. *Students know* how natural selection determines the differential survival of groups of organisms.

BI 8.b. *Students know* a great diversity of species increases the chance that at least some organisms survive major changes in the environment.

Variation within a species increases the chance that at least some organisms will be able to survive if the environment changes. Variation among species plays a similar role in the ability of organisms to survive major environmental changes, such as global changes in climate. The greater the variation among species, the greater the chance that at least some species will have traits that help them survive if major environmental changes occur.

Natural Selection and Differential Survival When an environment changes, only some individuals in a species may be able to survive. A difference in the ability to survive is referred to as differential survival. It is a measure of fitness, along with the ability to reproduce successfully. Differential survival can lead to a significant change in the traits of a species.

An example of this occurred in England during the 1800s, when air pollution from factories caused tree bark to darken. Before then, most of the moths in a particular species could usually avoid predators while they rested on the trunks and branches of trees. Like the trees, almost all the moths were light-colored, so they were hard for predators to spot. After the trees darkened, light-colored moths were much less likely to avoid predators while resting on trees. However, there were rare, dark-colored moths in the species that could avoid predators and survive. Differential survival of light- and dark-colored moths led to a significant change in the color of the moth species, as shown in Figure 4–5.

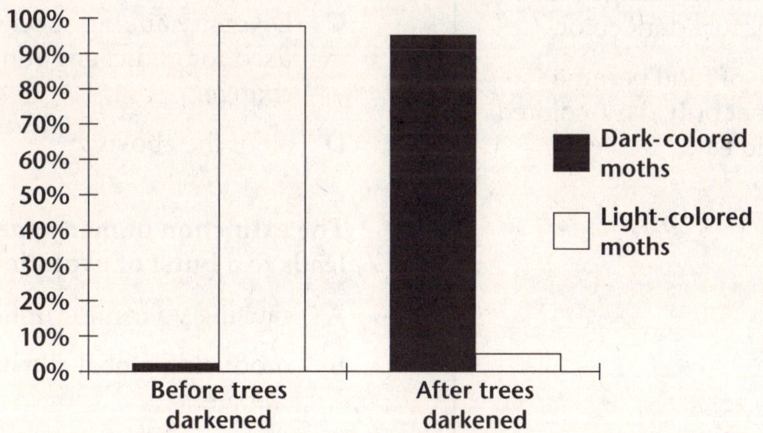

Figure 4–5 Differential survival in a moth species Differential survival of light-colored and dark-colored moths resulted in the species changing from mostly light-colored moths to mostly dark-colored moths.

Biology/Life Sciences Standards: Evolution

Diversity of Species Without variation in the species of moths in Figure 4–5, the change in environment might have resulted in the species going extinct. Similarly, a wide diversity of species helps ensure that some species will survive major changes in the environment.

Major environmental changes occurred several times in Earth's history. The changes led to mass extinctions. Huge numbers of species went extinct in a relatively short periods of time. However, because of the diversity of species, there were always some species able to survive the changes.

One mass extinction occurred about 65 million years ago. More than half of all plant and animal species went extinct. Scientists speculate that a combination of events—such as a huge asteroid striking Earth and major volcanic eruptions—caused a global climate change. The extinction of many species left habitats wide open for the relatively few species that survived. As a result, the mass extinction was followed by a burst of evolution that produced many new species.

Review Questions

20 In the example of moths in England during the 1800s, what environmental change led to natural selection for dark-colored moths?

A Air pollution made it harder for light-colored moths to breathe.

B A new type of predator moved into the area that preferred light-colored moths.

C The bark of trees changed from a light color to a dark color.

D A new type of food became available that only dark-colored moths could eat.

21 Which statement is true about diversity among species and environmental change?

A Diversity among species increases the chance that some species will survive environmental change.

B Diversity among species is a major cause of environmental change.

C Diversity among species can be used to predict environmental change.

D all of the above

22 The extinction of many species leads to a burst of evolution by

A causing volcanic eruptions.

B producing global climate change.

C leaving habitats open.

D making the extinct species more fit.

Biology/Life Sciences Standards: Evolution

BI 8.c. *Students know* the effects of genetic drift on the diversity of organisms in a population.

In small populations, the frequency of alleles can change by chance alone, even without natural selection. A change in allele frequencies that occurs by chance in small populations is called genetic drift. Genetic drift generally reduces diversity within a population.

How Genetic Drift Occurs Suppose a jar holds thousands of tiny beads, half of them red and half of them black. If you randomly removed hundreds of beads from the jar, chances are good that close to half would be red and close to half would be black. But what if you removed just ten beads from the jar? There is a good chance of a different outcome, such as three red beads and seven black beads. The smaller the sample of beads you remove, the more your beads may differ from the beads in the jar. For example, if you removed just two beads, there is good chance they would both be red or both be black.

In populations, adults pass alleles to gametes, some of which unite to form the individuals of the next generation. Which alleles go to particular gametes and which gametes unite to form the next generation are largely random events, like removing beads from a jar. In a small population, relatively few gametes (of the millions of gametes produced) actually unite to become part of the next generation. As a result, there is a good chance that the next generation will differ from the previous generation in the frequencies of alleles. The next generation may even be missing alleles that were present in the previous generation.

Genetic Drift and Diversity In this way, the frequency of a particular allele in a small population may rise or fall through time due to genetic drift. However, if the frequency of an allele falls below 50 percent (0.5), genetic drift is likely to reduce its frequency even more. Eventually, the allele is likely to disappear from the population's gene pool. This is why genetic drift generally reduces genetic diversity within a population.

There are two special cases in which genetic drift may reduce genetic diversity very quickly. One case occurs when a population goes through a sudden, drastic reduction in size, called a bottleneck. The other case occurs when a new population is founded by a very small number of individuals.

- The bottleneck effect happens when a disaster or similar event greatly reduces a population's size. The result is a much smaller population that is likely to have fewer alleles and different allele frequencies than the original population before the bottleneck.

- The founder effect occurs when a small group of individuals leaves a large population and founds a new population.

Biology/Life Sciences Standards: Evolution

The founding population is likely to have fewer alleles and different allele frequencies than the original large population. If more than one founding population leaves the same large population, the founding populations may also differ from one another in their allele frequencies. This is illustrated in Figure 4–6.

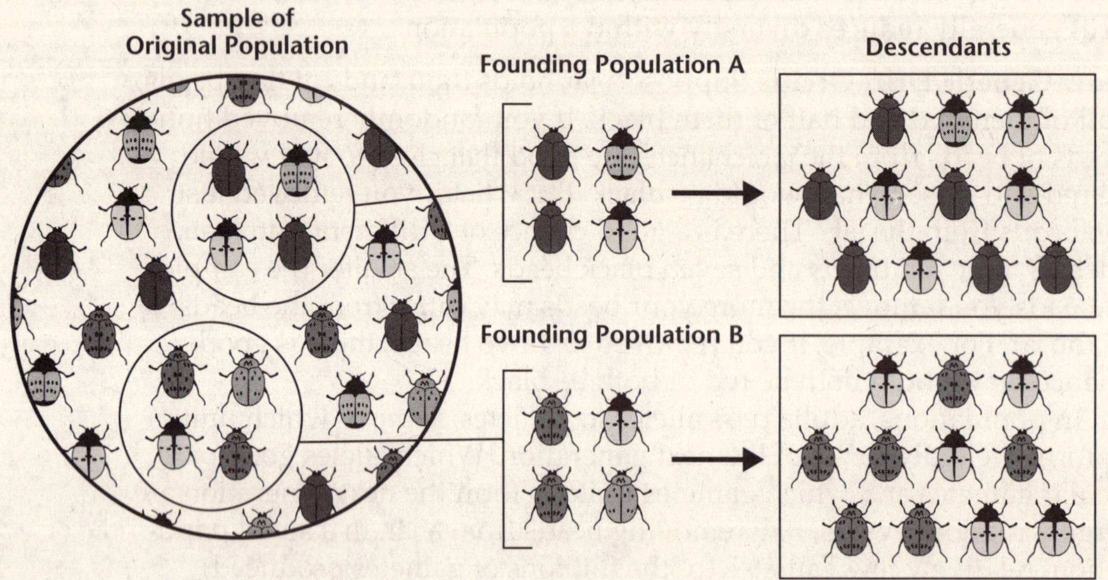

Figure 4–6 Founder effect and diversity in beetles Each founding beetle population has less diversity than the original population. However, there is marked diversity between the two founding populations.

Review Questions

23 Which factor determines whether genetic drift occurs in a population?

   A population size

   B allele frequencies

   C natural selection

   D mutation

24 How does genetic drift generally affect diversity in a population?

   A It increases diversity.

   B It has no affect on diversity.

   C It reduces diversity.

   D It creates more diversity.

25 A few birds were separated from their original large flock in a windstorm, and they formed their own small flock. This is an example of

   A founder effect.

   B natural selection.

   C bottleneck effect.

   D genetic diversity.

Biology/Life Sciences Standards: Evolution

BI 8.d. *Students know* reproductive or geographic isolation affects speciation.

A species is a group of similar organisms that can breed and produce fertile offspring together. Individuals who belong to the same species share a common gene pool. For a new species to evolve, a group of individuals from the species must become too different from the rest of the species to breed with them. This is called reproductive isolation. When reproductive isolation occurs between two groups, the two groups no longer share the same gene pool. They have become separate species.

Reproductive Isolation Reproductive isolation refers to the inability of individuals from different species to breed and produce fertile offspring together. Individuals in different species may be unable to breed together due to a variety of factors. The factors can be grouped into two categories: prezygotic factors and postzygotic factors.

- Prezygotic factors prevent individuals from mating and producing fertilized eggs, or zygotes. For example, secretions in the female reproductive tract of one species might be too acidic for sperm of another species to survive.

- Postzygotic factors prevent zygotes from surviving or becoming fertile adults if mating does occur between members of different species. For example, horses and donkeys, which belong to two different species, can mate and produce offspring, called mules. However, mules are not fertile. They are unable to breed with other mules or with horses or donkeys.

Geographic Isolation Reproductive isolation typically develops after a geographic barrier separates part of a species from the rest of the species range. This is called geographic isolation. The geographic barrier could be a river, mountain, or body of water. Geographic isolation may explain why many new species develop.

Consider the example shown in Figure 4–7. A mountain range formed on an island where there had once been only lowlands. The mountain range divided a species on the island into two separate populations, A and B. The mountains prevented members of the two populations from breeding together. The two populations had separate gene pools and evolved independently of one another.

Eventually, populations A and B became so different that members of the two populations could no longer breed and produce fertile offspring together—even if they were brought together in the same geographic area. They had become reproductively isolated from one another, not just geographically isolated. Each population had evolved into a separate species.

Biology/Life Sciences Standards: Evolution

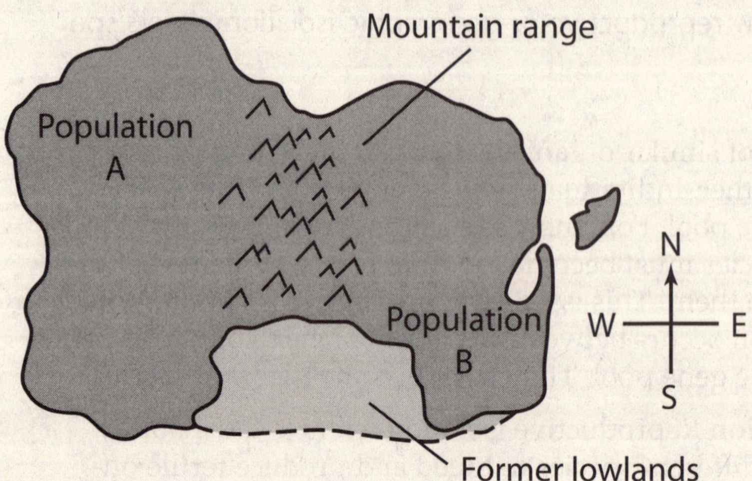

Figure 4–7 Geographic isolation After being isolated by a newly
formed mountain range, members of populations A and B no longer had
any contact with each other.

Review Questions

26 **Which statement is generally true about two different species?**

A   They are reproductively isolated from each other.

B   They are geographically isolated from each other.

C   They can mate with each other, but their offspring are not fertile.

D   They can breed together if they live in the same geographic area.

27 **Any factor that keeps individuals from breeding and producing fertile offspring together is called**

A   geographic isolation.

B   postzygotic isolation.

C   reproductive isolation.

D   prezygotic isolation.

28 **Birds from two similar species do not mate because they have different mating songs. This is an example of reproductive isolation due to a**

A   postzygotic factor.

B   breeding factor.

C   geographic factor.

D   prezygotic factor.

29 **Birds that Charles Darwin observed on the Galápagos Islands were ground birds that could not fly from one island to another. Bird populations on the different islands had different gene pools because of**

A   genetic isolation.

B   postzygotic isolation.

C   geographic isolation.

D   prezygotic isolation.

Biology/Life Sciences Standards: Evolution

7 3.c. *Students know* how independent lines of evidence from geology, fossils, and comparative anatomy provide the bases for the theory of evolution.

Charles Darwin first published his theory of evolution by natural selection in the 1860s. According to Darwin's theory, species change over time as natural selection makes them more fit for their environments. Evidence from several different areas of science supports Darwin's theory. Some of the evidence was known even before Darwin's time. Other evidence was gathered more recently, using modern technology. Evidence still is accumulating in support of Darwin's theory.

Evidence From Fossils Fossils are the preserved remains of once-living organisms. They typically consist of bones, teeth, or shells that were buried by sediments thousands or millions of years ago and gradually turned to rock. Fossils show what extinct organisms looked like and how they lived.

If scientists can determine how old fossils are, they can use the fossils to help trace the evolution of organisms through time. There are two general ways of determining the age of fossils: relative dating and absolute dating.

- Relative dating is based on geology. Rock layers closer to the surface formed more recently than rock layers deeper underground. Therefore, a fossil found in a rock layer near the surface is presumed to be younger than a fossil found in a deeper rock layer. Rock layers may also provide information about the physical environment and how it changed over time.

- Absolute dating estimates the actual age of fossils—not just which fossil is older or younger. There are several absolute dating methods, including radioactive dating. This method is based on the known rate of breakdown, or decay, of certain radioactive elements. Scientists measure the amount of radioactive decay that has occurred in a fossil and use the information to estimate about how long ago the fossil organism died.

Evidence From Comparative Anatomy Scientists have long known that many living things have similar structures. For example, even by Darwin's time, scientists knew that the limbs of all vertebrates (animals with backbones) have the same basic structure. This is illustrated in Figure 4–8. The similarity in limb structure suggests that all modern species of vertebrates are related. Related species, like related people, are descendants of a common ancestor.

Biology/Life Sciences Standards: Evolution

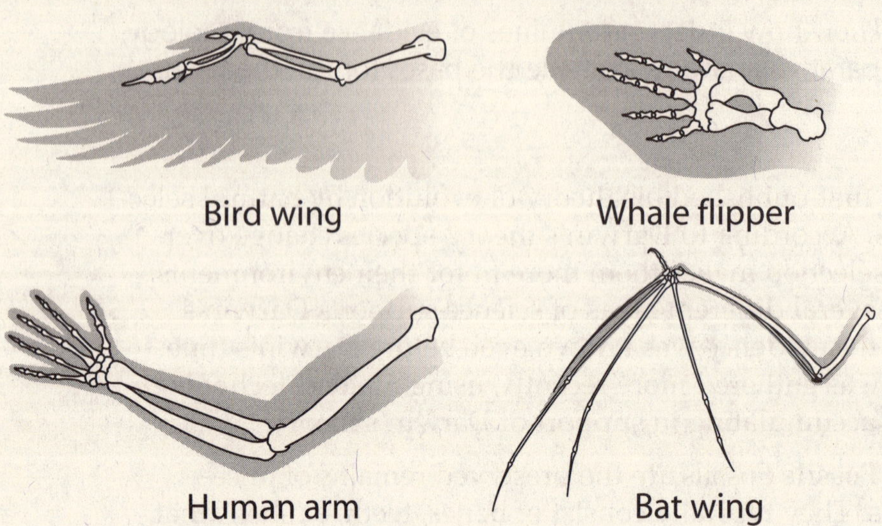

Figure 4–8 Limb structure of vertebrates Birds, whales, humans, and bats all have the same arrangement of bones in their upper limbs. This provides evidence that these modern organisms evolved from a common ancestor.

Most related organisms look more similar during early life stages than they do as adults. For example, in all vertebrate embryos, the same groups of cells develop in the same order and in similar patterns. This explains why all the vertebrates shown in Figure 4–8 have a similar limb structure. It also provides additional evidence that the species have a common ancestor.

Review Questions

30 According to Darwin's theory of evolution,

A species do not change over time unless they leave fossils behind.

B only fossils can provide evidence for the change in species over time.

C species change over time unless natural selection prevents it.

D natural selection improves a species's fitness over time.

31 Which statement is true about the relative dating of fossils?

A It is based on the decay of radio-active elements.

B It is based on knowledge of rock layers.

C It estimates the actual ages of fossils in years.

D It estimates how long ago fossil organisms died.

Biology/Life Sciences Standards: Evolution

32 To determine the actual age of fossils, scientists use

 A   absolute dating.

 B   geology.

 C   relative dating.

 D   comparative anatomy.

33 Chicken and rat embryos look very similar. This provides evidence that the two organisms

 A   are related.

 B   look very similar as adults.

 C   belong to the same species.

 D   have not evolved.

Biology/Life Sciences Standards: Evolution

BI 8.e. *Students know* how to analyze fossil evidence with regard to biological diversity, episodic speciation, and mass extinction.

All the fossils that have been found and analyzed by scientists make
up the fossil record. The fossil record provides evidence for the major
events in the history of life on Earth. It documents when the earliest
known life forms appeared on Earth and how life diversified through
time. It also shows that Earth went through several brief episodes during which vast numbers of species went extinct or huge numbers of new
species evolved. The fossil evidence for these major events in Earth's
biological history is the basis of the geologic time scale (see Figure 4–9).

Geologic Time Scale		
Era	**Period**	**Time (millions of years ago)**
Cenozoic	Quaternary	1.8 – present
Cenozoic	Tertiary	65 – 1.8
Mesozoic	Cretaceous	145 – 65
Mesozoic	Jurassic	208 – 145
Mesozoic	Triassic	245 – 208
Paleozoic	Permian	290 – 245
Paleozoic	Carboniferous	360 – 290
Paleozoic	Devonian	410 – 360
Paleozoic	Silurian	440 – 410
Paleozoic	Ordovician	505 – 440
Paleozoic	Cambrian	544 – 505
Precambrian Time	Vendian	650 – 544

Figure 4–9 The geologic time scale After Precambrian Time,
the geologic time scale is divided into eras. Each era is associated
with major events in the history of Earth's living things.

Biology/Life Sciences Standards: Evolution

Biological Diversity The earliest fossils of organisms date back to Precambrian Time. They were simple, single-celled organisms. By the start of the Paleozoic Era, the fossil record shows that life was already highly diverse. At that time, all life forms lived in the water. Eventually, an even greater diversity of life forms evolved to live on the land and in the air.

Mass Extinctions The fossil record shows that mass extinctions wiped out large percentages of species on Earth at several times in the past. For example, at the end of the Paleozoic Era, up to 95 percent of complex ocean species went extinct. At the end of the Mesozoic Era, more than 50 percent of all plant and animal species—including all the dinosaurs— went extinct. These and other mass extinctions were probably caused by a combination of several factors, such as large volcanoes erupting, continents moving, and sea levels changing.

Episodic Speciation The fossil record documents several dramatic episodes of rapid speciation, or evolution of new species. Some of these episodes followed mass extinctions. Each disappearance of so many species left habitats open and provided new opportunities for those species that survived. The result was a burst of evolution that produced many new species. For example, when dinosaurs went extinct at the end of the Mesozoic Era, it cleared the way for the evolution of modern species of mammals and birds.

Other periods of rapid speciation occurred when new traits, such as feathers and wings, evolved. The new traits let organisms exploit new habitats. For example, the evolution of feathers and wings allowed birds to fly and opened up the air to them. Many species of birds quickly evolved to take advantage of the new opportunities.

Review Questions

34 The earliest fossils show life probably first appeared on Earth during the

A Precambrian Time.

B Paleozoic Era.

C Mesozoic Era.

D Cenozoic Era.

35 The fossil record shows that half of all plants and animals went extinct at the end of the

A Precambrian Time.

B Paleozoic Era.

C Mesozoic Era.

D Cenozoic Era.

Biology/Life Sciences Standards: Evolution

36 What probably caused the mass extinctions documented by the fossil record?

A stability of Earth's surface

B evolution of major new traits

C episodes of rapid speciation

D major changes on Earth's surface

37 When would you expect to see fossil evidence of many new species?

A following a mass extinction

B shortly before a mass extinction

C during a period of stable environment

D before the evolution of a major new trait

Biology/Life Sciences Standards: Evolution

***BI 8.f.** *Students know* how to use comparative embryology, DNA or protein sequence comparisons, and other independent sources of data to create a branching diagram (cladogram) that shows probable evolutionary relationships.

A staggering diversity of organisms lives on Earth. As many as 100 million different species may exist today. Even more species have gone extinct over Earth's long history. To make sense of the tremendous diversity of living things, biologists must classify organisms in some way.

Classification Systems Early biologists classified organisms based on how similar they looked. They based the comparisons on a wide variety of obvious physical traits in adult organisms. Now, most biologists classify organisms based on traits that reveal evolutionary relationships. Evolutionary classifications are based on comparisons of embryos, DNA, proteins, or other traits that show genetic relatedness.

Comparative Embryology Many organisms that look very different as adults are more similar when you compare them at earlier stages of life. For example, the embryos of mammals, birds, and reptiles look very similar and share certain features, such as gill slits, that are not apparent in the adult organisms. The similarities provide evidence that the organisms are related. They show that the organisms shared a common ancestor at some time in the past.

DNA and Protein Sequences The genetic material, or DNA, provides the most direct evidence for evolutionary relationships. DNA molecules contain a sequence of smaller molecules called bases, which make up the genetic code. The more similar the DNA base sequences of two species, the more recently they shared a common ancestor, and the more closely related they are.

Proteins also provide evidence of evolutionary relationships. Proteins consist of amino acid sequences, and amino acid sequences are encoded in the base sequences of DNA. The more similar the amino acid sequences of two species, the more similar their DNA base sequences, and the more closely related the species are. Organisms as different as humans and yeasts make some of the same proteins. This indicates that even these organisms share a common ancestor.

Cladograms To represent evolutionary relationships among organisms, many biologists use diagrams called cladograms A cladogram is a branching diagram that shows lines of evolutionary descent.

Biology/Life Sciences Standards: Evolution

An example of a cladogram is shown in Figure 4–10. In this example, the cladogram is based on traits, such as segmentation, that had a major evolutionary impact by leading to new lines of descent. Both crabs and barnacles have bodies that are divided into segments and both types of organisms periodically shed, or molt, their external skeleton. Limpets, on the other hand, do not have either of these important traits. This suggests that barnacles and crabs shared a common ancestor more recently than either did with limpets.

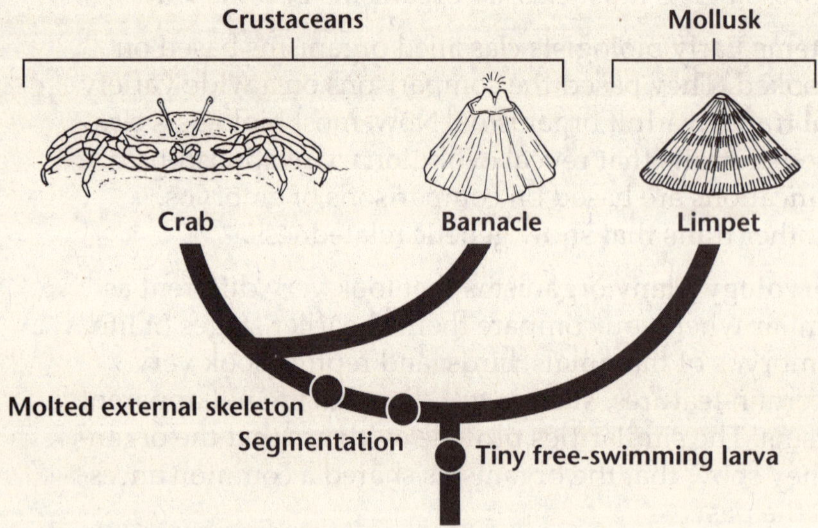

Figure 4–10 Cladogram Although barnacles look more like limpets than crabs, a comparison of other traits shows that barnacles and crabs are more closely related.

Review Questions

38 Evolutionary classifications of organisms may be based on comparisons of

A DNA.

B proteins.

C embryos.

D all of the above

39 The more similar the DNA base sequences of two species, the

A less closely related they are in evolutionary terms.

B more recently they shared a common ancestor.

C less similar their protein sequences are likely to be.

D longer it has been since they shared a common ancestor.

Biology/Life Sciences Standards: Evolution

40 **Cladograms are based on traits that**

  A reveal evolutionary relationships.

  B lead to extinction of species.

  C make unrelated organisms look similar.

  D appear only in adults of the species.

41 **Why does the cladogram in Figure 4–10 group barnacles with crabs instead of limpets?**

  A Barnacles look more like crabs than like limpets.

  B Limpets seem to resemble crabs more than barnacles.

  C Barnacles and crabs share important traits not found in limpets.

  D Limpets do not have a free-swimming larva stage.

Biology/Life Sciences Standards: Evolution

***BI 8.g.** *Students know* how several independent molecular clocks, calibrated against each other and combined with evidence from the fossil record, can help to estimate how long ago various groups of organisms diverged evolutionarily from one another.

Mutations are random changes in an organism's genetic material, or DNA. Some mutations are neutral, which means they have no effect on the fitness of the individuals that carry them. Neutral mutations do not increase or decrease in frequency through time because of natural selection. Instead, different neutral mutations accumulate gradually in a species's gene pool. Comparisons of neutral mutations can be used to estimate how long two or more species have been evolving independently of each other.

Neutral Mutations Neutral mutations in a given gene are thought to accumulate at about the same rate in different species. However, because mutations are random changes in DNA, different neutral mutations in the same gene are likely to accumulate in different species. The number of different neutral mutations that have accumulated in two species can be used to estimate the length of time that the two species have had separate gene pools. This is the basis of molecular clocks.

Molecular Clocks A molecular clock is a model that uses neutral mutations to measure evolutionary time. Figure 4–11 illustrates how a molecular clock works. The figure shows the accumulation of neutral mutations in the same gene in three species that descended from a common ancestral species. Species B and C share more neutral mutations with each other than either species shares with species A. On this basis, species B and C have a more recent common ancestor. Scientists can estimate about how long it has been since the species separated from each other, if the rate of accumulation of neutral mutations is known for that gene.

Some genes accumulate neutral mutations faster than others. Therefore, different genes provide different molecular clocks. Different molecular clocks help scientists study a variety of evolutionary events. For example, genes in which neutral mutations accumulate more rapidly are more useful for timing recent events. Therefore, a different molecular clock would be used to compare bird species, which shared a recent common ancestor, than to compare humans and yeasts, which shared a much more distant common ancestor.

Biology/Life Sciences Standards: Evolution

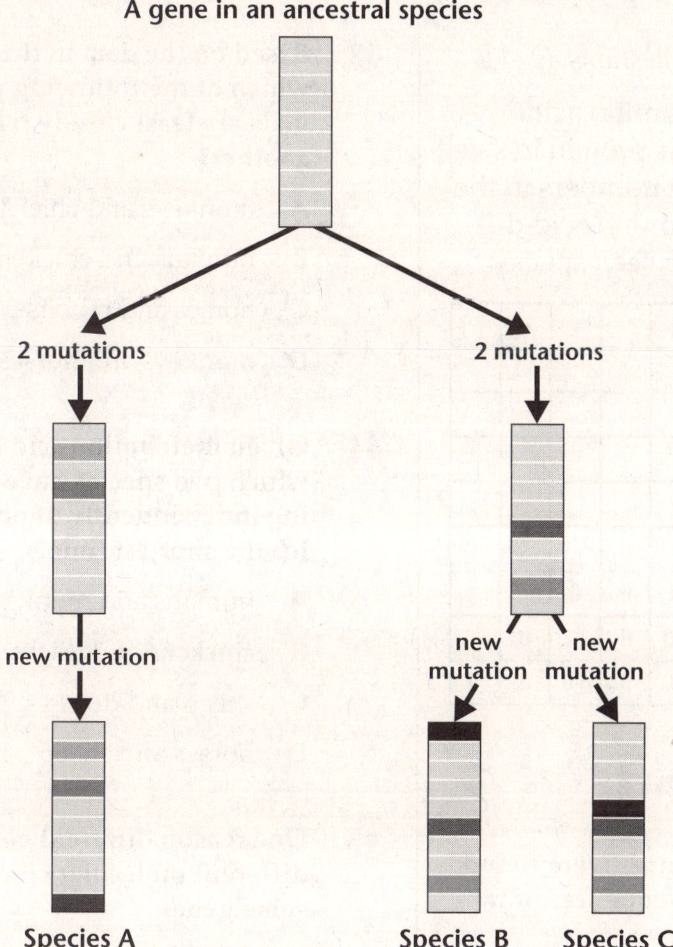

Figure 4–11 Accumulation of neutral mutations
Species A has been evolving independently of Species B
and C for a longer time than Species B and C have been
evolving independently of each other.

Amino acid sequences of proteins can also be used as the basis for molecular clocks. Amino acid sequences are encoded in DNA, so changes in amino acid sequences reflect changes (mutations) in DNA. The greater the differences in amino acid sequences of different species, the longer the species have been evolving independently of one another.

Molecular Clocks and the Fossil Record The timing of evolutionary events with molecular clocks generally agrees with estimates made on the basis of the fossil record. However, molecular clocks usually give more reliable and precise estimates than estimates based on fossils. Information from molecular clocks is especially useful in understanding evolutionary events that occurred during periods for which there are gaps in the fossil record.

Biology/Life Sciences Standards: Evolution

Review Questions

Use the table to answer Questions 42–44.

Scientists analyzed the amino acid sequences of a particular protein in several animal species. The numbers in the table show how many amino acid differences were found between species.

	Human	Monkey	Sheep	Horse	Dog	Rabbit	Kangaroo	Chicken	Duck
Human	0								
Monkey	1	0							
Sheep	10	9	0						
Horse	12	11	3	0					
Dog	11	10	3	6	0				
Rabbit	9	8	4	6	5	0			
Kangaroo	10	11	6	7	7	6	0		
Chicken	13	12	9	11	10	8	12	0	
Duck	11	10	8	10	8	6	10	3	0

42 How many differences were found in the amino acid sequences of rabbits and dogs?

A 0

B 5

C 6

D 7

43 Based on the data in the table, which of the following pairs of animals are least closely related to one another?

A monkeys and chickens

B humans and chickens

C horses and rabbits

D monkeys and horses

44 Given their amino acid differences, which two species have been evolving independently of one another for the shortest time?

A humans and monkeys

B chickens and ducks

C sheep and dogs

D horses and sheep

45 One reason different genes provide different molecular clocks is that some genes

A do not accumulate neutral mutations.

B show up in organisms without mutations.

C accumulate neutral mutations faster than other genes.

D accumulate neutral mutations only in a few species.

Biology/Life Sciences Standards: Physiology

7 5.a. *Students know* plants and animals have levels of organization for structure and function, including cells, tissues, organs, organ systems, and the whole organism.

Living things with many cells, such as plants and animals, are called multicellular organisms. These organisms have several levels of organization. At the lowest level are cells. Next are tissues, followed by organs, and then by organ systems. At the highest level is the organism. The levels of organization explain how the many cells of a multicellular organism can work together.

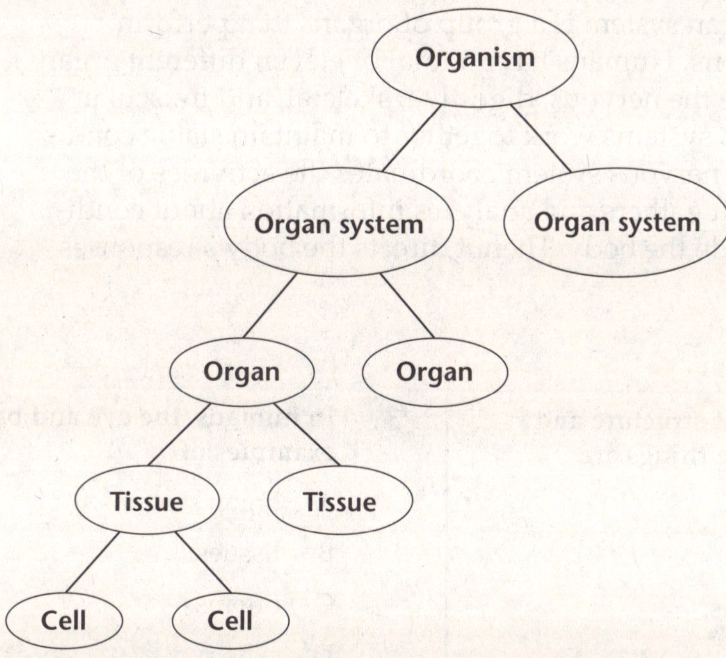

Figure 5–1 Levels of organization of a multicellular organism The trillions of cells in humans and other complex organisms are arranged in tissues. Tissues are arranged in organs, and organs are arranged in organ systems. Organ systems make up the organism.

Cell The cell is the basic unit of structure and function in all living things. In multicellular organisms, individual cells usually are specialized. A specialized cell has a unique structure that allows it to perform a particular function. Examples of specialized cells in humans include nerve cells and skin cells. Nerve cells are specialized to carry messages. Skin cells are specialized to protect the body.

Tissue A tissue is a group of cells that perform a single function. In humans, there are four basic types of tissues: epithelial, connective, nervous, and muscle tissues.

Biology/Life Sciences Standards: Physiology

- Epithelial tissues make up membranes, such as those that cover the inside and outside surfaces of the body.
- Connective tissues support the body and connect its parts.
- Nervous tissues carry messages throughout the body.
- Muscle tissues, along with bones, allow the body to move.

Organ An organ is a group of tissues that work together to perform a single function. For example, the eye is an organ made up of epithelial, connective, nervous, and muscle tissues. All the different tissues work together to perform the single function of sight.

Organ System An organ system is a group of organs that perform closely related functions. Humans have a total of eleven different organ systems. They include the nervous, digestive, skeletal, and muscular systems. All the organ systems work together to maintain stable conditions in the body. The nervous system coordinates the activities of the other organ systems. It gathers and analyzes information about conditions inside and outside the body. Then it directs the body's responses.

Review Questions

1 The basic units of structure and function in living things are

   A tissues.

   B cells.

   C organ systems.

   D organs.

2 Which type of human tissue supports the body?

   A epithelial tissue

   B connective tissue

   C nervous tissue

   D muscle tissue

3 In humans, the eye and brain are examples of

   A organ systems.

   B tissues.

   C organs.

   D cells.

4 Which statement is true about the organ systems of multicellular organisms?

   A They are made up of groups of cells that perform a single function.

   B They are organized into tissues and cells.

   C They work together to maintain stable conditions in the body.

   D They consist of tissues that work together to perform a single function.

Biology/Life Sciences Standards: Physiology

BI 9.b. *Students know* how the nervous system mediates communication between different parts of the body and the body's interactions with the environment.

BI 9.d. *Students know* the functions of the nervous system and the role of neurons in transmitting electrochemical impulses.

BI 9.e. *Students know* the roles of sensory neurons, interneurons, and motor neurons in sensation, thought, and response.

Multicellular organisms have a communication system that lets their many cells work together. The communication system consists of specialized cells that carry messages. In humans, these cells are mainly nerve cells. Nerve cells make up the tissues and organs of the nervous system.

Nervous System The human nervous system controls and coordinates all the body's functions in response to conditions both inside and outside the body. The nervous system has two major parts: the central nervous system and the peripheral nervous system.

- The central nervous system consists of the brain and spinal cord. It receives and analyzes information from all over the body. It also sends messages to the body about how to respond.

- The peripheral nervous system consists of a system of interconnected nerve cells throughout the body. It transmits information from nerves in sense organs, such as the eyes and ears, to the central nervous system. It also transmits information from the central nervous system to organs and glands in the body.

Consider what happens when you put your hand in bath water to test the temperature. Nerves in your skin sense the water temperature and send a message about the temperature through peripheral nerves to the spinal cord. The spinal cord transmits the message to the brain. The brain analyzes the message and decides on a response. Then the brain sends a message about the response through the spinal cord to peripheral nerves in your hand. Your hand turns the faucet and adjusts the water temperature.

Messages are carried in the nervous system in the form of electrochemical signals, called nerve impulses. A nerve impulse flows through the nervous system like electric current through a wire. Nerve cells transmit the impulses from cell to cell.

Neurons Nerve cells are also called neurons. There are three types of neurons: sensory neurons, motor neurons, and interneurons. The three types differ in the direction that they carry nerve impulses.

Biology/Life Sciences Standards: Physiology

- Sensory neurons carry impulses from the sense organs to the spinal cord and brain.
- Motor neurons carry impulses from the brain and spinal cord to muscles and glands.
- Interneurons carry impulses between sensory neurons and motor neurons.

Figure 5–2 shows a typical neuron. The largest part of the neuron is the cell body, which contains the nucleus. Attached to the cell body are short branches called dendrites. The dendrites carry nerve impulses from the environment or from other neurons and toward the cell body. Also attached to the cell body is a single, long fiber called an axon. The axon carries impulses away from the cell body and toward other cells. The axon ends in small swellings called axon terminals.

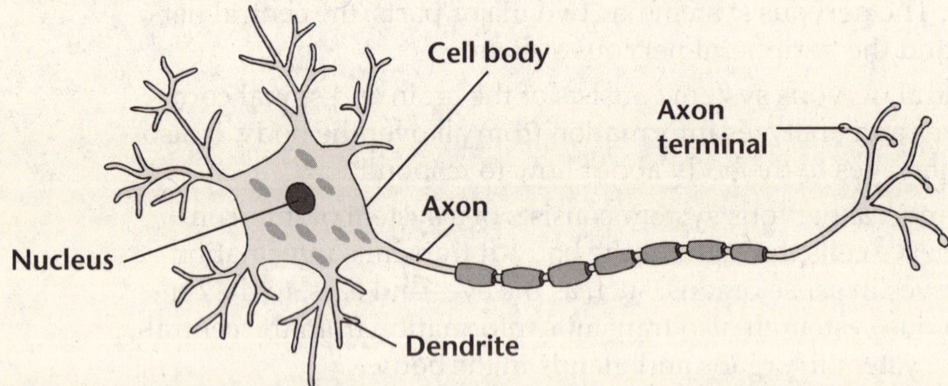

Figure 5–2 Neuron A typical neuron may have dozens of dendrites, but it usually has only one axon.

Nerve Impulse A neuron at rest has a positive charge outside the cell membrane and a negative charge inside the cell membrane. A nerve impulse begins when stimulation from another neuron or the environment causes positively charged particles, called ions, to move across the cell membrane into the neuron. The ions make the inside of the membrane more positively charged than the outside. This change in charge is the nerve impulse.

Once the nerve impulse begins in this way, it travels rapidly down the axon away from the cell body and toward the axon terminals. The movement of the impulse is like the fall of a row of dominoes. An impulse at any point on the membrane causes an impulse at the next point on the membrane. When an impulse reaches an axon terminal, it is passed to another cell.

Biology/Life Sciences Standards: Physiology

Synapse The location where the nerve impulse is passed to another cell is called the synapse (see Figure 5–3). At the synapse, a space known as the synaptic cleft separates the axon terminal from the next cell. When an impulse arrives, chemicals called neurotransmitters are released from tiny sacs in the axon terminal. The chemicals travel across the synaptic cleft to the next cell. They attach to the cell membrane and let positive ions pass through the membrane into the second cell. This stimulates the second cell, and a new impulse begins.

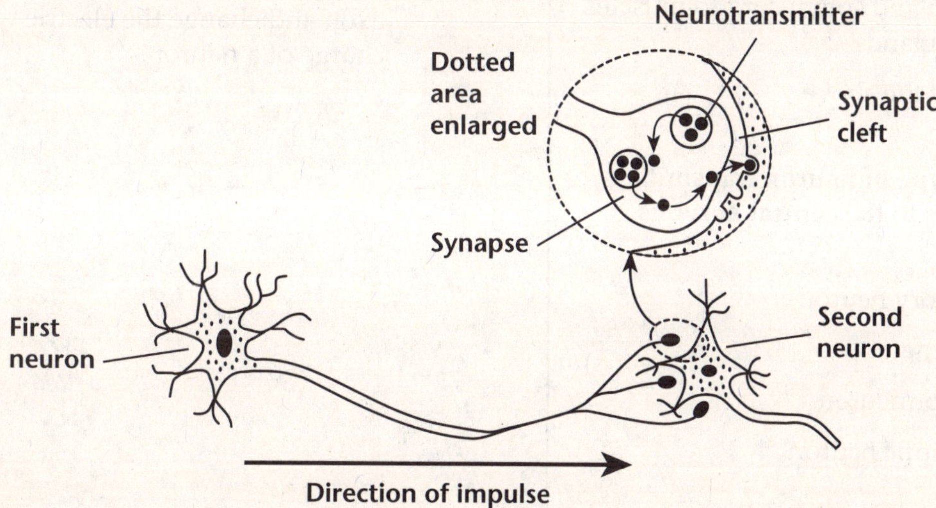

Figure 5–3 Synapse At the synapse, neurotransmitter molecules carry a nerve impulse from one neuron to the next.

Review Questions

5 **Which statement is true about the nervous system?**

  A It is made up of cells called peripheral cells.

  B It has two major parts: the brain and the central nervous system.

  C Its messages are carried by the bloodstream.

  D It controls functions throughout the body.

6 **What is a role of the central nervous system?**

  A receiving messages from sense organs

  B receiving messages from the brain

  C transmitting messages from sense organs

  D transmitting messages to the brain

Biology/Life Sciences Standards: Physiology

7 **What is the function of motor neurons?**

   A carrying impulses from sensory neurons to interneurons

   B carrying impulses from sense organs to the spinal cord and brain

   C carrying impulses from the brain and spinal cord to muscles and glands

   D all of the above

8 **Which type of neuron transmits messages to the central nervous system?**

   A sensory neuron

   B interneuron

   C motor neuron

   D synaptic neuron

9 **A nerve impulse begins when**

   A positive ions move across the cell membrane of a neuron.

   B neurotransmitters flow down an axon of a neuron.

   C dendrites let negative ions pass through an axon of a neuron.

   D negative ions flow down an axon and change the electric charge of a neuron.

Biology/Life Sciences Standards: Physiology

7 5.c. *Students know* how bones and muscles work together to provide a structural framework for movement.

The skeletal system is made up of bones that protect and support the body. Bones meet at joints. Some joints, called moveable joints, allow bones to move. The elbow is an example of a moveable joint. Bones move at moveable joints when muscles apply force to the bones.

Bones and Skeletal Muscles The muscles that move bones are called skeletal muscles. Skeletal muscles are attached to bones by tough tissues called tendons. Skeletal muscles work by contracting, or getting shorter. When the muscles contract, they cause the tendons to pull on the bones.

The bones at a joint work like a lever. The joint between the two bones acts as the fulcrum—the fixed point around which the lever moves. When muscles contract, they provide the force needed to move the lever.

Muscle Pairs Individual skeletal muscles can pull bones in only one direction when they contract. Therefore, most skeletal muscles must work in pairs to move bones in more than one direction. When one muscle in a pair contracts, the other muscle relaxes. Then the first muscle relaxes, while the other muscle contracts. The muscles of the upper arm, shown in Figure 5–4, are an example of opposing muscles that work together in this way. This pair of muscles, the triceps and biceps, moves the bones of the arm at the elbow joint.

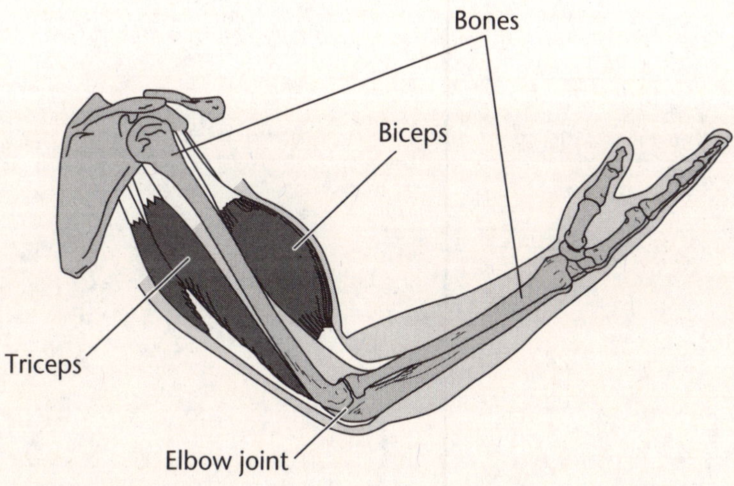

Figure 5–4 Opposing muscles When the biceps muscle contracts, the arm bends at the elbow. When the triceps muscle contracts, the arm straightens out.

Biology/Life Sciences Standards: Physiology

Review Questions

10 What provides the force to move bones?

   A tendons

   B skeletal muscles

   C levers

   D joints

11 Most skeletal muscles must work in pairs because individual muscles

   A can move bones in only one direction.

   B are too weak to move bones by themselves.

   C can contract or relax but not both.

   D can pull bones in only two directions.

Biology/Life Sciences Standards: Physiology

***BI 9.h.** *Students know* the cellular and molecular basis of muscle contraction, including the roles of actin, myosin, Ca^{2+}, and ATP.

Muscles are a type of tissue that helps the body move. There are three different types of muscle tissues: skeletal, smooth, and cardiac. Each type of muscle tissue is specialized for a particular type of movement. For example, skeletal muscle tissue is specialized for voluntary movement, such as typing or dancing. Skeletal muscles usually are attached to bones. When skeletal muscles contract, or shorten, the force of the contraction makes the bones move.

Structure of Skeletal Muscles Skeletal muscles are made up of long, slender cells known as muscle fibers. Each muscle fiber is made up of many smaller structures called filaments. Thick filaments alternate with thin filaments. Thick filaments consist mostly of the protein myosin. Thin filaments consist mostly of the protein actin.

How Skeletal Muscles Contract During a muscle contraction, myosin attaches to binding sites on actin, as shown in Figure 5–5. This creates cross-bridges between the thick and thin filaments in the muscle fiber. Energy from ATP molecules causes the cross-bridges to change shape. The shifting cross-bridges pull on the thin filaments and make them move. The thin filaments slide over the thick filaments, causing the muscle fiber to shorten, or contract.

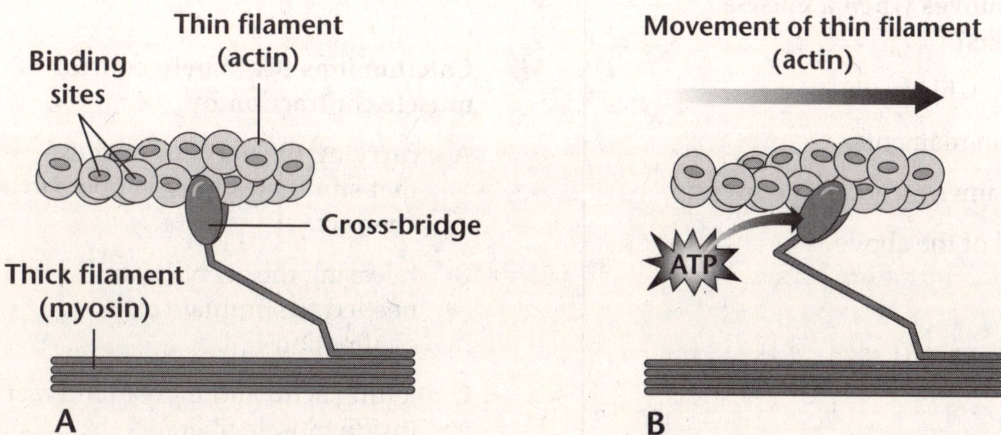

Figure 5–5 Muscle contraction (A) A cross-bridge forms between a thick filament and a thin filament. (B) Energy from ATP changes the shape of the cross-bridge, making the thin filament slide over the thick filament.

Biology/Life Sciences Standards: Physiology

Control of Muscle Contraction The contraction of skeletal muscle fibers is under the control of nerve cells called motor neurons. A motor neuron stimulates a muscle fiber to contract by releasing the chemical acetylcholine. Acetylcholine carries a nervous impulse from the motor neuron to the muscle fiber. The impulse causes calcium ions (Ca^{2+}) to be released within the muscle fiber. Calcium ions are needed for actin and myosin to interact. The muscle fiber remains contracted as long as the motor neuron releases acetylcholine.

Review Questions

12 **Which statement is true about the structure of a muscle fiber?**

  A It is a long, slender filament inside a muscle cell.

  B It is a thin filament made of the chemical myosin.

  C It is a thick fiber made of the protein actin.

  D It is a muscle cell containing both thick and thin filaments.

13 **What moves when a muscle contracts?**

  A thick filaments

  B thin filaments

  C filaments containing myosin

  D all of the above

14 **What is the role of ATP in muscle contraction?**

  A It attaches to binding sites on actin and forms cross-bridges.

  B It carries nervous impulses from neurons to muscle fibers.

  C It provides the energy that causes cross-bridges to change shape.

  D It moves when cross-bridges between filaments change shape.

15 **Calcium ions (Ca^{2+}) help control muscle contraction by**

  A carrying the nervous impulse that stimulates muscle fibers to contract.

  B releasing the acetylcholine needed to stimulate a contraction.

  C letting actin and myosin interact inside muscle fibers.

  D creating cross-bridges between thick and thin filaments in muscle fibers.

Biology/Life Sciences Standards: Physiology

7 6.j. *Students know* that contractions of the heart generate blood pressure and that heart valves prevent backflow of blood in the circulatory system.

The circulatory system consists of the heart, blood vessels, and blood. The heart pumps the blood through the blood vessels. Blood vessels that carry blood away from the heart are called arteries. The pumping action of the heart creates pressure inside the arteries and other blood vessels. This pressure helps keep the blood flowing. Blood flows through the system in just one direction because the heart contains valves that prevent blood from flowing backward.

The Heart The heart is a hollow organ made up mostly of cardiac muscle. As shown in Figure 5–6, the heart is divided into four separate areas, called chambers. The top two chambers are known as atria (singular: atrium), and the bottom two chambers are known as ventricles. Blood enters the heart through the atria. The atria contract and squeeze the blood into the ventricles. Then the ventricles contract and squeeze the blood into the arteries.

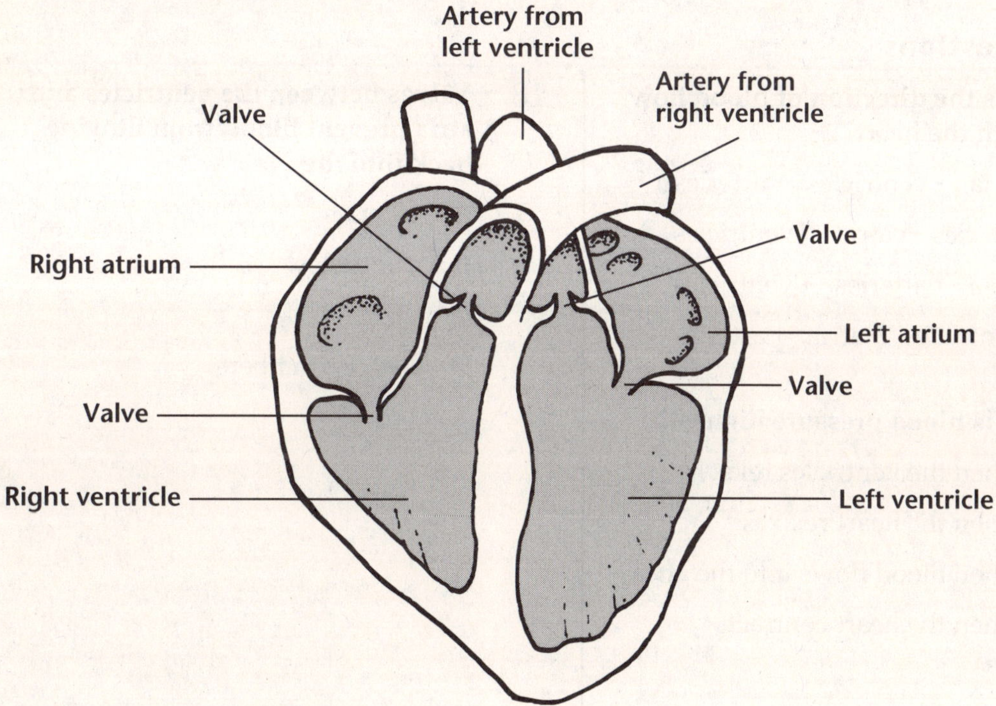

Figure 5–6 Human heart The heart is an efficient pump that keeps blood moving through the circulatory system.

Biology/Life Sciences Standards: Physiology

Blood Pressure The force of the blood on the inside of artery walls is known as blood pressure. Blood pressure is highest when the heart contracts. It decreases when the heart relaxes between contractions. However, the blood in the circulatory system remains under some pressure even between contractions. Without any pressure, blood would stop flowing through the circulatory system.

Heart Valves The heart contains four flaps of tissue called valves. There is a valve on each side of the heart between the atrium and ventricle. There is also a valve between each ventricle and the artery that leaves it. The valves keep blood moving in one direction, like traffic on a one-way street. The one-way flow of blood makes the heart a more efficient pump.

When the atria contract, the valves between the atria and ventricles are held open by the force of the flowing blood. Just before the ventricles contract, these two valves close and prevent the blood from flowing back into the atria. At the same time, the valves between the ventricles and arteries open, allowing the blood to leave the heart. When the ventricles relax, the valves to the arteries close again and prevent the blood from flowing back into the heart.

Review Questions

16 **What is the direction of blood flow through the heart?**

   A   atria → ventricles → arteries

   B   arteries → atria → ventricles

   C   atria → arteries → ventricles

   D   ventricles → atria → arteries

17 **When is blood pressure highest?**

   A   when the ventricles relax

   B   when the heart relaxes

   C   when blood flows into the atria

   D   when the heart contracts

18 **Valves between the ventricles and atria prevent blood from flowing back into the**

   A   arteries.

   B   ventricles.

   C   atria.

   D   lower chambers.

Biology/Life Sciences Standards: Physiology

BI 9.a. *Students know* how the complementary activity of major body systems provides cells with oxygen and nutrients and removes toxic waste products such as carbon dioxide.

Cells need oxygen and nutrients in order to function. Cells also release toxic waste products, including carbon dioxide. Four major body systems work together to provide the substances that cells need and to remove the wastes that cells produce. The four body systems are the digestive, respiratory, circulatory, and excretory systems.

Four Major Body Systems and Their Functions

Body System	Functions
Digestive system	• Breaks down food into nutrients that cells can use • Absorbs nutrients into the blood
Respiratory system	• Absorbs oxygen from the air into the blood • Releases carbon dioxide from the blood into the air
Circulatory system	• Transports nutrients and oxygen to cells throughout the body • Transports wastes such as carbon dioxide from the cells
Excretory system	• Filters wastes from the blood • Excretes the wastes from the body in urine

Digestive System The digestive system includes the mouth, stomach, small intestine, and several other structures. The digestive system breaks down food into simpler nutrient molecules. The simpler molecules can be absorbed by the blood and used by the cells for energy and other vital functions.

Digestion of food takes place in the mouth, stomach, and small intestine. Absorption of nutrients takes place mainly in the small intestine. The surface of the small intestine is folded and covered with tiny "fingers," called villi. The folds and villi provide a huge surface area for the absorption of nutrient molecules into the blood. The molecules enter the blood by crossing the thin walls of tiny blood vessels, called capillaries, which surround the villi.

Respiratory System The respiratory system includes the nose and lungs and the air passages connecting them. The respiratory system exchanges oxygen and carbon dioxide between the blood and the air. Gas exchange takes place in the lungs, in millions of tiny saclike structures known as alveoli.

Biology/Life Sciences Standards: Physiology

When a person inhales, air enters the nose and travels to the lungs. Oxygen in the inhaled air dissolves in moisture on the surfaces of the alveoli. The oxygen enters the blood through the thin walls of capillaries surrounding the alveoli. Carbon dioxide in the blood crosses the capillary walls in the opposite direction—from the blood to the air in the lungs. The carbon dioxide leaves the body when the air in the lungs is exhaled.

Circulatory System The circulatory system consists of the heart, blood vessels, and blood. The heart pumps blood through the blood vessels to all parts of the body. Nutrients enter the blood in the small intestine, and oxygen enters the blood in the lungs. The nutrients and oxygen are carried by the blood to cells throughout the body.

Waste products such as carbon dioxide enter the blood from cells. The blood carries the wastes to other major body systems for removal from the body. The blood carries carbon dioxide to the lungs, where it is exhaled into the air. The blood carries other waste products to the excretory system.

Excretory System The excretory system includes the kidneys and urinary bladder. One of the main functions of the excretory system is to remove waste products from the blood. The two kidneys filter wastes from the blood and produce urine, which contains wastes and excess water. The urinary bladder stores the urine until it is excreted, or passed from the body.

Review Questions

19 Which body systems work together to provide nutrients to cells?

   A excretory and circulatory

   B digestive and circulatory

   C respiratory and circulatory

   D digestive and excretory

20 The respiratory system helps remove the waste products of cells by

   A absorbing oxygen from the air into the blood.

   B transporting the wastes from the cells to the lungs.

   C releasing carbon dioxide from the blood into the air.

   D filtering the wastes from the blood.

21 What is the *main* function of the excretory system?

   A transporting wastes from cells and excreting them from the kidneys

   B excreting wastes from cells and transporting them to the kidneys

   C filtering wastes from the blood and excreting them in urine

   D transporting wastes to the kidneys and filtering them from urine

Biology/Life Sciences Standards: Physiology

***BI 9.f.** *Students know* the individual functions and sites of secretions of digestive enzymes (amylases, proteases, nucleases, lipases), stomach acid, and bile salts.

The digestive system breaks down food into simpler molecules that can be absorbed by the blood and used by the cells. Digestion occurs in the mouth, stomach, and small intestine. Other organs also play a role in digestion by secreting substances that help break down food. These substances include digestive enzymes, stomach acid, and bile salts.

Digestive Enzymes Enzymes are proteins that speed up chemical reactions in the body. Digestive enzymes speed up chemical reactions in which food is broken down into simpler molecules. The table shows the sites of activity of digestive enzymes and their roles in digestion.

Digestive Enzymes

Site of Activity	Enzyme	Role in Digestion
Mouth	Salivary amylase	Begins to break down carbohydrates
Stomach	Pepsin	Begins to break down proteins
Small intestine (from the pancreas)	Pancreatic amylase	Continues the breakdown of carbohydrates
	Trypsin	Continues the breakdown of proteins
	Nuclease	Breaks down nucleic acids
	Lipase	Breaks down fats
Small intestine (from cells lining the small intestine)	Maltase, sucrase, lactase	Complete the breakdown of carbohydrates
	Peptidase	Completes the breakdown of proteins

Digestive enzymes can be classified by the type of molecules they break down. For example, enzymes called amylases break down carbohydrates such as starch. Enzymes called proteases, such as pepsin and trypsin, break down proteins, or polypeptides. Nuclease enzymes break down nucleic acids (DNA and RNA), and lipases break down fats.

Mouth and Stomach Digestion begins in the mouth. Salivary glands in the mouth secrete an amylase enzyme in saliva. This enzyme, called salivary amylase, breaks down starches into sugars.

Digestion continues in the stomach. The stomach lining contains millions of glands, called gastric glands, that release hydrochloric acid and pepsin. Pepsin breaks down proteins into smaller polypeptides.

Biology/Life Sciences Standards: Physiology

The hydrochloric acid provides an acidic environment, which pepsin needs in order to work.

Small Intestine Digestion is completed in the small intestine, mainly in the first third of the small intestine, which is known as the duodenum. This is also where most digestive enzymes enter the small intestine. The enzymes are produced by the pancreas or by cells lining the duodenum. In addition, the liver produces a substance that aids in digestion in the duodenum.

- The liver secretes bile, a fluid consisting of lipids and salts. Bile salts act like detergent, dissolving and breaking up droplets of fat. This makes it easier for lipase enzymes to reach and break down fat molecules.

- The pancreas secretes pancreatic amylase, which continues the breakdown of carbohydrates. It also secretes trypsin, which continues the breakdown of proteins. In addition, the pancreas secretes nuclease, which breaks down nucleic acids, and lipase, which breaks down fat.

- Cells lining the duodenum secrete maltase, sucrase, and lactase. All three enzymes are amylases, and they complete the breakdown of carbohydrates. Cells lining the duodenum also secrete peptidase, a protease that completes the breakdown of proteins.

Review Questions

22 **Which enzyme begins the digestion of carbohydrates?**

    A   peptidase

    B   salivary amylase

    C   maltase

    D   sucrase

23 **Which type of digestive enzyme helps break down proteins?**

    A   lipase

    B   protease

    C   amylase

    D   nuclease

24 **What role does stomach acid play in digestion?**

    A   It lets pepsin work.

    B   It helps break down fat.

    C   It helps break down sugar.

    D   It dissolves fat droplets.

Biology/Life Sciences Standards: Physiology

25 The pancreas aids in digestion by secreting the enzymes

  A   maltase, sucrase, lactase, and pancreatic protease.

  B   pancreatic protease, pepsin, nuclease, and trypsin.

  C   pancreatic amylase, trypsin, nuclease, and lipase.

  D   peptidase, trypsin, nuclease, and pancreatic amylase.

26 How are bile salts involved in digestion?

  A   They start the break down of carbohydrates.

  B   They make the stomach acidic so pepsin can work.

  C   They complete the break down of nucleic acids.

  D   They dissolve and break up fat droplets.

Biology/Life Sciences Standards: Physiology

***BI 9.g.** *Students know* the homeostatic role of the kidneys in the removal of nitrogenous wastes and the role of the liver in blood detoxification and glucose balance.

Homeostasis is the process of keeping the body's internal conditions stable. For example, all organisms produce wastes, some of which are toxic. Removing toxic wastes from the blood and excreting them from the body is part of homeostasis. Keeping blood levels of sugar (glucose) and other nutrients fairly constant is also part of homeostasis. The liver and kidneys play important roles in these aspects of homeostasis.

Liver The liver is a large organ located near the stomach. It helps maintain homeostasis in two major ways. One way is helping to keep the level of glucose in the blood relatively constant. As shown in Figure 5–7, when glucose rises in the blood, the liver takes up glucose. The glucose is stored in the liver as a starch called glycogen. When glucose falls in the blood, the liver breaks down glycogen and releases glucose back into the blood.

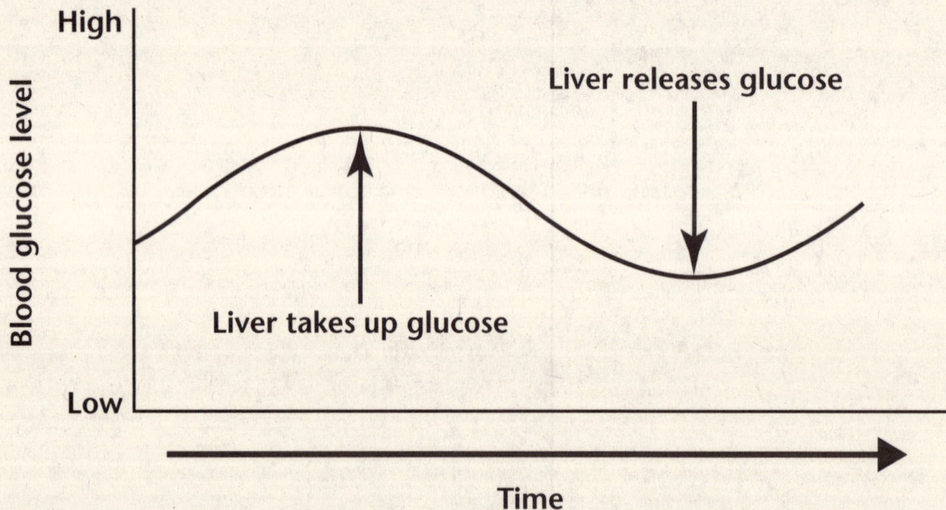

Figure 5–7 The liver and glucose balance The liver helps keep the blood glucose level stable.

The other major way the liver helps maintain homeostasis is by removing toxins from the blood. For example, when cells of the body break down polypeptides (from proteins), excess amino acids are released into the blood. The liver takes up the excess amino acids and converts them into other useful compounds. Poisonous nitrogen wastes are also produced in this process, but the liver quickly converts them into urea. Urea is a nitrogen-containing compound that is constantly filtered from the blood by the kidneys.

Biology/Life Sciences Standards: Physiology

Kidneys Filtering urea from the blood is one of the ways that the kidneys help maintain homeostasis. The two kidneys are the major organs of the excretory system. They are located on either side of the spinal column near the lower back. A tube, called the ureter, joins each kidney to a saclike organ called the urinary bladder.

When blood enters the kidneys, many tiny structures called nephrons filter urea from the blood and form urine. The purified blood is returned to circulation. The urine passes through the ureter to the urinary bladder. The bladder collects the urine until it is excreted from the body.

Review Questions

27 **Homeostasis is the process of**

- **A** filtering glucose from blood.
- **B** removing amino acids from urine.
- **C** keeping internal conditions stable.
- **D** converting glycogen to glucose.

28 **How does the liver help keep the blood glucose level stable?**

- **A** by releasing glucose when the blood glucose level rises
- **B** by taking up glucose when the blood glucose level rises
- **C** by releasing glycogen when the blood glucose level rises
- **D** by taking up glycogen when the blood glucose level falls

29 **The liver converts poisonous nitrogen wastes into**

- **A** urea.
- **B** urine.
- **C** amino acids.
- **D** glycogen.

30 **How is urea removed from the blood?**

- **A** The liver converts urea into nitrogen wastes.
- **B** The liver breaks down urea into other useful compounds.
- **C** The kidneys convert urea to amino acids the body can use.
- **D** The kidneys filter urea from the blood and excrete it in urine.

Biology/Life Sciences Standards: Physiology

BI 9.c. *Students know* how feedback loops in the nervous and endocrine systems regulate conditions in the body.

***BI 9.i.** *Students know* how hormones (including digestive, reproductive, osmoregulatory) provide internal feedback mechanisms for homeostasis at the cellular level and in whole organisms.

The endocrine system is made up of glands that secrete their products into the blood. These products, called endocrine hormones, deliver messages to other cells throughout the body. The secretion of hormones by endocrine glands is controlled by feedback loops that may include other endocrine glands and the nervous system.

Endocrine Glands and Hormones There are ten human endocrine glands. They include the hypothalamus, pituitary gland, and thyroid gland. The hypothalamus secretes hormones that control the pituitary gland. The pituitary gland secretes hormones that control most of the other endocrine glands, including the thyroid gland. The thyroid gland secretes a hormone that controls the rate of activities in body cells.

Endocrine hormones are carried by the blood to cells everywhere in body. However, only certain cells, called target cells, respond to the hormones. Target cells have molecules, known as receptors, on their cell membranes. The receptors let particular hormones bind to the membranes. When a hormone binds to a cell membrane at a receptor, it can control activities of the cell. Cells without receptors are not affected by the hormones.

Hypothalamus The nervous and endocrine systems work together to regulate conditions in the body. The two systems interact through the hypothalamus. The hypothalamus is part of the brain as well as an endocrine gland. As part of the brain, the hypothalamus is influenced directly by impulses from the nervous system. The hypothalamus is also influenced by hormones and other substances in the blood. The hypothalamus, in turn, controls the pituitary gland. Hormones secreted by the hypothalamus travel to the pituitary gland and stimulate the pituitary gland to either start or stop releasing its hormones.

Feedback in the Endocrine System The endocrine system is regulated by feedback loops that help maintain homeostasis, or a stable internal environment. Feedback occurs when an increase or decrease in a substance "feeds back" to stop or start the process that produces the substance. Figure 5–8 shows how feedback controls the thyroid gland.

Biology/Life Sciences Standards: Physiology

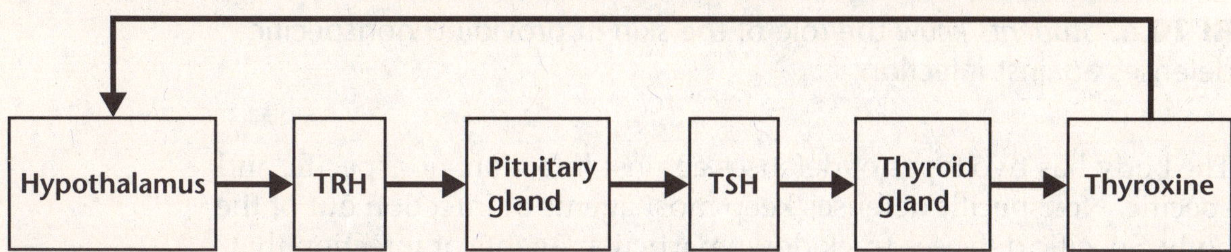

Figure 5–8 Control of the thyroid gland The thyroid gland is controlled by a feedback loop that includes the hypothalamus and pituitary gland.

The hypothalamus secretes a hormone called thyrotropin-releasing hormone (TRH). TRH stimulates the pituitary gland to secrete one of its hormones, thyroid-stimulating hormone (TSH). TSH, in turn, stimulates the thyroid to secrete its hormone, thyroxine. The level of thyroxine in the blood feeds back to control the secretion of TRH by the hypothalamus. When the level of thyroxine is low, the hypothalamus secretes TRH. As the level of thyroxine rises, the hypothalamus stops secreting TRH.

Similar feedback loops control the secretion of many other hormones, including those that regulate digestion, reproduction, and the amount of water in the blood. For example, when the water content of the blood is low, the pituitary gland secretes antidiuretic hormone (ADH). ADH stimulates the kidneys to remove less water from the blood. As the water content of the blood rises, the pituitary stops secreting ADH.

Review Questions

31 **What do pituitary hormones directly control?**

   A the hypothalamus

   B other endocrine glands

   C the secretion of TRH

   D the rate of cell activities

32 **The nervous and endocrine systems interact through the**

   A hypothalamus.

   B pituitary gland.

   C thyroid gland.

   D kidneys.

33

The diagram shows the feedback loop that controls the amount of water in blood. Which choice correctly completes the feedback loop?

   A pituitary gland

   B thyroid gland

   C hypothalamus

   D thyroxine

Biology/Life Sciences Standards: Physiology

BI 10.a. *Students know* the role of the skin in providing nonspecific defenses against infection.

The body has two types of defenses against infection: nonspecific and specific. Nonspecific defenses keep most agents of infection out of the body. Specific defenses track down particular agents of infection that have managed to get past the nonspecific defenses and invade the body. Unlike specific defenses, nonspecific defenses do not distinguish between one kind of infectious agent and another. For example, nonspecific defenses do not distinguish between different kinds of bacteria. The body's most important nonspecific defense is the skin.

The Skin as a Barrier The body's first line of defense against infection is keeping infectious agents out of the body. The skin plays the primary role in this line of defense by acting as a barrier against infection. Very few infectious agents can penetrate the skin.

The importance of the skin as a barrier against infection becomes obvious when the skin is broken by a cut or other injury. When that happens, infectious agents such as bacteria can enter the body and multiply. As the bacteria increase in number, they cause symptoms of infection, such as swelling, redness, and pain.

The skin is made up of two layers: the epidermis and the dermis. These layers are shown in Figure 5–9. Both layers play a role in the first line of defense.

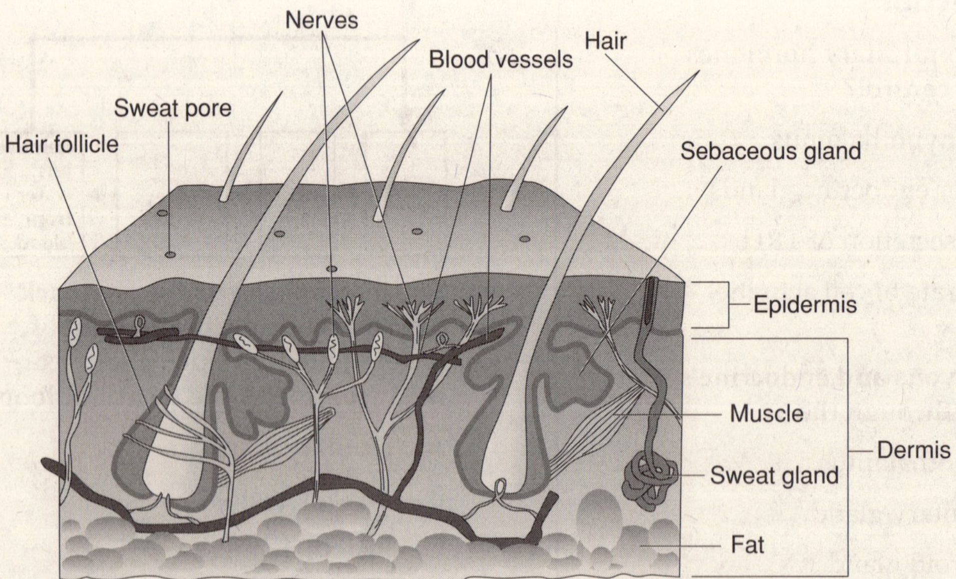

Figure 5–9 The skin The epidermis provides a tough covering that few infectious agents can penetrate. The dermis produces oil and sweat that make the surface of the skin too acidic for many bacteria.

Biology/Life Sciences Standards: Physiology

Epidermis The epidermis is the outer layer of the skin. The lower part of the epidermis is made up of living cells that rapidly divide and create new cells. The new cells push older cells toward the surface of the skin. Before the older cells die, they make keratin—a tough, fibrous protein. Dead cells and keratin make up the upper part of the epidermis. They form a tough covering that keeps out most agents of infection.

Dermis The dermis is the inner layer of the skin. It contains sebaceous glands, sweat glands, and several other structures. Sebaceous glands produce oil that keeps the surface of the skin flexible and waterproof. Sweat glands produce sweat that helps keep the body cool. Oil and sweat cause the surface of the skin to be acidic. The acidic environment kills many bacteria that come into contact with the skin.

Review Questions

34 Which statement is true about non-specific defenses?

  A They keep most agents of infection out of the body.

  B They do not work against bacteria and other infectious agents.

  C They play a minor role in the body's defense against infection.

  D They distinguish between different kinds of infectious agents.

35 Where is keratin found in the skin?

  A in the lower part of the dermis

  B in the upper part of epidermis

  C between the dermis and epidermis

  D in new cells that are dividing rapidly

36 Oil and sweat on the skin help defend against infection by making the skin's surface

  A flexible.

  B cool.

  C acidic.

  D tough.

Biology/Life Sciences Standards: Physiology

BI 10.d. *Students know* there are important differences between bacteria and viruses with respect to their requirements for growth and replication, the body's primary defenses against bacterial and viral infections, and effective treatments of these infections.

Both bacteria (singular: bacterium) and viruses can be pathogens, or agents of disease. However, the two types of pathogens have important differences in their needs. They also cause disease in different ways, and the body responds to them differently as well. In addition, treatments vary for infections caused by bacteria and infections caused by viruses. These differences between bacteria and viruses are summarized in the table.

Bacteria and Viruses as Agents of Infection

Type of Pathogen	What It Is	How It Causes Disease	How the Body Responds	How Infections Are Treated
Virus	Tiny particle containing genetic material	Invades and destroys cells	Interferon production	Antiviral drugs
Bacterium	Single-celled living organism	Breaks down tissues for food or releases toxins	Inflammatory response	Antibiotic drugs

Viruses Viruses are tiny particles that invade and replicate (make copies of themselves) inside living cells. Viruses do not have cells, so they must depend on the cells of living organisms for their needs. A virus attaches to the surface of a cell, inserts its genetic material into the cell, and takes over the cell's structures to produce viral proteins and to replicate. This usually destroys the infected cell.

Viruses can infect the cells of nearly every type of organism, including plants, animals, and bacteria. Viruses that infect human cells cause a wide range of diseases. Human diseases caused by viruses include the common cold, influenza, warts, and AIDS.

When viruses enter the human body and infect cells, the infected cells may produce special proteins. The proteins are called interferons, because they "interfere" with the viruses. Interferons do not kill viruses, but they prevent viruses from replicating and infecting other cells. This may slow down and eventually stop the spread of the virus through the body.

Antibiotic drugs have no effect on viruses. However, antiviral drugs have been developed to fight some viruses. The drugs generally prevent viruses from invading and replicating inside cells.

Biology/Life Sciences Standards: Physiology

Bacteria Bacteria are microorganisms that lack a cell nucleus. Unlike viruses, bacteria do not need to invade cells in order to replicate. As living cells, bacteria have all the structures they need for reproduction and other vital processes. Instead, bacteria cause disease in other ways— either by breaking down tissues for food or by releasing toxins.

Most bacteria are harmless to humans, but some cause disease. Typically, the diseases caused by bacteria are serious. They include diphtheria, botulism, anthrax, and strep throat.

When bacteria enter the body, the body's first reaction may be the inflammatory response. The inflammatory response is an early, nonspecific reaction to tissue damage caused by injury or infection. As part of the inflammatory response, large white blood cells called phagocytes "eat up" invading bacteria.

Bacterial infections can be treated with antibiotics. Antibiotics are drugs that kill microorganisms such as bacteria without harming the cells of the infected organism. Antibiotics work by interfering with the cell processes of the microorganisms.

Review Questions

37 **How do viruses cause disease?**

   A by breaking down tissues for food

   B by invading and destroying cells

   C by releasing toxins in cells

   D by interfering with antibiotics

38 **Cells infected with viruses may produce**

   A interferons.

   B antibiotics.

   C phagocytes.

   D antivirals.

39 **An example of a human bacterial disease is**

   A AIDS.

   B warts.

   C influenza.

   D strep throat.

40 **Which statement about antibiotics is true?**

   A Antibiotics do not affect viruses.

   B Antibiotics do not harm the cells of infected organisms.

   C Antibiotics kill bacteria.

   D all of the above

Biology/Life Sciences Standards: Physiology

BI 10.b. *Students know* the role of antibodies in the body's response to infection.

BI 10.c. *Students know* how vaccination protects an individual from infectious diseases.

The immune system defends the body against specific pathogens, such as particular viruses or bacteria. The immune system's reaction to infection is called the immune response. A substance that triggers the immune response is known as an antigen. Proteins on the surfaces of viruses, bacteria, and other pathogens can be antigens. Certain cells of the immune system produce substances that recognize and bind to specific antigens. The substances are called antibodies. By binding to antigens, antibodies disable and help destroy the pathogens.

Antibodies When pathogens invade the body, their antigens are recognized as foreign invaders by a few cells of the immune system. These cells, called B cells, divide rapidly, resulting in large numbers of B cells that recognize the antigen. Some of these B cells release antibodies. The antibodies are carried in the blood and in lymph fluid, which flows through tissues. The antibodies bind to pathogens that are circulating in these fluids.

Each antibody is specific for a particular type of antigen. It has two antigen-binding sites, as shown in Figure 5–10. After antibodies bind with the antigens on a pathogen, the pathogen can no longer harm the body. Pathogens with antibodies also attract phagocytes, the white blood cells that "eat up" pathogens.

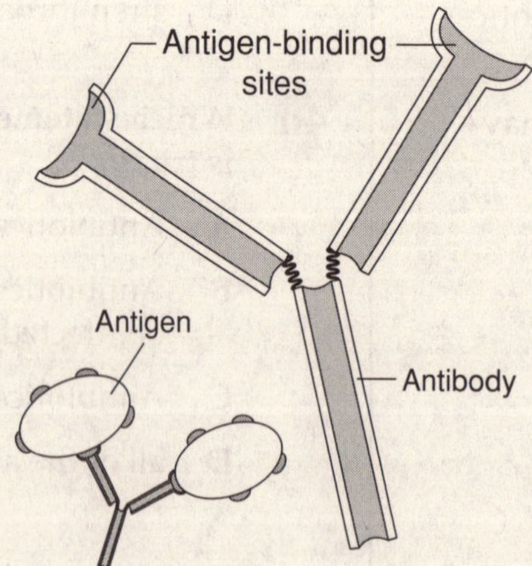

Figure 5–10 Antibody An antibody has two identical antigen-binding sites. The sites bind to only a particular type of antigen.

Biology/Life Sciences Standards: Physiology

Immunity After an individual has been exposed to a pathogen and produced antibodies to it, some of the B cells "remember" how to produce the antibodies. This greatly reduces the chance that the pathogen will be able to cause disease in that individual again. If the same pathogen enters the body a second time, antibodies will be produced so quickly that the pathogen will be destroyed before it can multiply and cause disease. The ability of the body to resist a particular pathogen in this way is called immunity.

Vaccination Immunity to many pathogens can also be achieved by vaccination. Vaccination is the injection of a weakened pathogen into an organism in order to produce immunity to that pathogen. The pathogen is too weak to cause disease, but its antigens stimulate the immune system to make B cells capable of producing antibodies against it. The B cells are ready to produce antibodies if the actual pathogen ever enters the body.

Review Questions

41 A substance that triggers the immune response is known as a(an)

    A antibody.

    B antigen.

    C B cell.

    D phagocyte.

42 How do antibodies help fight infection?

    A by guarding body cells

    B by producing B cells

    C by binding to antigens

    D by "eating up" pathogens

43 The ability of the immune system to quickly produce antibodies to a particular pathogen is called

    A immunity.

    B vaccination.

    C disease.

    D infection.

44 A weakened pathogen is injected in a vaccination because the weakened pathogen can

    A compete with regular pathogens.

    B stimulate an immune response.

    C cause a weaker form of disease.

    D force B cells to produce antigens.

Biology/Life Sciences Standards: Physiology

***BI 10.f.** *Students know* the roles of phagocytes, B-lymphocytes, and T-lymphocytes in the immune system.

The immune system helps the body fight infections and diseases such as cancer. Three important types of immune system cells are phagocytes, B-lymphocytes, and T-lymphocytes. Phagocytes destroy foreign particles, including pathogens such as bacteria. Phagocytes may also trigger B- or T-lymphocytes to help fight infection. When B- or T-lymphocytes respond to an infection, immunity may develop. Immunity is the ability to resist future infections by a particular pathogen.

Phagocytes Phagocytes are white blood cells that engulf and digest particles in body fluids and tissues. The particles may be foreign cells (such as bacteria), cancerous cells, dead cells, or debris. The process in which this occurs is called phagocytosis. The process is shown in Figure 5–11.

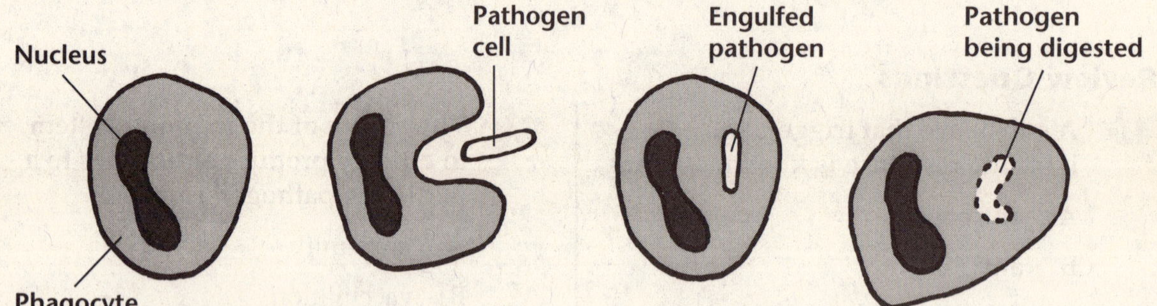

Figure 5–11 Phagocytosis A phagocyte finds and engulfs a pathogen. Then the phagocyte kills the pathogen by digesting it.

Phagocytes may also trigger an immune response. When phagocytes engulf and digest foreign cells such as bacteria, the phagocytes express the foreign antigens on their surface. Phagocytes expressing foreign antigens may stimulate B- or T-lymphocytes to respond to the pathogen.

B-Lymphocytes B-lymphocytes are also called B cells. If foreign antigens stimulate B cells, the B cells divide rapidly and produce large numbers of two different types of B cells: plasma cells and memory B cells.

- Plasma cells are the B cells that release antibodies in body fluids. The antibodies fight infection by binding to antigens on the surfaces of pathogens. Once the pathogens have been destroyed, the plasma cells die out and antibody production stops.

- Memory B cells remain after the infection is over. They can quickly respond to the pathogen if it ever invades the body again, resulting in immunity to the pathogen. Memory B cells provide immunity to pathogens in body fluids. This type of immunity is called humoral immunity.

Biology/Life Sciences Standards: Physiology

T-Lymphocytes T-lymphocytes are also called T cells. If foreign antigens stimulate T cells, the T cells divide and produce four different types of T cells: helper T cells, killer T cells, suppressor T cells, and memory T cells.

- Helper T cells activate killer T cells. Helper T cells also produce memory T cells.

- Killer T cells bind to cells containing the pathogen. They break open the cell membranes and kill the cells. Any pathogens inside the cells are also killed.

- Suppressor T cells release a substance that shuts down killer T cells after they fight the infection.

- Memory T cells, like memory B cells, remain after the infection is over. They can quickly respond to the pathogen if it ever invades again, resulting in immunity. Memory T cells provide immunity against pathogens inside living cells. This type of immunity is called cell-mediated immunity.

Review Questions

45 **Phagocytes can trigger an immune response by**

   A expressing foreign antigens on their surface.

   B releasing antibodies into body fluids.

   C secreting substances that shut down killer T cells.

   D providing immunity against pathogens inside living cells.

46 **Which type of immune system cell is involved in humoral immunity?**

   A killer T cells

   B memory T cells

   C suppressor T cells

   D memory B cells

47 **Which type of immune system cell invades and destroys infected cells?**

   A killer T cells

   B memory B cells

   C helper T cells

   D plasma cells

48 **Memory T cells provide immunity against pathogens that are**

   A in the blood.

   B outside cell membranes.

   C in body fluids.

   D inside living cells.

Biology/Life Sciences Standards: Physiology

BI 10.e. *Students know* why an individual with a compromised immune system (for example, a person with AIDS) may be unable to fight off and survive infections by microorganisms that are usually benign.

The immune system normally defends the body against a wide range of pathogens. However, the immune system may be damaged, or compromised, by disease. Infection with HIV, the virus that causes AIDS, is a major cause of a compromised immune system. People with a compromised immune system may be unable to fight off pathogens that are usually harmless to people with a healthy immune system.

HIV and the Immune System HIV, or human immunodeficiency virus, infects and destroys immune system cells called helper T cells. Helper T cells play a key role in cell-mediated immunity. This type of immunity defends against pathogens, such as viruses, that invade living cells.

When an HIV virus attacks a helper T cell, it binds to the cell membrane and enters the cell. Once the virus is inside the cell, it uses the cell's structures to make new viruses. Then the virus destroys the cell. The new viruses are released into the bloodstream. They travel through the blood, infecting and destroying other helper T cells.

As an HIV infection progresses, more helper T cells are destroyed. Doctors determine the number of helper T cells in the blood of people with HIV infections to monitor how far their infections have progressed. The fewer helper T cells in the blood, the more advanced the infection (see Figure 5–12).

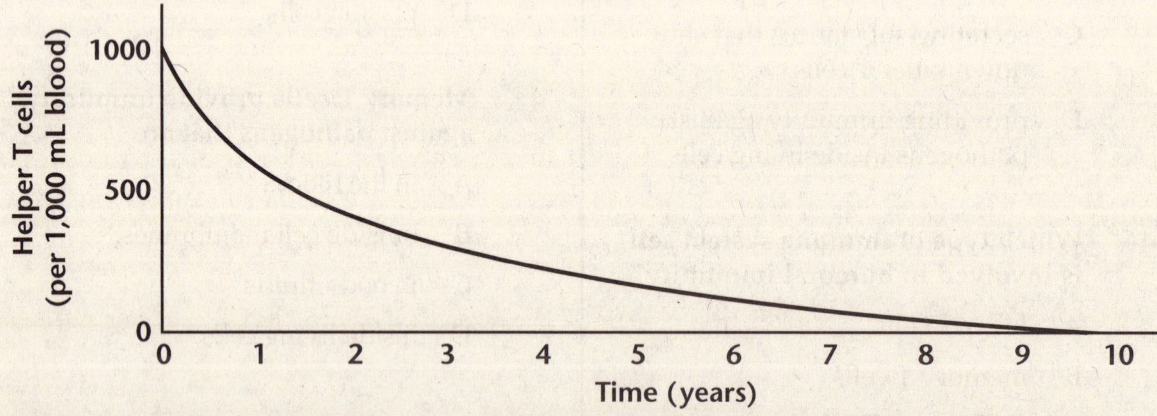

Figure 5–12 Helper T cells in a person with an untreated HIV infection Before being infected with HIV, a healthy person has about 1,000 helper T cells in each cubic milliliter of blood. During the first year or two after being infected with HIV, the number of helper T cells falls to about half the normal number. By seven or eight years after being infected, the number of helper T cells falls below 200 per cubic milliliter. At this point, opportunistic diseases start to appear.

Biology/Life Sciences Standards: Physiology

Opportunistic Diseases As the immune system becomes increasingly compromised by HIV, the body becomes more and more susceptible to diseases that seldom show up in people with a healthy immune system. Such diseases are called opportunistic diseases. Opportunistic diseases include a rare skin cancer, called Kaposi's sarcoma, and an unusual pneumonia, called *Pneumocystis carinii* pneumonia. When a person infected with HIV develops one or more opportunistic diseases, the person is considered to have AIDS. Opportunistic diseases—not the HIV virus—are generally the cause of death in people with AIDS.

Although opportunistic diseases are often associated with AIDS, they are not limited to people with HIV infections. People who have had an organ transplant may be given drugs to suppress their immune system. This is done to prevent the immune system from attacking and rejecting the transplanted organ. Because of the drugs, these people are also susceptible to opportunistic diseases.

Review Questions

49 **What does HIV do to helper T cells?**

A   It destroys them.

B   It activates them.

C   It makes them immune.

D   It causes them to multiply.

50 **People with AIDS develop opportunistic diseases because they have**

A   a compromised immune system.

B   very few helper T cells.

C   weakened cell-mediated immunity.

D   all of the above

51 **Which statement is true about opportunistic diseases?**

A   They occur only in people with AIDS.

B   They include rare forms of cancer and pneumonia.

C   They are caused by the AIDS virus.

D   They occur in everyone who has an HIV infection.

Investigation and Experimentation

7 7.c. Communicate the logical connection among hypotheses, science concepts, tests conducted, data collected, and conclusions drawn from the scientific evidence.

Science is an organized way to find out about the natural world. The goals of science are to find answers to questions and to develop explanations for observations.

Observations, Inferences, and Hypotheses Scientific thinking usually begins with observations—information learned using the senses. For example, *the aquarium plants are turning brown* is an observation. An inference is a logical interpretation of an observation. *The aquarium plants are dying* is an inference that might be made based on the observation that the plants are turning brown and the knowledge that healthy plants are green. Observations, along with logic and prior knowledge about science concepts, can be used to develop a hypothesis, or a possible explanation for an observation or scientific question. *The aquarium plants are dying because they are not getting enough light* is a hypothesis. This possible explanation for the observation can be tested scientifically.

Conducting a Test An experiment is a scientific test that is used to find out if a hypothesis is correct. To test the hypothesis that aquarium plants die if they do not get enough light, an experiment might expose aquarium plants to different amounts of light. If all of the other conditions are kept the same, the difference in the aquarium plants will be due to the differences in the amount of light they received.

The information collected during the experiment is called data (singular: datum). Observations and measurements are common types of data gathered during an experiment. Data tables and graphs are an organized way to record and present data. Other data are recorded in the form of diagrams or drawings.

Drawing Conclusions The data from an experiment are used to evaluate the hypothesis and draw conclusions. The data may allow the researcher to conclude that the hypothesis was supported. For example, the experiment with aquarium plants may lead to the conclusion that aquarium plants need 6 hours of light each day to stay healthy. The hypothesis that the aquarium plants were dying because they did not get enough light was supported. On the other hand, data from an experiment may not support the hypothesis. Often, the data and conclusions from one experiment lead to another question, as shown in Figure 6–1. Conclusions are considered valid when the experiment was properly designed, the data were correctly recorded, and the experiment can be repeated with similar results. Conclusions should be questioned if they mix fact and opinion or are based on small sample sizes.

Investigation and Experimentation

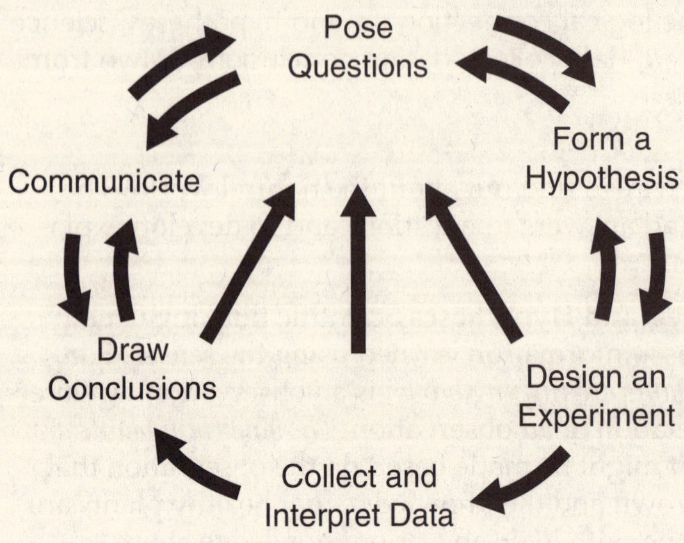

Figure 6–1 Scientific inquiry Finding answers to scientific questions can be accomplished in many different ways.

Review Questions

1 Which is the best description of a hypothesis?

- **A** a logical interpretation of an observation
- **B** a possible explanation for an observation
- **C** a piece of information gathered using the senses
- **D** a set of information collected during an experiment

2 During an experiment, a student measured the temperature of a beaker of water every 10 minutes. What word best describes this group of measurements?

- **A** data
- **B** hypothesis
- **C** inference
- **D** conclusion

3 A scientific study showed that the depth at which some microscopic producers were found in a lake varied from day to day. On clear days, they were found at an average of 6 meters below the surface of the water. On cloudy days they were found at an average depth of 1 meter below the surface. Which hypothesis would be supported by these data?

- **A** Precipitation affects the location of microscopic producers.
- **B** Wind currents affect the location of microscopic producers.
- **C** Nitrogen concentration affects the location of microscopic producers.
- **D** Light intensity affects the location of microscopic producers.

Investigation and Experimentation

4   **Caloric Content of Foods**

Food	Calories per Ounce
Protein	147
Fat	271
Carbohydrate	152

A student investigated the amount of energy contained in different kinds of foods. One ounce each of foods high in protein, carbohydrate, and fat were burned separately in a calorimeter to determine their caloric content. The student's results are shown in the data table. Which statement represents a valid conclusion based on these data?

A   An ounce of fat contains about twice as many Calories as an ounce of protein.

B   Foods high in protein are a better source of energy than foods high in carbohydrates.

C   Foods containing carbohydrates taste better than foods containing fat or protein.

D   Proteins and carbohydrates provide the most Calories per ounce.

Investigation and Experimentation

BIIE 1.a. Select and use appropriate tools and technology (such as computer-linked probes, spreadsheets, and graphing calculators) to perform tests, collect data, analyze relationships, and display data.

Various tools and technology can be used to collect and analyze scientific data. Computer-linked probes, spreadsheets, and graphing calculators are three examples of tools and technology used during scientific investigations.

Tools for Gathering Information Computer-linked probes are tools used to collect data during investigations. These devices transmit information directly to a computer or calculator. A pH probe is an example of a computer-linked probe used in science. This device measures the pH of a solution and records and displays the information on a calculator or computer. A temperature probe can be used in place of a standard thermometer. This device measures temperature and relays the information to a computer or calculator.

Tools for Recording and Analyzing Information Graphing calculators are calculators that generate graphs based on information that is input by hand or through a computer-linked probe. Graphing calculators are useful tools for analyzing trends in data.

Spreadsheets are computer programs used to record and manipulate data. A spreadsheet appears as rows and columns of cells. Each cell is simply a box into which a number can be entered. The cells in a spreadsheet can be linked by mathematical formulas. For example, a particular cell might contain the sum of the numbers in two other cells. Spreadsheets are a powerful way to predict how a change in one piece of datum will affect other data.

Review Questions

5 Temperature probes, pH probes, and other types of computer-linked probes are most useful for

   A   gathering data.

   B   analyzing data.

   C   making graphs.

   D   drawing conclusions.

6 A computer program designed for the manipulation of data is called a

   A   probe.

   B   trend.

   C   spreadsheet.

   D   graph.

Investigation and Experimentation

8 9.c. Distinguish between variable and controlled parameters in a test.

In science, testing a hypothesis often involves designing an experiment. The factors in an experiment that can change are called variables. In a controlled experiment, only one variable is changed, or tested, at a time.

Variables and Controls In a controlled experiment, one factor, or parameter, is changed at a time. The plants in Figure 6–2 are a part of a controlled experiment to find out if temperature affects the rate of plant growth. In an experiment the variable that is intentionally changed is called the manipulated variable. In this case, the manipulated variable is temperature. The variable that changes in response to the manipulated variable is the responding variable. In this experiment, the responding variable is the rate of plant growth.

In order to make valid conclusions, all other variables in the experiment should be controlled, or kept the same. Notice that both plants shown in Figure 6–2 are the same variety and receive the same color of light. Other variables that need to be controlled in this experiment include the amount of water each plant receives and the type of soil in which each plant grows.

In a carefully controlled experiment, the changes in the responding variable can be attributed to changes in the manipulated variable. If more than one variable is changed at a time, there is no way to be sure what caused any changes in the responding variable.

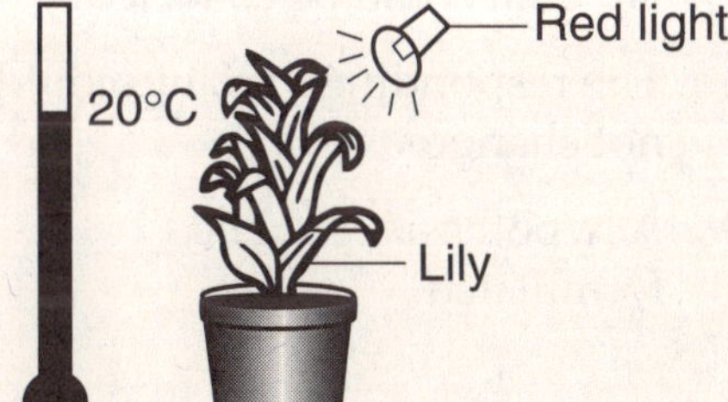

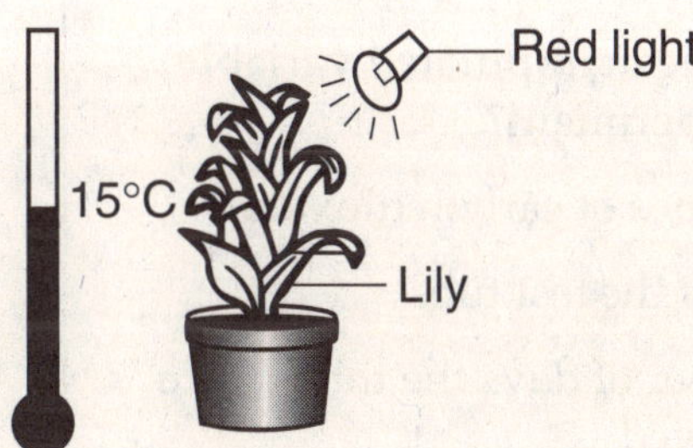

Figure 6–2 A controlled experiment In a controlled experiment, only one variable, or parameter, is changed at a time.

Investigation and Experimentation

Review Questions

Use the diagram to answer questions 7 and 8.

Two test tubes, A and B, were set up as shown in the diagram below. Bromthymol blue, which turns from blue to yellow in the presence of carbon dioxide, was added to the water at the bottom of each tube before the tubes were sealed. The tubes were maintained at the temperatures shown for six days. A student observed and recorded the color of the water in each tube to check for the presence of carbon dioxide.

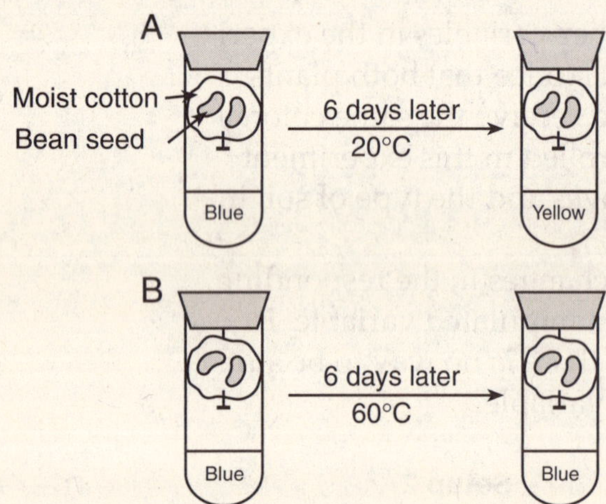

7 **What is the manipulated variable in this experiment?**

A   presence of carbon dioxide

B   size of the test tube

C   number of days the tubes were observed

D   temperature

8 **What is the responding variable in this experiment?**

A   presence of carbon dioxide

B   size of the test tube

C   number of days the tubes were observed

D   temperature

9 **In an experiment to find out how the intensity of exercise affects heart rate, the manipulated variable is**

A   the number of individuals participating in the experiment.

B   the amount of data collected.

C   the final heart rate after exercise.

D   the intensity of exercise.

10 **What would happen if an experiment included two manipulated variables?**

A   A valid conclusion could not be made.

B   No data could be collected.

C   The responding variable could not change.

D   A hypothesis could be formulated.

Investigation and Experimentation

BIIE 1.b. Identify and communicate sources of unavoidable experimental error.

In scientific experiments, sources of error are factors or conditions that cause data to be incorrect. Some types of error, such as planning an experiment that is not controlled, can be avoided. Other types of errors are unavoidable.

Sources of Experimental Error After an experiment is performed, it is important to review the data and procedures to determine possible sources of error. Experimental error can result from human mistakes or malfunction of equipment.

Measurement is one source of unavoidable experimental error. Every measurement made during a scientific experiment is a possible source of error. One cause of errors in measurement is limitations in measuring devices. For example, a thermometer might have a marking for each degree. Any measurement that falls between two degree marks cannot be made with total certainty. A thermometer marked in intervals of tenths of degrees will cause less measurement error, but again, if a measurement is not exactly on a tenth of a degree mark, some error in the measurement will occur. Figure 6–3 shows a student making a measurement with a meter stick. His measurements could have errors due to the limitations of the meter stick, human error in reading the measurement, or mistakes when recording the data.

Figure 6–3 Experimental error Measurements are one source of unavoidable experimental error.

Investigation and Experimentation

Error can also occur when a small group of objects studied does not accurately represent the whole group. Sample size, or the number of objects tested in an experiment, is an important consideration when analyzing sources of error. Suppose you were testing the effect of sunlight on plant growth. If only two plants were used—one that receives 8 hours of sunlight each day and one that receives 2 hours of sunlight each day—differences in the rate of plant growth might be due to differences in the individual plants, rather than the differences in the amount of light received. Using a larger number of plants in each group and averaging the rates of growth would provide more reliable results.

Review Questions

Use the diagram to answer Questions 11 and 12.

A student used this group of plants to see how a particular fertilizer affected plant growth. The five experimental plants all received fertilizer. The five control plants received distilled water. The student recorded the average growth of each group of plants once a week.

11 **What change would make the data from this experiment more reliable?**

A including a greater number of plants in each group

B reporting the growth of individual plants rather than group averages

C changing more than one variable in this experiment

D estimating the amount of plant growth rather than measuring

12 **When the student was preparing the plants for this experiment, she used a balance to be sure each plant was planted in the same mass of soil. The balance she used measures mass to the nearest gram. How could this student reduce the unavoidable error in her measurements?**

A use a centimeter ruler instead of the balance

B estimate the mass of soil rather than measuring

C use a balance that measures to the nearest five grams

D use a balance that measures to the nearest tenth of a gram

Investigation and Experimentation

13 **Experimental error can result from**

   A limitations in measuring devices.

   B malfunction of equipment.

   C human mistakes.

   D all of the above

14 **During an investigation, a student noticed that the balance he was using was not working properly. What should he do?**

   A Communicate this source of error when reporting his results.

   B Average the data so there is less error.

   C Avoid mentioning this error, because every experiment has error.

   D Ignore the problem with the balance because he had a large sample size.

Investigation and Experimentation

8 9.b. Evaluate the accuracy and reproducibility of data.

After an investigation, the data collected should be evaluated for accuracy and reproducibility. Valid conclusions can only be made using data that are both accurate and reproducible.

Accuracy Data that are accurate are close to the true, or correct, value. The accuracy of data can be evaluated by comparison to an accepted value or the results of other researchers. In the peer review process, researchers evaluate the accuracy of data obtained by other researchers.

Reproducibility Precision refers to how close a group of measurements are to one another. Precision is a measure of the reproducibility of data. Imagine measuring the width of a leaf three times. If all three measurements are very close to the same value, the data have a high level of precision. However, this does not imply that the measurements are accurate. Data can be precise but not accurate.

Neither precise nor accurate   **Precise but not accurate**   **Both precise and accurate**

Figure 6–4 Accuracy and precision Valid conclusions can be drawn only if data are both accurate and precise.

Figure 6–4 uses darts on a dartboard to model the ideas of accuracy and precision. The first dartboard shows darts thrown in a way that was neither accurate (not close to the bulls eye) nor precise (not reproducible). The middle dart board shows darts with a high level of precision. Notice that the darts are all in a very similar position. However, the darts were not thrown accurately. The darts on the third dart board model both accuracy and precision.

In science, data must be both accurate and precise in order to be useful. Carefully performing measurements with high-quality measuring tools improves accuracy and precision of measurements. Repeating each measurement several times allows the precision of the measurements to be evaluated.

Investigation and Experimentation

Review Questions

15 A student stated that his results for a particular measurement had a high degree of accuracy. How could he be sure of the accuracy of his results?

A by making sure that the measurements were reproducible

B by comparing his measurements to an accepted value

C by comparing his results to the results he had hoped to get

D by repeating the measurement several more times

16 A student measured the mass of a soil sample several times. The measurements she recorded were 25.2 g, 35.1 g, 20.3 g, and 19.9 g. The actual mass of the sample is 30 g. Which statement best describes this student's results?

A both accurate and precise

B accurate but not precise

C precise but not accurate

D neither accurate nor precise

Use the table to answer Questions 17 and 18.

A group of students measured the temperature of a water sample from a pond ecosystem. Each student took a turn measuring the water temperature and recording his or her results. The table below shows the students' measurements.

Temperature of the Water in Stillwater Pond

Student #	Temperature Reading
1	15.6 °C
2	15.0 °C
3	15.3 °C
4	15.5 °C

17 This group's data are precise, or very close to one another. A high degree of precision is an indicator of

A the correctness of the measurements.

B the reproducibility of the data.

C the accuracy of the group's results.

D the importance of the data.

18 What other information is needed to determine the accuracy of these students' temperature measurements?

A the type of thermometer used for the measurements

B the results of groups that studied other ponds

C the actual temperature of the pond water

D the total number of students in the class

Investigation and Experimentation

BIIE 1.c. Identify possible reasons for inconsistent results, such as sources of error or uncontrolled conditions.

After an experiment, it is useful to evaluate both the accuracy and the precision of the data obtained. Results that are inconsistent indicate that the data lack accuracy, precision, or both. These data will not be useful for making a valid conclusion. What are some factors that can lead to inconsistent results during a scientific investigation?

Sources of Error Identifying possible sources of error is an important step in all investigations. When an investigation has results that are inconsistent with an accepted value (the results are not accurate) or inconsistent among a group or class (the results are not precise), it becomes especially important to find the reasons for the inconsistency. Some error is unavoidable in every measurement, but measurement is also a source of avoidable error. Improperly reading the volume of a liquid using a graduated cylinder is a potential source of error in many investigations. Figure 6–5 shows a liquid in a graduated cylinder. Notice that the top surface of the liquid is curved. This curve is called a meniscus. To obtain the correct measurement, the graduated cylinder should be placed on a level surface. The meniscus should be viewed at eye level. The volume of the liquid is read at the bottom of the meniscus.

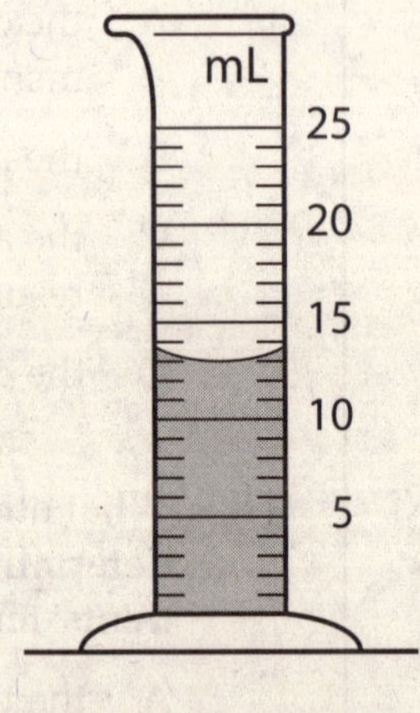

Figure 6–5 Graduated cylinder Reading a graduated cylinder properly can help reduce error in an investigation.

Investigation and Experimentation

A small sample size can also lead to inconsistent results if the sample used in the investigation does not accurately reflect the entire group. Suppose you are testing the pH of one soil sample from a forest ecosystem. Using one sample to determine the pH of the soil in the entire ecosystem could lead to results that are inconsistent with the correct value. Measuring the pH of a large number of samples from various parts of the ecosystem would lead to more reliable results.

Uncontrolled Conditions The results of an experiment might also be inconsistent if the experimental conditions are not carefully controlled. Imagine an experiment to measure how temperature affects the growth of a fruit fly population. A controlled experiment would consist of two fruit fly populations placed at two different temperatures, with all other conditions being the same. If other conditions, such as the size of the container or type of food, vary between the two populations, the results will probably not be consistent with accepted values or with other groups performing the same experiment.

Another important factor in a controlled experiment is the control group, in which no variable is manipulated. If experimental results cannot be compared to a control, there is no way to determine if changes in the manipulated variable caused any changes in the responding variable.

Review Questions

19

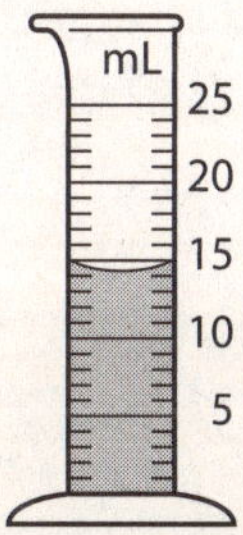

What is the correct measurement for the volume of this liquid?

A   15 mL

B   14 mL

C   15 L

D   14 L

20 In an experiment to measure the rate at which seeds geminate in soils with different pH levels, a student placed one seed in each of three pots of soil. Each pot of soil had a different pH. In every other way, the seeds and pots were kept in the same conditions. This student's results were not consistent with those of other students in the class. What is one way that this student could obtain more consistent results?

A   use a larger sample size

B   control the experimental conditions

C   change another variable in addition to the pH of the soil

D   record data from the experiment more frequently

Investigation and Experimentation

21 A student performed an experiment to determine if treating tomato plants with an auxin (a plant growth hormone) would make them grow faster. The student treated 500 tomato plants with auxin and measured the plants' growth several times. The results are shown in the table below.

Days	Average Stem Height (cm)
1	10
5	13
10	19
15	26
20	32
25	40

Identify one definite source of error in this student's experiment.

A small sample size

B lack of a control group

C incorrect hypothesis

D malfunctioning equipment

Investigation and Experimentation

6 7.e. Recognize whether evidence is consistent with a proposed explanation.

BIIE 1.d. Formulate explanations using logic and evidence.

If the data from an investigation are evaluated and found to be reliable, the data can then be used to develop an explanation of the results. This explanation, or conclusion, is considered valid if it is a logical interpretation of reliable data.

Formulating Explanations Scientific experiments begin with a hypothesis—a possible explanation for a set of observations or a scientific question. The experiment is a method of gathering information to find out if the hypothesis is supported or refuted. A conclusion is a statement that explains the results of the experiment in light of the original hypothesis.

For example, a student had the following hypothesis: Enzymes produced by human cells are most active at 37°C. The student carried out a controlled experiment to test his hypothesis. After evaluating his data, he found that the data support his hypothesis. His conclusion, that enzymes produced by human cells are most active at 37°C, is based on reliable data from a controlled experiment.

Evaluating Evidence and Explanations Part of scientific thinking is evaluating the explanations and conclusions made by others. Explanations are valid only when they are based on reliable data, so evaluating the experimental design and data used to make a conclusion is a good first step in evaluating a conclusion. For example, a conclusion based on data obtained from a very small sample or an uncontrolled experiment may not be valid. Experiments and results must also be reproducible in order for conclusions to be considered valid.

Explanations must be logical and based on the data obtained. Imagine if the student described above had made this conclusion: Enzymes produced by human cells work best at 37°C and a pH of 7. This conclusion is not supported by the student's data because he did not measure the effect of pH on enzyme activity. Conclusions should pertain only to the information collected in the experiment.

Investigation and Experimentation

Review Questions

22 **Temperature and Bacterial Growth**

Temperature (°C)	Bacterial Growth (Number of Colonies)	
	Strain A	Strain B
25	10	11
28	10	7
31	11	3
34	12	0

A student experimented to determine how the growth of two strains of bacteria was affected by temperature. The results are shown in the table. What is a valid conclusion this student could make using these data?

A   Bacteria grow best at 25°C.

B   Strain A grows better at 34°C.

C   Bacteria cannot grow at 34°C.

D   Strain A grows best in the dark at 34°C.

23 A student conducted an original, well-designed experiment carefully following proper scientific procedure. In order for the student's conclusions to be considered valid, the experiment should

A   contain several manipulated variables.

B   support the original hypothesis.

C   be repeated to verify the results.

D   be conducted by a professional scientist.

24 To investigate the effect of a substance on plant growth, two bean seeds of the same species were grown under identical conditions with Substance X added to the soil of one of the plants. At the end of two weeks, the plant grown with Substance X was 12.5 centimeters tall, and the plant grown without Substance X was 12.2 centimeters tall. The researcher concluded that the presence of Substance X causes plants to grow taller. Why should the validity of this conclusion be questioned?

A   The experiment did not include a control.

B   The sample size was too small.

C   The researcher did not start with a scientific question.

D   The researcher did not measure the effect of Substance X.

25 A student tossed a coin five times and observed the results of four tails and one head. He concluded that when a coin is tossed, there is an 80% chance of getting a tail and a 20% chance of getting a head. What reason might another student have to question the validity of this conclusion?

A   The experiment should not have included more than two tosses.

B   The weight of the coin was not taken into consideration.

C   The surface the coin landed on was not taken into consideration.

D   The experiment should have included many more tosses.

Investigation and Experimentation

BIIE 1.e. Solve scientific problems by using quadratic equations and simple trigometric, exponential, and logarithmic functions.

Scientific problem-solving often involves the use of mathematical formulas and equations. Understanding certain mathematical concepts is essential for gaining an understanding of some scientific concepts.

Quadratic Equations A quadratic equation is a mathematical equation that includes at least one variable raised to the second power (squared) and no variables raised to a power higher than two. An equation such as $y = 5x^2$ is a quadratic equation. This equation can be solved by inserting a known value for one of the variables and solving for the value of the other variable.

Quadratic equations are applied in many ways in science. The Hardy-Weinberg equation, $p^2 + 2pq + q^2 = 1$ (or 100%), is a quadratic equation used in population genetics. In this case, the variables refer to the frequency of particular alleles in a population. The equation can be solved to find the percentage of genotypes and phenotypes in a population.

Trigometric Functions Relationships between the size of the angles and the lengths of the sides of a right triangle can be expressed in ratios, which are called trigometric ratios. Trigonometry has many applications in science, especially in astronomy. Trigometric ratios are used by astronomers to determine the distance to stars.

The Pythagorean theorem is an equation that describes the relationship of the lengths of the sides of a right triangle (one that contains a 90° angle). Using the equation $a^2 + b^2 = c^2$, in which a and b represent the length of the right triangle's legs and c represents the length of the triangle's hypotenuse, the unknown length of a triangle's side can be determined. Imagine a right triangle with the leg lengths of 6 m and 8 m. The length of the hypotenuse can be determined in the following way:

$$a^2 + b^2 = c^2$$

$$(6 \text{ m})^2 + (8 \text{ m})^2 = c^2$$

$$36 \text{ m}^2 + 64 \text{ m}^2 = c^2$$

$$100 \text{ m}^2 = c^2$$

$$10 \text{ m} = c$$

Investigation and Experimentation

Exponential Functions Exponents are a method of expressing a number multiplied by itself a certain number of times. For example, 4^3 is a way of writing $4 \times 4 \times 4$. In this example, the number 4 is called the base. The number 3 is called the exponent.

In science, the numbers used to describe objects are sometimes very large or very small. Scientific notation utilizes exponents to express these numbers. Numbers written in scientific notation are expressed as the product of a number (usually between 1 and 10) and 10 raised to an exponent. The following table show numbers expressed in standard notation and scientific notation.

Standard Notation	Scientific Notation
3,000	3.0×10^3
47,000,000	4.7×10^7
0.00013	1.3×10^{-4}

Logarithmic Functions Logarithms are another way to use exponents. In base 10 (the most common way that numbers are expressed), a logarithm is simply the exponent to which 10 must be raised to result in a particular number. For example, the log of 100 is 2, because 2 is the exponent to which 10 is raised to obtain a result of 100.

In science, logarithms are utilized when a great range of values need to be described on a single scale. The Richter scale, which measures earthquake intensity, is a logarithmic scale. That means each number on the Richter scale is a log. So, an earthquake with an intensity of 3 on the Richter scale is 10 times more powerful than an earthquake with an intensity of 2. The pH scale is another example of a logarithmic scale used in science. Each number on the pH scale is a log that indicates the concentration of H^+ ions in a solution.

Investigation and Experimentation

Review Questions

26 In a population, the frequency of the dominant allele, represented by the variable p, is 30% (0.30). The frequency of the recessive allele, represented by q, is 70% (0.70). Use the Hardy-Weinberg equation $p^2 + 2pq + q^2 = 1$ to find the percentage of the population with the genotype pq.

A 9%

B 42%

C 49%

D 100%

27 A right triangle has a hypotenuse that is 20 mm long and one leg that is 12 mm long. Use the Pythagorean theorem ($a^2 + b^2 = c^2$) to find the length of the other leg.

A 16 mm

B 400 mm

C 8 mm

D 544 mm

28 How would the number 56,000,000 be expressed in scientific notation?

A 5.6^7

B 5.6^{-7}

C 5.6×10^7

D 5.6×10^{-7}

29 In base 10, what is the value of log 5?

A 500

B 1,000

C 100,000

D 500,000

Investigation and Experimentation

BI 1.f. Distinguish between hypothesis and theory as scientific terms.

In science, hypotheses are used to guide and plan experiments and investigations. The results of many observations, experiments, and investigations are used to develop scientific theories.

Hypothesis A hypothesis is a possible explanation for a set of observations or a scientific question. Hypotheses are developed using careful observations, prior knowledge, and logical inferences. Charles Darwin made a set of observations about the diversity of living things on Earth. Using his prior knowledge and logical inferences, he developed the hypothesis that living things change over time. Note that this hypothesis is a possible explanation for his observations. For a hypothesis to be useful in science, it should be testable by experimentation or investigation.

Scientific Theories A theory is a well-tested explanation that unifies a broad range of observations. Not only do theories explain past observations, they can also be used to predict what will happen in new situations. The word *theory* is sometimes used in everyday conversation to describe an idea that has not been tested. This is quite different from the scientific use of the word *theory*.

Accepted scientific theories are continually re-examined by scientists. New research and new technologies can result in evidence that supports an existing theory. Sometimes the new evidence requires that an existing theory be modified or changed completely. Although scientific theories are well-supported and carefully developed, they are not considered unchangeable.

Charles Darwin's hypothesis that life changes over time led to the development of the theory of evolution. This theory was developed using evidence from several areas of science. As new technology has been developed, further support for the theory of evolution has been added.

Investigation and Experimentation

Review Questions

30 **Which of the following is the best description of a hypothesis?**

   A a possible explanation for a set of observations or a scientific question

   B a series of inferences about a variety of topics

   C a well-tested explanation that unifies many observations

   D a set of observations about one area of study

31 **Darwin's observations led to his hypothesis that living things change over time. Why is this considered a hypothesis?**

   A It is a possible explanation for a series of observations.

   B It is a good guess based on a single observation.

   C It is a well-tested explanation for observations.

   D It is an idea that is not possible to investigate.

32 **Why does a scientific theory take longer to develop than a hypothesis?**

   A Many investigations and experiments are required to develop a theory.

   B Time-consuming observations are not required for making a hypothesis.

   C A theory cannot be developed until it is unchangeable.

   D A hypothesis is just a guess, so it can be developed quickly.

33 **Which statement about scientific theories is correct?**

   A All scientific theories are unchangeable.

   B All scientific theories are well-tested.

   C All scientific theories have been recently developed.

   D All scientific theories are untested ideas.

Investigation and Experimentation

BIIE 1.g. Recognize the usefulness and limitations of models and theories as scientific representations of reality.

Models and theories are tools used in science to explain observations and to predict what will happen in new situations. Although models and theories have many uses in science, they also have some limitations.

Models Scientific models are representations of an object or situation. Models are particularly useful for studying complex or dangerous situations or objects that cannot be observed directly.

Figure 6–6 is a model of a DNA molecule. It allows the structure of DNA to be observed and studied. The DNA model is an example of a physical model—an actual object used to represent an object that is too large, small, or dangerous to be actually observed. Mathematical models are equations or formulas that show relationships between two or more variables. The Hardy-Weinberg equation, used in population genetics, is an example of a mathematical model. Computer simulations are another type of model used in science. A computer simulation is a computer program that can be used to simulate a variety of situations. For example, a computer simulation that models stream flow can be used to predict how quickly pollutants will move in a stream. A conceptual model shows ideas in the form of a diagram.

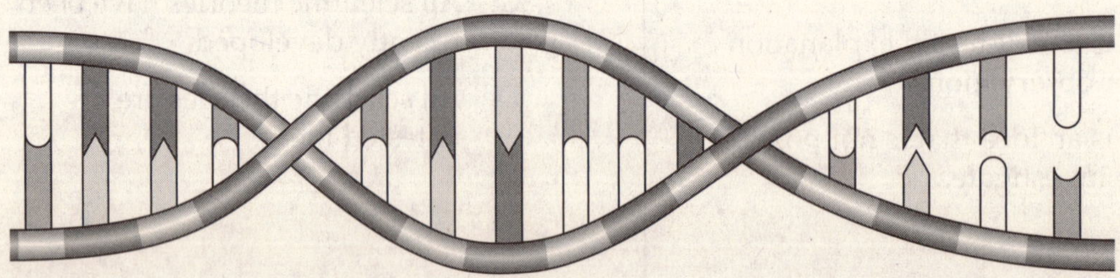

Figure 6–6 A physical model Actual DNA molecules are difficult to study because of their small size. This physical model allows the structure of DNA to be observed easily.

Although models are a useful tool, models do have limitations. Models are never a perfect substitute for studying an actual object or situation. A model might be limited because it includes only a portion of a complex situation. There may be other differences between a model and the actual object it represents. For example, the DNA model shown in Figure 6–6 does not show how DNA interacts with other molecules present within cells.

Investigation and Experimentation

Theories Scientific theories are well-tested explanations that unify a broad range of observations. Theories are a powerful tool for explaining observations. Theories are also useful for making predictions. For example, a scientist can make predictions about how a species of animal will respond to a change in the environment based on the theory of evolution.

Theories also have limitations. An established theory can lead scientists to doubt or ignore observations that do not agree with the theory. In this way, scientific investigations are occasionally limited by the presence of an established theory.

Review Questions

34 In which situation would a physical model be most useful?

A measuring different rates of bird flight

B studying the interaction of two biological molecules

C examining the weight differences of children in a variety of cities

D measuring the effect of rainfall on crop growth

35 What is a common limitation of computer models?

A They are too large to be useful for most people.

B They are never accurate.

C They cannot include every aspect of extremely complex situations.

D They are always much smaller than the actual object they model.

36

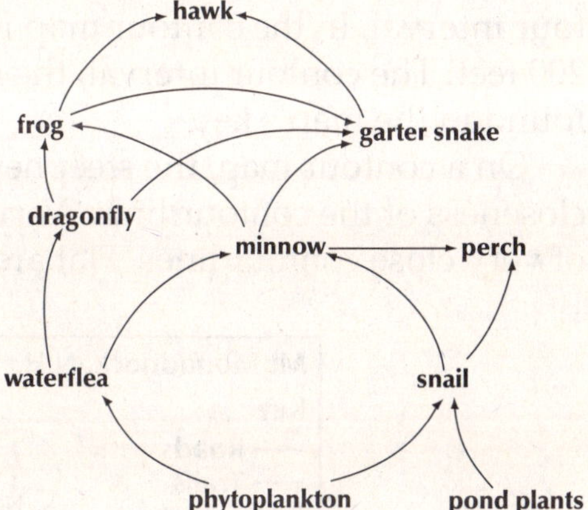

The food web diagram shown here is a model used to provide information about an actual food web in an ecosystem. Why is this model useful for learning about feeding relationships in an ecosystem?

A It shows the actual number of living things in the ecosystem.

B It gives information about a complex situation that is difficult to observe.

C It provides information about feeding relationships in all ecosystems.

D It explains every aspect of the complex feeding relationships in an ecosystem.

Investigation and Experimentation

BIIE 1.h. Read and interpret topographic and geologic maps.

Maps are physical models of Earth's surface. Different kinds of maps provide different kinds of information about the features of Earth's surface.

Topographic Maps A topographic map is a type of map that shows the elevations of different points on Earth's surface. An example of a topographic map is shown in Figure 6–7. The lines on the map, called contour lines, connect points that have the same elevation. Some of the contour lines are slightly thicker and are marked with a number. These are the index contours. The number marked on the index contour indicates elevation.

The difference in elevation between contour lines is called the contour interval. In the contour map in Figure 6–7, the contour interval is 200 feet. The contour interval, the map's scale, and the compass rose are found in the map's key.

On a contour map, the steepness of the terrain is indicated by the closeness of the contour lines. Very steep areas are indicated by a series of very close contour lines. Flat areas have relatively few contour lines.

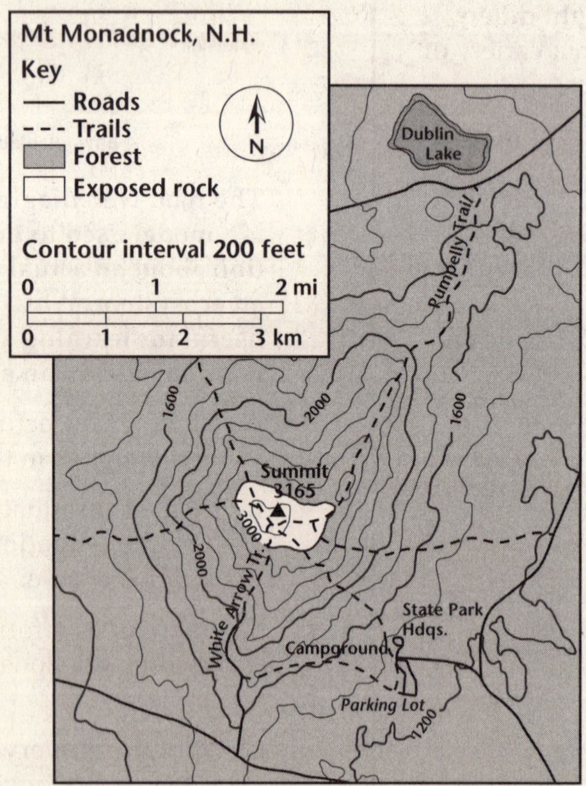

Figure 6–7 A topographic map Contour lines on topographic maps connect areas of equal elevation.

Investigation and Experimentation

Geologic Maps Information about the location of various rocks, minerals, and faults is found on a geologic map. These maps use different colors to indicate different types of bedrock. Faults are indicated with lines on geologic maps. Geologic maps can be used to determine potential locations of groundwater or valuable minerals. Geologic maps can also be used to predict potential hazards, such as sites of possible earthquake activity.

Review Questions

Use the diagram to answer Questions 37 and 38.

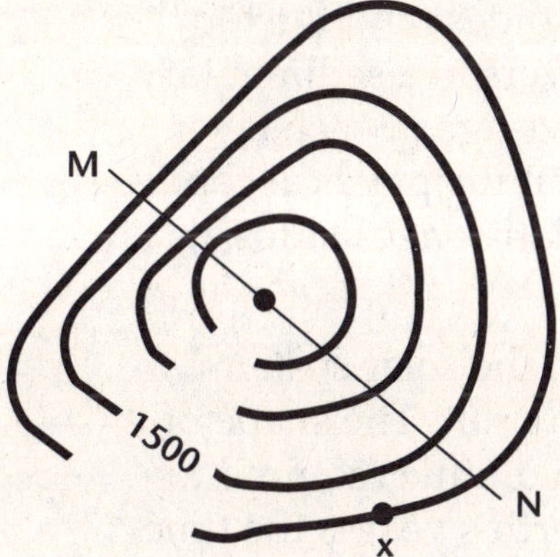

Contour interval = 15 meters

37 Along line M-N on the map, which of the following would the profile most closely resemble?

A 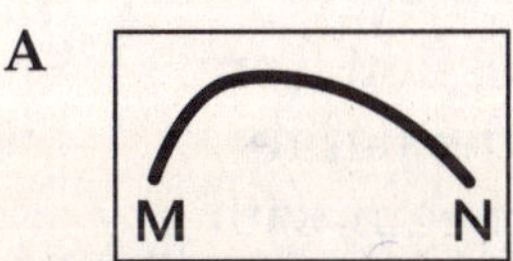

B 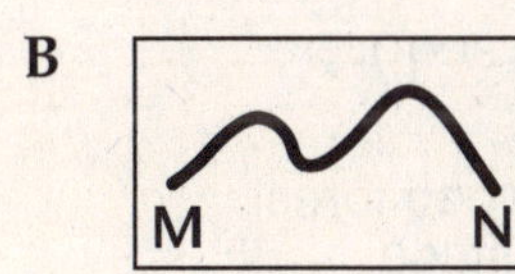

C 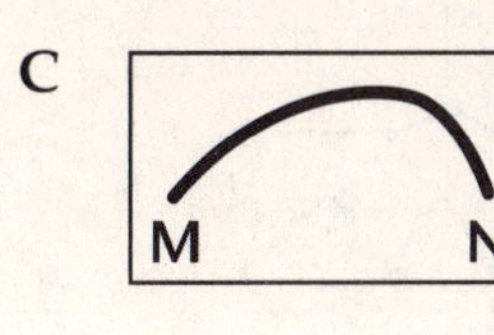

D 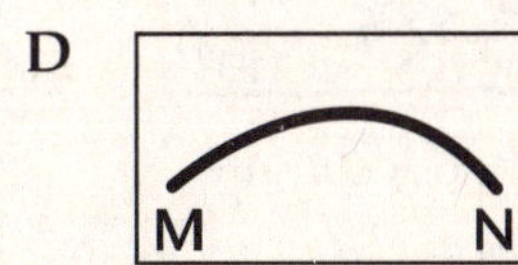

38 What is the elevation of the point marked *x* on the map?

A   1400 meters

B   1485 meters

C   1500 meters

D   1555 meters

39 Areas of differing color on a geologic map represent

A   different-sized faults.

B   different elevations.

C   different kinds of bedrock.

D   different cities and towns.

40 What information is *least* likely to be found on a geologic map?

A   elevations of various landforms

B   possible locations of mineral resources

C   sites of potential earthquake activity

D   potential locations of groundwater

Investigation and Experimentation

BIIE 1.i. Analyze the locations, sequences, or time intervals that are characteristic of natural phenomena (e.g. relative ages of rocks, locations of planets over time, and succession of species in an ecosystem).

Natural processes often occur in predictable ways. The locations, sequences, and time intervals associated with various processes can be used to learn more about past events and to predict how these events will proceed in the future.

Relative Ages of Rocks Layers of sedimentary rock accumulate over time. Each layer builds upon the previous layer. In an undisturbed sedimentary formation, the bottom layer of rock is the oldest and the top layer is the newest. The vertical sequence of the layers in a sedimentary rock formation can be used to determine the relative age of each layer. This information can be applied to learn more about the physical conditions at various times in Earth's history and the relative ages of fossils found in the rock layers.

Locations of the Planets Over Time The planets in the solar system move around the sun in a regular pattern called an orbit. The shape of each planet's orbit is an ellipse, or oval. The length of time required to complete one orbit varies from planet to planet. Earth's year is the time it takes for planet Earth to travel one time around the sun.

Succession of Species in an Ecosystem The series of predictable changes that occur in a community of living things is called ecological succession. Succession can result from slow changes in the physical environment or an abrupt change, such as a forest fire.

Figure 6–8 shows the series of changes in ecological succession from bare soil to a forest community. The changes represented in the figure occur over a time period of many years. Succession can also begin with bare rock. As soil gradually accumulates, the needs of other living things can be met. These changes occur in a regular and predictable sequence.

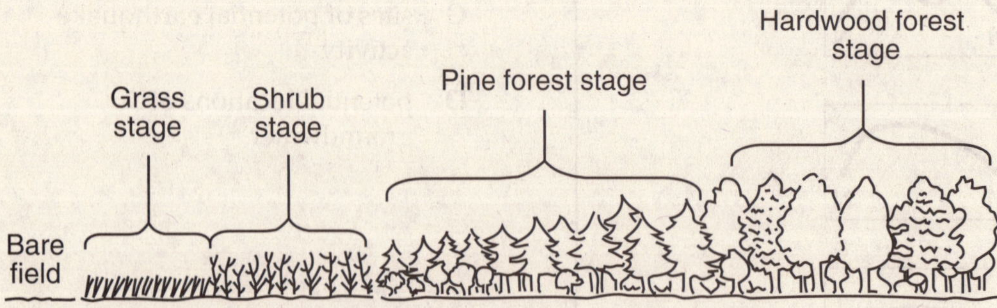

Figure 6–8 Ecological succession The predictable series of changes that occur in an ecosystem are called ecological succession.

Investigation and Experimentation

Review Questions

41 Information about the vertical sequence of sedimentary rock layers can be used to

A find the absolute age of each rock layer.

B determine the relative age of each rock layer.

C examine succession in ecosystems.

D determine the absolute age of a fossil.

42 How much time does it take Earth to travel once around the sun?

A one hour

B one day

C one month

D one year

43 What is ecological succession?

A the series of predictable changes that occurs in a community of living things

B a series of random changes that occurs in a community of living things

C the evolution of a particular species in an ecosystem

D the orderly formation of rock in an ecosystem

44 When a stable forest community is destroyed by fire, the community is usually

A not restored.

B restored in a series of successive changes.

C restored only if humans plant trees.

D changed to a permanent grassland.

Investigation and Experimentation

6 7.c. Construct appropriate graphs from data and develop qualitative statements about the relationships between variables.

Graphs are used in science to show relationships between variables and to reveal trends and patterns in data. There are three kinds of graphs that scientists often use: line graphs, bar graphs, and circle graphs. Each kind of graph is used to show different kinds of data.

Line Graphs A line graph is a used to show how a responding variable changes when the manipulated variable is changed. The line graph in Figure 6–9 shows how the percent of seeds germinated changes as temperature changes. In this experiment, temperature is the manipulated variable, and seed germination is the responding variable. This graph makes it easy to see the trends in the data obtained for these two types of seeds. Statements about the relationships between the variables can be developed using the information shown on the graph. For example, *peach seeds germinate best at about 9°C* is a statement that can be made about the information on the graph.

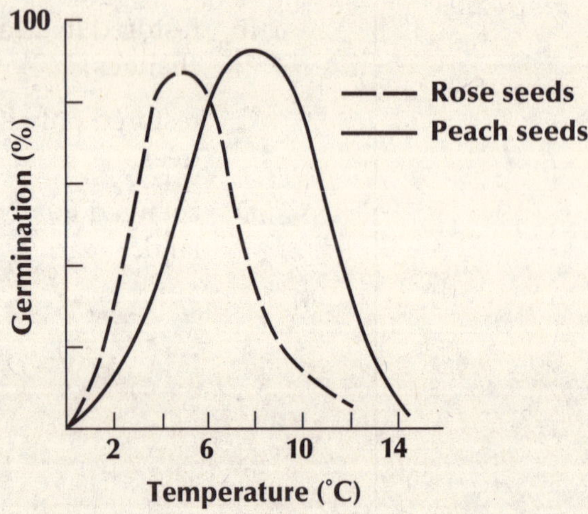

Figure 6–9 Line graph Changes in the responding variable are shown on a line graph.

A line graph is constructed using horizontal and vertical axes. The name of the manipulated variable is used to label the horizontal axis. The name of the responding variable is used to label the vertical axis. An appropriate scale must be chosen for each axis so the entire data set can be shown. The experimental data can then be plotted on the graph. After all of the data points are in place, a line of best fit is drawn to show the pattern in the data. Note that some of the data points might fall above or below the line of best fit.

Investigation and Experimentation

Bar Graphs A bar graph is used to compare data that fall into distinct categories. Figure 6–10 is an example of a bar graph. This graph displays data from an experiment in which the concentration of different ions were measured inside and outside of a cell. Note that the horizontal axis describes the categories of data, which in this case are different ions.

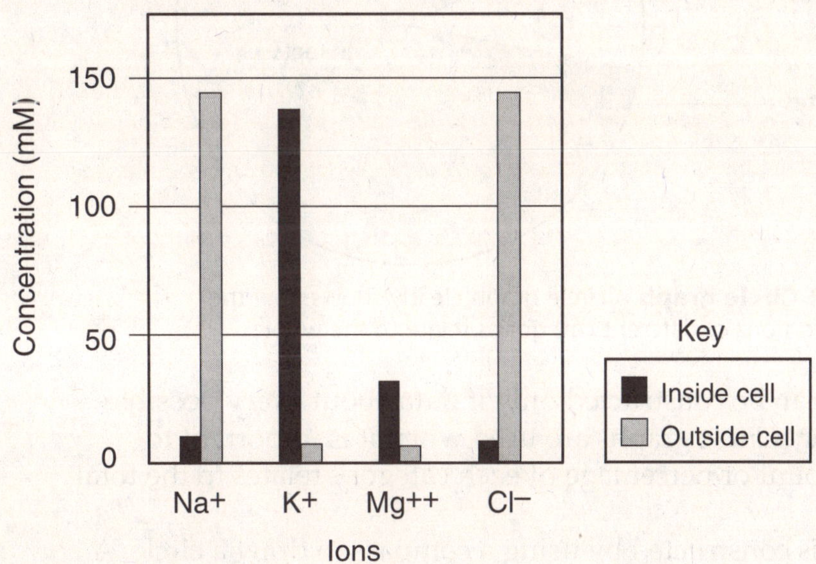

Figure 6–10 Bar graph When data are in distinct categories, a bar graph can be useful for making comparisons.

To make a bar graph, data must be divided into categories. The horizontal axis is labeled with each individual category as well as a term used to describe all of the categories. The data for each category are displayed using a bar, or a double bar, as shown in the Figure 6–10.

Comparisons between the data groups are easily visualized using a bar graph. For example, it is easy to see that Na+ ions are much more likely to be found outside a cell than inside a cell and that K+ ions are more likely than Na+ ions to be found inside a cell.

Circle Graphs A circle graph is used to show how the relative proportions of different categories relate to the whole. Figure 6–11 is a circle graph that shows the relative proportions of different types of animals in the animal kingdom.

Investigation and Experimentation

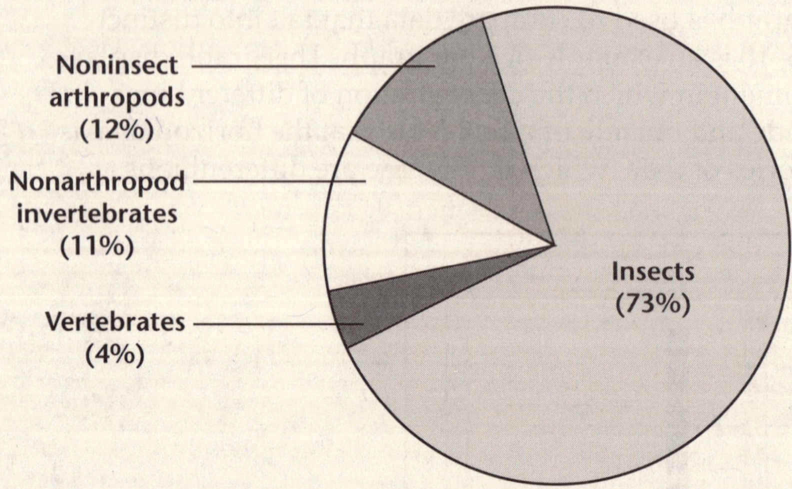

Figure 6–11 Circle graph A circle graph clearly shows how the relative proportions of different categories relate to the whole.

A circle graph can be constructed only if data about every possible category are known. Circle graphs are used when it is important to show how the amount or percentage of each category relates to the total or whole.

A circle graph is constructed by using a compass to draw a circle. A ruler is then used to draw a line from the center of the circle to a point at the top. The size of the sections of the circle graph can be calculated mathematically. Recall that a circle graph shows how data in each category are related to a whole. So, each category represents a certain percentage of the whole. In the example shown, insects are 73% of all animals. To draw a section that is 73% of the circle, the percentage must be converted to a number of degrees. A complete circle contains 360°. Multiplying 73% by 360° gives the result of 263°. Measuring 263° from the starting line using a protractor shows how large the section for insects should be. This method is used to determine the size of the section for each category. Because circle graphs always show portions of a whole, the categories always add up to 100%, or 360°.

Investigation and Experimentation

Review Questions

45 A student investigated the effect of temperature on the action of an enzyme that is contained in stomach fluid. Test tubes 1–5 were identically prepared to measure the amount of digestion at a variety of different temperatures. Each tube contained a certain number of milligrams of egg white, which was measured again at the conclusion of the experiment. The best graph of the results of the investigation would be made by plotting the data on which set of axes?

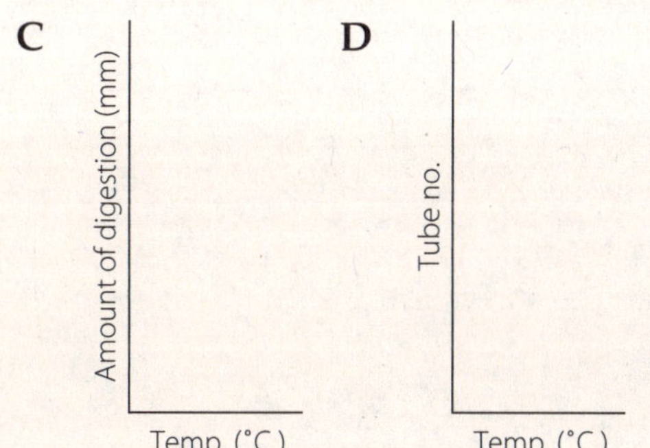

46

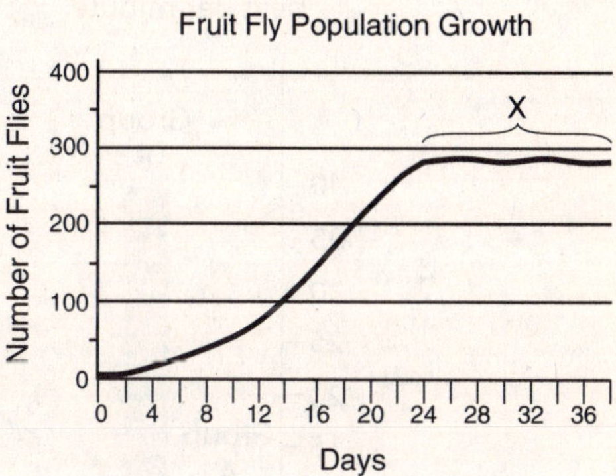

What statement best summarizes the relationship between variables shown in this graph?

A The fruit fly population increased constantly.

B The fruit fly population was unchanged throughout the investigation.

C The fruit fly population increased and then remained constant.

D The fruit fly population increased and then decreased dramatically.

Investigation and Experimentation

47

Average heart
beat per minute

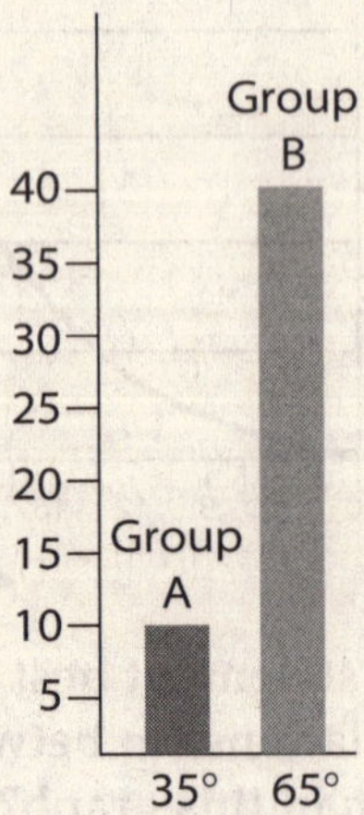

A student used this graph to show the results of an investigation on the effect of temperature on the heart rate of frogs. Why is a bar graph the best choice for showing these data?

A   because the data show change over time

B   because the data are divided into categories

C   because it was important to show how the parts relate to the whole

D   because there was no manipulated variable in the investigation

48 **For what set of data would a circle graph be the most useful?**

A   data that show how a plant's growth is affected by fertilizer

B   data that describe the amount of rainfall each day for seven days

C   data that show how a wheat field is divided to grow three varieties of wheat

D   data that describe the change in an enzyme's activity as temperature increases

Investigation and Experimentation

BIIE 1.j. Recognize the issue of statistical variability and the need for controlled tests.

Statistics is the area of mathematics that involves describing and evaluating numerical data. It includes a set of mathematical tools that can be used to analyze the data obtained during scientific investigations and experiments. Mean, median, and mode are measures of central tendency—statistical calculations that determine a value that best represents an entire data set. Range and deviation are calculations that measure the variability of a data set.

Statistical Variability An investigation compared how two different fertilizers affected plant growth. The two sets of plants were measured after one week, and the amounts of growth were recorded in the following data table:

Fertilizer Effect on Plant Growth

Fertilizer A		Fertilizer B	
Plant #	Growth (cm)	Plant #	Growth (cm)
1	2	1	5
2	8	2	6
3	10	3	6
4	9	4	7
5	1	5	6

By examining these two data sets, it is clear to see that these two fertilizers are not equally effective for promoting consistent plant growth. However, both of these data sets have a mean of 6 cm. (The mean is calculated by adding all of the values and dividing by the total number of data points.) An analysis of these data sets that included only the mean could be misleading.

Measures of variability can be used to describe how spread out the values in a data set are. The range of a data set is calculated in the following way:

Range = Greatest Value – Least Value

The data set for Fertilizer A has a range of 9 cm; the data set for Fertilizer B has a range of 2 cm. Reporting the range of a data set allows the consistency of the data to be evaluated.

Investigation and Experimentation

Average deviation of a data set is another measure of variability. It describes the average distance of the values in the data set from the mean. Recall that the mean of both of these data sets is 6 cm. To determine the average deviation, the distance of each data point from the mean is totaled and divided by the total number of data points.

Fertilizer Effect on Plant Growth

Fertilizer A			Fertilizer B		
Plant #	Growth (cm)	Difference from Mean (cm)	Plant #	Growth (cm)	Difference from Mean (cm)
1	2	4	1	5	1
2	8	2	2	6	0
3	10	4	3	6	0
4	9	3	4	7	1
5	1	5	5	6	0
		Total = 18 18 ÷ 5 = 3.6			Total = 2 2 ÷ 5 = 0.4

So, the average deviation of the data set for Fertilizer A is 3.6 cm. The average deviation for the data set for Fertilizer B is 0.4 cm.

Although plants grown with both fertilizers grew an average of 6 cm, Fertilizer B gave much more consistent results. Understanding the statistical variability of a data set is important when analyzing data and drawing conclusions.

Controlled Tests Although understanding the variability in the data sets from the two types of fertilizers is an important part of analyzing the data obtained in this investigation, no conclusion about the effectiveness of these fertilizers can be drawn using these data. Because no control data are provided, there is no way to compare the plant growth with the fertilizers to plant growth without fertilizers. A valid conclusion would require data describing a third set of plants, grown in identical conditions, without any fertilizer added.

Investigation and Experimentation

Review Questions

49

Day	Air Temperature (°C)
1	14
2	17
3	18
4	12
5	13
6	15
7	16

The table contains data about a forest ecosystem collected over a seven-day time period. What is the range of this data set?

A 6 °C

B 12 °C

C 5 °C

D 18 °C

50 What information does the average deviation of a data set provide?

A the reliability of the data

B the value that best describes the entire data set

C the variability of the data set

D the difference between the greatest and least data points

51

Data Set 1	Species A	4.5 cm
		5.2 cm
		4.3 cm
		6.7 cm
		4.3 cm
Data Set 2	Species B	2.5 cm
		7.3 cm
		4.5 cm
		3.2 cm
		7.5 cm

A student measured 5 individuals in two different species of worms. The lengths of the worms are recorded in the data table. What is the best summary of these data sets?

A Data Set 1 and Data Set 2 have the same mean and range.

B Data Set 1 has less variability than Data Set 2.

C Data Set 1 has a greater mean than Data Set 2.

D Data Set 1 has a greater average deviation than Data Set 2.

52 Why is a control group an important part of an experiment?

A It allows the variability of the data to be measured.

B It determines the mean value of the data set.

C It allows the data to be compared to a reference point.

D It determines the range of the data set.

Investigation and Experimentation

BIIE 1.k. Recognize the cumulative nature of scientific evidence.

The word *science* can be used to describe an organized method of studying the natural world. It also describes the body of knowledge that has been developed about the natural world. This body of knowledge, which has accumulated over time, continues to grow and change.

Scientific Knowledge Accumulates Over Time The overall body of scientific knowledge grows and changes over time. Scientific ideas are constantly re-examined and refined. New techniques, technologies, and observations continually provide new data, which may or may not support existing theories and concepts.

The development of the cell theory is an example of the accumulation of scientific knowledge over time. The development of a new technology—the microscope—allowed scientists to examine living things more closely than ever before. Early microscopes, like the one shown in Figure 6–12, led to the discovery of cells. The work of several scientists led to the development of the cell theory, a fundamental concept of biology. Knowledge about cells did not stop accumulating when the cell theory was developed. Instead, a tremendous amount of information about cells has been discovered since the development of the cell theory. As new technologies allow cells to be studied in new ways, this body of knowledge will continue to grow.

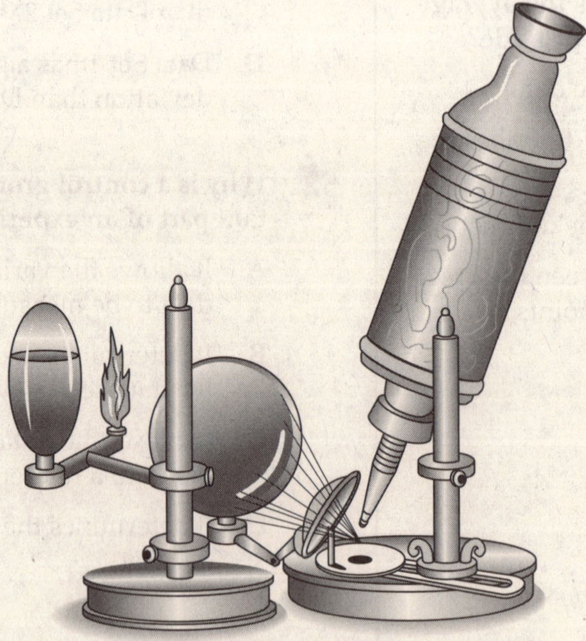

Figure 6–12 An early microscope The microscope is an example of a technology that led to new scientfic knowledge.

Investigation and Experimentation

The theory of evolution is another example of the way in which scientific knowledge accumulates over time. The theory of evolution was developed using Darwin's observations and a wide range of information previously developed by others. New techniques and technologies in fields such as molecular biology have allowed the theory of evolution to be added to and refined over time.

Review Questions

53 **Which is the best description of scientific knowledge?**

   A It rarely changes.

   B It has all been discovered.

   C It accumulates over time.

   D It is not affected by new technology.

54 **Why are scientific theories and concepts continually modified over time?**

   A Early scientists were not careful researchers.

   B New technology and techniques allow new observations.

   C Older scientific knowledge is not accurate.

   D Early scientists did not use technology.

55 **Knowledge about the cells that make up the human body**

   A continues to accumulate.

   B is unchanged since the development of the cell theory.

   C is not related to early scientific knowledge about cells.

   D is complete and unchanging.

56 **The theory of evolution was developed**

   A using only Darwin's observations.

   B without the use of any other scientific knowledge.

   C using Darwin's observations and previously existing scientific knowledge.

   D by Darwin and has not been reexamined since that time.

Investigation and Experimentation

BIIE 1.I. Analyze situations and solve problems that require combining and applying concepts from more than one area of science.

Science is a body of knowledge that describes the natural world. Biology, the study of life, is just one aspect of science. Understanding concepts in one area of science often requires the application of concepts from other areas of science. Biochemistry, evolution, and ecology are just three examples of ways that scientific concepts from more than one area of science are combined. Almost all topics of scientific study integrate concepts from more than one area of science.

Biochemistry Chemical reactions that occur within cells are essential to life processes. Biochemistry is the application of chemical principles to living systems. Understanding processes such as photosynthesis, cellular respiration, and the action of enzymes requires the use of concepts from both biology and chemistry.

Evolution The study of evolution incorporates concepts from many fields, including geology and molecular biology. The geologic time scale combines information about living things and the physical history of Earth. Molecular biology has given rise to a set of techniques that enable the molecular similarities and differences of living things to be more closely examined.

Ecology The study of ecology requires an understanding of concepts from several areas of science. Recall that ecology is the study of interactions among organisms and between organisms and their environment. An understanding of concepts in earth science is essential to an understanding of the nonliving environment. Ecology also incorporates concepts from meteorology, chemistry, and biology.

Review Questions

57 Food webs and food chains model the flow of matter and energy through ecosystems. Understanding the processes by which living things use matter and energy requires knowledge of

   A chemistry and biology.

   B meteorology and biology.

   C geology and chemistry.

   D meteorology and geology.

58 Determining the relative age of fossils is a technique used to learn about living things that requires a knowledge of

   A physics.

   B molecular biology.

   C chemistry.

   D geology.

Investigation and Experimentation

BIIE 1.m. Investigate a science-based societal issue by researching the literature, analyzing data, and communicating the findings. Examples of issues include irradiation of food, cloning of animals by somatic cell nuclear transfer, choice of energy sources, and land and water use decisions in California.

Science and technology have a huge impact on society. In many cases, scientific knowledge and technological developments have greatly improved the quality of human life. Innovations, such as antibiotics and seat belts, have saved countless lives. In some cases, however, it is more difficult to determine if new knowledge or a new technology is beneficial or harmful to society.

Science-Based Issues There are a great number of science-based issues that impact society. Irradiation of food is a technology that uses radiation to reduce the presence of harmful bacteria and parasites on food. Although this technique can benefit human health, some individuals remain concerned about the safety of irradiated food.

Genetic engineering is a set of techniques used to manipulate genetic material. The potential benefits and drawbacks of these techniques are the subject of much debate. Cloning animals is just one aspect of genetic engineering. Animals are cloned by transferring the nucleus of an adult animal's body cell into an egg cell that has had its nucleus removed. This fused cell is then implanted into an adult female, where it develops into a young animal genetically identical to the adult from which the nucleus was taken. Animals have been successfully cloned, but the clones have shown a tendency to develop health problems. Animal cloning raises the possibility of human cloning, an idea that raises serious ethical questions.

Science-based issues that affect society are not only found in biology. The use of energy, land, and water resources are also issues that impact society. Scientific knowledge contributes to the understanding of the choices that can be made concerning the use of resources, however, there are often no clear-cut "right" answers to these issues.

Investigating the Issues Developing an informed opinion about science-based issues requires time and effort. These issues do not usually have clear-cut right or wrong answers. A careful review of reliable information using library and Internet resources is a good first step toward understanding these issues. Each written source should be carefully evaluated for reliability and bias, or a particular point of view. Analyzing data available from scientific studies can also help to clarify a science-based issue.

Investigation and Experimentation

After careful research and evaluation of the information, an informed opinion can be developed. Opinions about scientific issues can then be communicated to others in the school or community. For example, you may wish to write a letter to the editor of the school or local newspaper to share your opinions about an environmental issue. Writing letters to elected officials is a way to communicate your views with those in government. Sharing informed opinions is a way to help influence decisions about important science-based issues.

Review Questions

59 **Science-based issues that impact society**

   A only occur in the field of biology.

   B usually do not have clear-cut right and wrong answers.

   C cannot be researched or investigated.

   D are never the subject of unbiased research.

60 **Your opinion about the use of natural resources**

   A should be developed using careful research.

   B should not be based on scientific facts.

   C should always agree with your friends' opinions.

   D should be developed without careful thought.

Investigation and Experimentation

BIIE 1.n. Know that when an observation does not agree with an accepted scientific theory, the observation is sometimes mistaken or fraudulent (e.g. the Piltdown Man fossil or unidentified flying objects) and that the theory is sometimes wrong (e.g. the Ptolemaic model of the movement of the Sun, Moon, and planets).

Scientific theories are well-tested explanations that unify a broad range of observations. When a new observation does not fit with an established theory, the observation may be wrong. It could also mean that the theory is invalid, and needs to be modified or changed completely.

Fraudulent or Mistaken Observations Observations that do not agree with an accepted theory may be fraudulent or intentionally misleading. One notable example of a fraudulent observation was the discovery of the fossilized remains known as Piltdown Man. In 1911 and 1912, a fossilized jaw and skull that appeared to be from a very early human were found in Piltdown, England. These fossils appeared to come from much earlier in Earth's history than expected, and cast some doubt on the established theory of evolution. Technologies developed in the 1950's finally revealed that the Piltdown Man fossil was a hoax. The fossils were treated with chemicals to make them appear much older than they actually were.

Some observations that do not agree with an accepted theory are the result of honest mistakes or naive beliefs. Jean-Baptist Lamark proposed that through the use or disuse of organs, organisms acquired or lost traits during their lifetimes. As shown in Figure 6–13, he mistakenly believed that these acquired or lost traits could be passed to offspring. This idea was eventually discarded as more information was gathered about evolution and genetics.

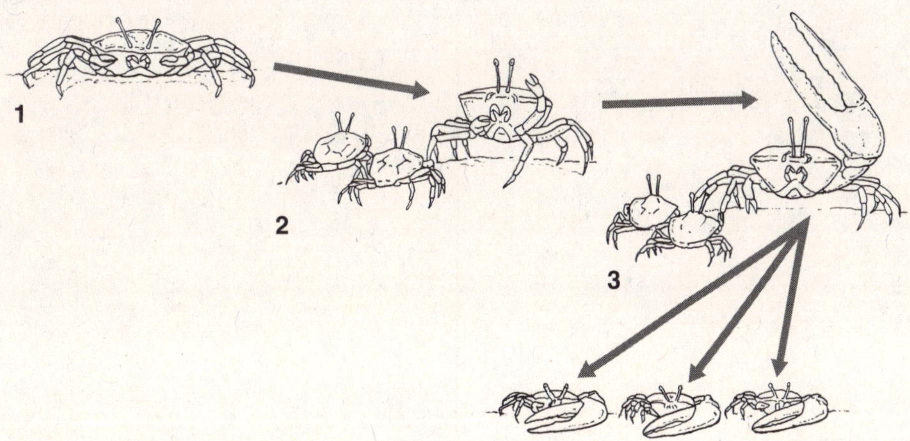

Figure 6–13 Inheritance of acquired traits Lamark thought that the use or disuse of an organ led to a change in that organ that was then passed on to offspring. His idea was found to be incorrect.

Investigation and Experimentation

Changes to Theories Sometimes observations result in the modification or complete revision of an existing theory. An example of a theory that was completely changed is the theory of a geocentric (Earth-centered) universe. Early Greek astronomers developed the theory of an Earth-centered universe. The geocentric model was further refined by Ptolemy, a Greek astronomer. It was not until the 16th and 17th centuries that new observations led scientists to question this theory. The development of the telescope allowed observations to be made that showed the sun is the center of the solar system. The new observations resulted in change to an existing theory.

Review Questions

61 Observations that do not agree with an existing scientific theory

A are always fraudulent.

B always cause an existing theory to be modified.

C are always mistaken.

D mean that the theory might need to be changed.

62 Observations that led to changes in the geocentric model of the universe

A were made using newer technology.

B were not correct.

C agreed with the existing theory.

D were the result of fraud.

Biology/Life Sciences Standards: Practice Test

1 In plant and animal cells, chromatin is found in the

A cytoplasm.

B nucleus.

C nucleolus.

D ribosomes.

2 In both plants and animals, sugar molecules are broken down and carbon dioxide and energy are released in the process of

A cellular respiration.

B breathing.

C glycolysis.

D photosynthesis.

3 Which of the following statements correctly describes the relationship between photosynthesis and cellular respiration?

A The products of each process provide the reactants needed for the other process.

B The products for both processes are the same.

C The reactants for both processes are the same.

D There is no relationship between the two processes.

4 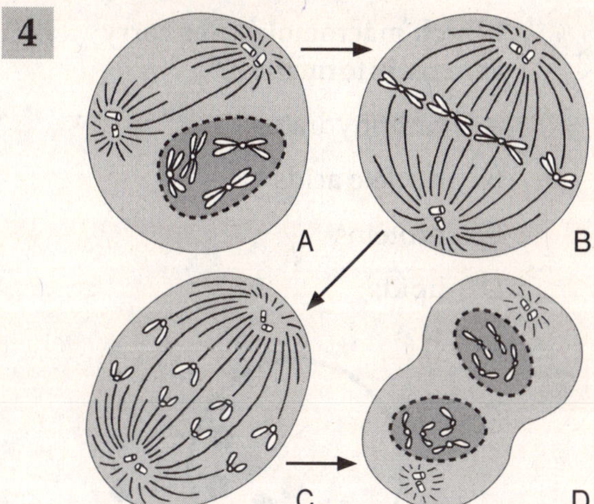

The drawings show the four phases of mitosis. Which phase is represented by drawing B?

A telophase

B prophase

C anaphase

D metaphase

5 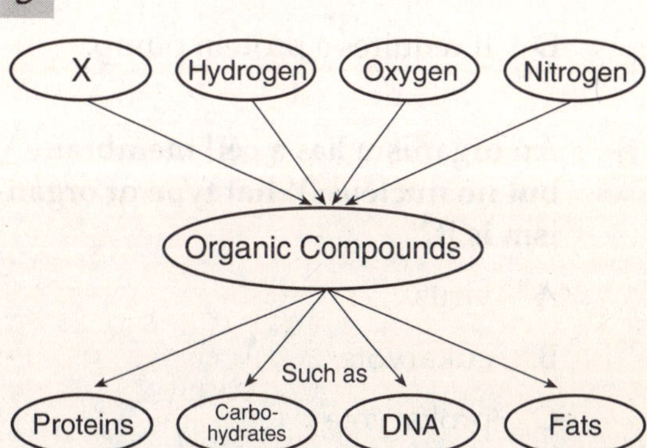

The diagram shows the elements that make up organic molecules. Which element is represented by the letter X?

A glucose

B sodium

C carbon

D chlorine

Biology/Life Sciences Standards: Practice Test

6 **Which macromolecules carry genetic information?**

A   carbohydrates

B   nucleic acids

C   proteins

D   lipids

7

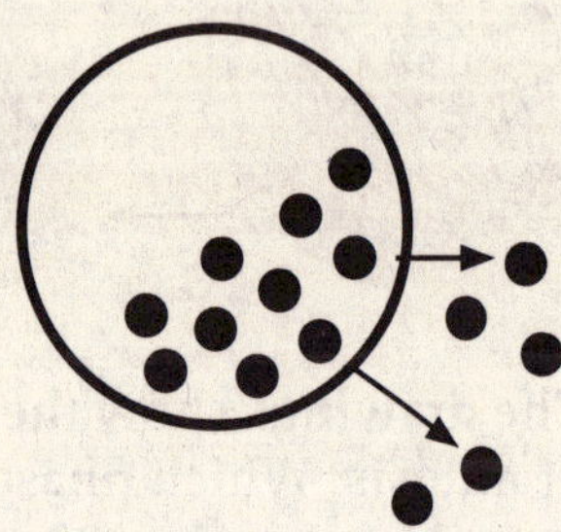

The diagram shows dissolved substances crossing a cell membrane. What is true about the process shown in the diagram?

A   It is called diffusion.

B   It is called active transport.

C   It requires energy.

D   It requires a protein pump.

8 **An organism has a cell membrane but no nucleus. What type of organism is it?**

A   virus

B   eukaryote

C   prokaryote

D   any of the above

9 **What is the structure of a typical virus?**

A   a core of cytoplasm surrounded by cell membrane

B   a core of genetic material surrounded by a protein coat

C   a core of protein surrounded by a nuclear membrane

D   a core of nucleic acid surrounded by a lipid membrane

10 **During the light-dependent reactions of photosynthesis,**

A   light is given off by chloroplasts.

B   energy is stored in ATP and NADPH.

C   ATP is converted to NADPH.

D   carbon dioxide is released.

11 **What is an advantage of sexual reproduction over asexual reproduction?**

A   It allows for much faster reproduction.

B   It takes full advantage of a favorable environment.

C   It increases the chances of organisms adapting to changing environments.

D   It always produces offspring that are genetically identical to the parents.

12 **An example of a human trait that is controlled by more than one gene is**

A   earlobe attachment.

B   ABO blood type.

C   eye color.

D   all of the above

Biology/Life Sciences Standards: Practice Test

13

Phenotype	Allele Combination(s)
Phenotype 1	A_1A_1 or A_1A_2
Phenotype 2	A_2A_2

The table shows phenotypes and allele combinations for a trait that is controlled by a gene with two alleles, A_1 and A_2. Based on the information in the table, you can conclude that

A both forms of the trait are always expressed.

B the A_1 allele is dominant to the A_2 allele.

C the A_2 allele is expressed whenever it is present.

D both alleles are expressed in the phenotype when present.

14 Which cell structure includes all of the others?

A gene

B DNA

C nucleus

D chromosome

15 What is one way that meiosis differs from mitosis?

A Meiosis is involved in asexual reproduction.

B Meiosis occurs only in reproductive cells.

C Meiosis produces a total of two daughter cells.

D Meiosis occurs before chromosomes replicate.

16

	W	w
W		
w		

A Punnett square can be used to show possible combinations of alleles in zygotes of a particular cross. The Punnett square shows a cross between two parents with the same combination of alleles for a gene. What combinations of alleles *not* found in the parents are possible in zygotes produced by this cross?

A *WW* and *Ww*

B *Ww* and *ww*

C *ww* and *WW*

D none

17

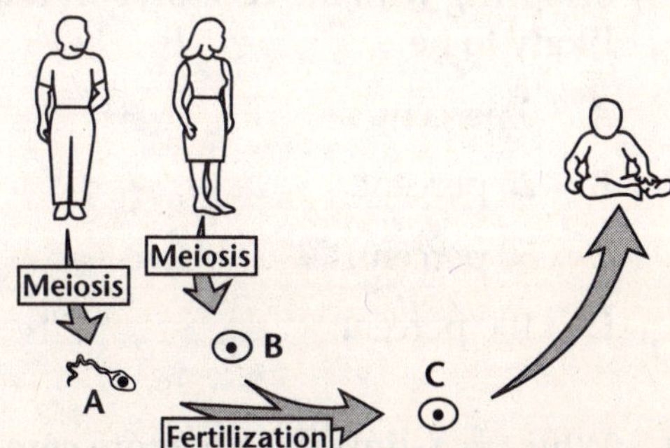

Both parents in the diagram have 23 pairs of chromosomes—or 46 chromosomes altogether—in each body cell. Which choice gives the correct number of chromosomes in each cell identified in the diagram?

A A = 46, B = 46, C = 46

B A = 23, B = 23, C = 46

C A = 46, B = 46, C = 92

D A = 23, B = 23, C = 23

Biology/Life Sciences Standards: Practice Test

18 Genes on the Y chromosome are important for the normal development of

A both boys and girls.

B girls only.

C neither boys nor girls.

D boys only.

19

	T	t
t		
t		

The Punnett square shows a cross between two parents for a gene with two alleles, *T* and *t*. The gene controls an autosomal trait, and *T* is dominant to *t*. If you completed the Punnett square, you could determine that the percentage of offspring with the recessive trait is likely to be

A 0 percent.

B 25 percent.

C 50 percent.

D 100 percent.

20 Why are X-linked traits more common in males than in females?

A All alleles on the X chromosome are dominant.

B All alleles on the Y chromosome are recessive.

C A recessive allele on the X chromosome always produces the trait in a male.

D Any allele on the Y chromosome will be recessive to the same allele on the X chromosome.

21 What is the function of RNA?

A storing genetic information in the nucleus

B using genetic information in DNA to make proteins

C passing genetic information to offspring in gametes

D all of the above

22 Chains of small molecules called amino acids form important macromolecules called

A proteins.

B carbohydrates.

C nucleotides.

D nucleic acids.

23 How do herbivores get the energy they need to survive?

A by converting solar energy to chemical energy

B by eating producers

C by hunting and eating prey

D by breaking down wastes and dead organisms

Biology/Life Sciences Standards: Practice Test

24

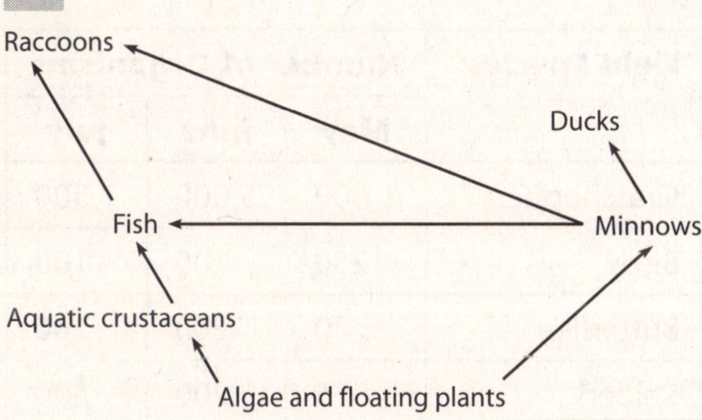

This food web diagram shows how matter and energy are transferred between living things in an ecosystem. Which of the following is a producer in this ecosystem?

A fish

B raccoon

C aquatic crustacean

D floating plant

25 **The living things in an ecosystem depend on one another in many ways. What is the *main* reason that the number of plants in an ecosystem determines the number and variety of animals the ecosystem can support?**

A Plants convert solar energy to chemical energy.

B Plants release carbon dioxide.

C Plants absorb oxygen.

D Plants release water through transpiration.

26 **The abiotic factors in an ecosystem include all of the nonliving things in an area. The amount of minerals, humus, and pH are all characteristics of which abiotic factor?**

A air

B soil

C water

D climate

27

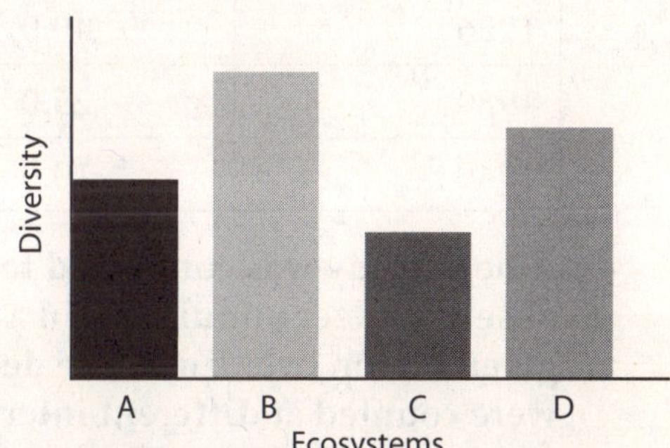

The biodiversity of an ecosystem is the sum total of the different kinds of living things in an area. Different ecosystems have different levels of biodiversity. Which ecosystem is *most* stable and *most* able to withstand a pest or disease?

A A

B B

C C

D D

Biology/Life Sciences Standards: Practice Test

28

Deer Population Changes 1900–1940

Year	Deer Population (thousands)
1900	3.0
1910	9.5
1920	65.0
1924	100.0
1926	40.0
1930	25.0
1940	10.0

A field study was conducted to observe a deer population in a given region over time. The deer were counted at different intervals over a period of 40 years. At some times during this 40-year period, deer hunting was permitted. At other times, deer hunting was prohibited. A summary of the collected data is presented in the table. During which time period did the greatest increase in the deer population occur?

A   1900 - 1910

B   1910 - 1920

C   1920 - 1930

D   1930–1940

29

Field Species	Number of Organisms		
	May	June	July
Grasshoppers	1,000	5,000	1,500
Birds	250	100	100
Butterflies	70	200	60
Spiders	75	200	500

Population size is affected by birth rate, death rate, immigration, and emigration. For which population did the number of births and immigrations exceed the number of deaths and emigrations for the entire time period studied?

A   grasshoppers

B   birds

C   butterflies

D   spiders

30   Water cycles between living things and the nonliving environment. Which of the following processes moves water from an organism to the nonliving environment?

A   precipitation

B   transpiration

C   fixation

D   evaporation

Biology/Life Sciences Standards: Practice Test

31 Human activity can have an impact on the cycles of matter that occur in ecosystems. Burning of fossil fuels has the *greatest* impact on which of these cycles?

A   nitrogen

B   water

C   carbon

D   oxygen

32

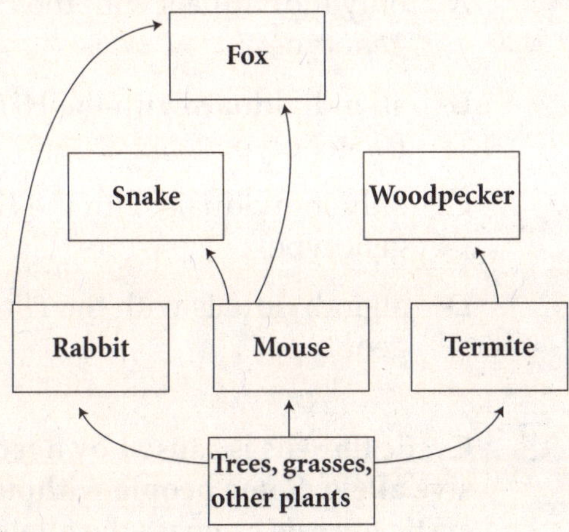

Food webs show the feeding relationships in an ecosystem. How would a dramatic change in the populations of trees, grasses, and other plants impact the other populations in this food web?

A   This change would impact only the rabbit, mouse, and termite populations.

B   This change would impact all of the other populations in the food web.

C   This change would impact none of the other populations in the food web.

D   This change would impact the only the snake and woodpecker populations.

33 Which statement best explains why there are relatively few third-level consumers in most ecosystems?

A   Energy is lost at each tropic level, so there is a limited amount of energy available to third-level consumers.

B   Third-level consumers are less efficient than other organisms at recycling energy.

C   The energy in an ecosystem does not flow to the third-level consumers in the food web.

D   Energy is recycled only by decomposers, so the number of third-level consumers that can survive is limited.

34 Which of the following is produced by mutation and needed for evolution to occur?

A   stability in the gene pool of a species

B   additional DNA in an organism

C   a struggle for existence

D   genetic variation in organisms

Biology/Life Sciences Standards: Practice Test

35 According to Darwin's theory of natural selection, what must occur for natural selection to take place?

  A Organisms within a population do not compete among themselves.

  B Traits that an organism develops in its lifetime are inherited by its offspring.

  C All individuals in a population have the same number of offspring.

  D Some individuals inherit traits that make them more fit than other individuals.

36

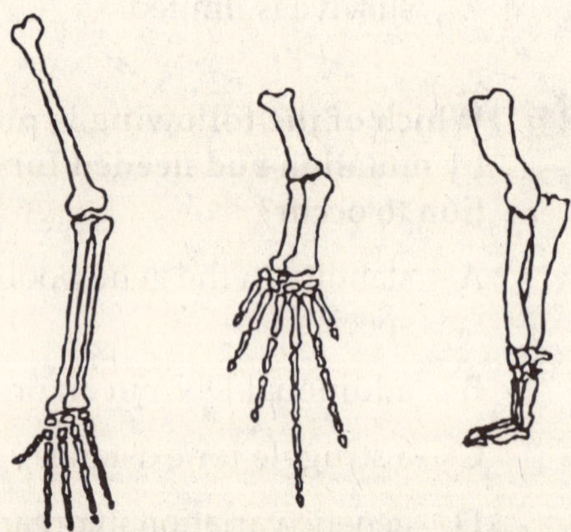

The diagram shows the forelimb bones of three present-day species of mammals. The number and arrangement of the bones provide evidence that these three species

  A descended from a common ancestor.

  B have the same genetic makeup.

  C obtain food in the same ways.

  D are not genetically related.

37 Suppose that tall plants are more likely to survive and reproduce than short plants because they receive more sunlight. Height in some plants is controlled by a single gene with two alleles, H and h. Allele H is dominant and controls the tall form of the trait. Which individuals in a population of these plants would be favored by natural selection?

  A only individuals with the HH genotype

  B all individuals with the HH or Hh genotype

  C only individuals with the Hh genotype

  D all individuals with the Hh or hh genotype

38 Cystic fibrosis is caused by a recessive allele. Some people without cystic fibrosis can pass the allele for the disorder to their offspring. This happens because these people have a

  A homozygous genotype.

  B heterozygous genotype.

  C recessive genotype.

  D variable genotype.

39 A change in the genetic material that occurs during DNA replication is called

  A natural selection.

  B genetic drift.

  C evolution.

  D mutation.

Biology/Life Sciences Standards: Practice Test

40

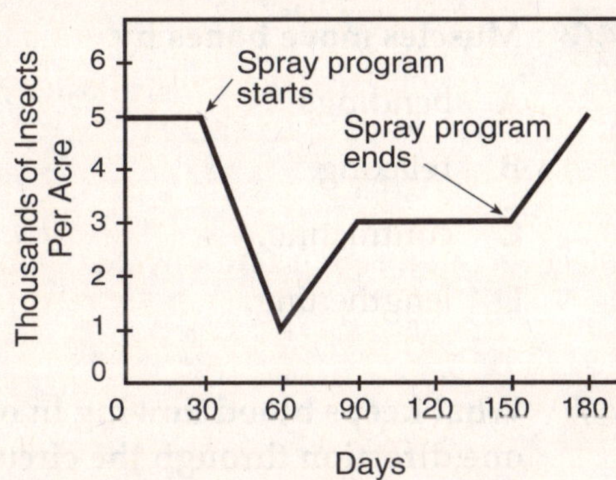

The graph shows the numbers of insects in an area on different days before, during, and after an insecticide spray program. Which statement best explains why some insects survived after the spray program first started and why the population began to make a comeback.

A The spray program was an environmental change to which all adult insects were already adapted.

B A natural variation existed within the insect population that allowed some individuals to survive and reproduce.

C The spray program killed plants that only some of the insects relied upon for food.

D Most of the insects were resistant to the insecticide due to an earlier spray program.

41

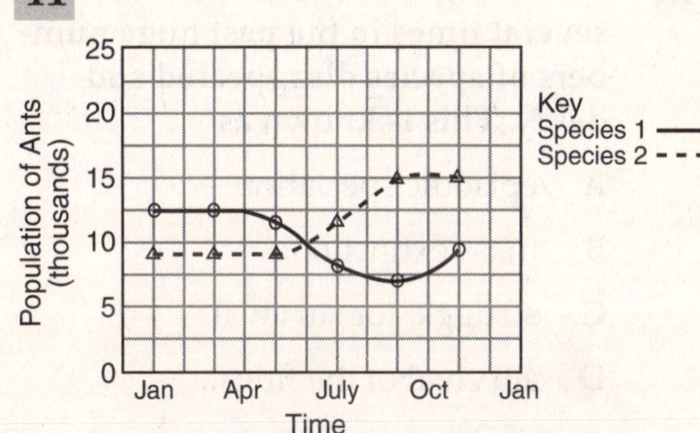

The graph shows populations of two species of ants. Ants in Species 2 have a thicker outer covering than ants in Species 1. The outer covering of ants helps them avoid drying out. The population changes shown in the graph are *most likely* due to

A an increase in food sources for both species from April through July.

B a disease that killed off Species 2 at the beginning of May.

C weather that was dryer than normal from April through September.

D an increase in mutations in Species 1 starting in June.

42 The chance that some species will survive a major environmental change is greater when

A there is diversity among species.

B species show little variation.

C there are just a few different species.

D species are already well adapted.

Biology/Life Sciences Standards: Practice Test

43 According to the fossil record, at several times in the past huge numbers of species disappeared suddenly. This is known as

A   episodic speciation.

B   mass extinction.

C   struggle for survival.

D   survival of the fittest.

44 The earliest fossils showing that ocean life was already highly diverse come from the

A   Cenozoic Era.

B   Mesozoic Era.

C   Paleozoic Era.

D   Precambrian Time.

45

Type of Tissue	Function
Connective tissue	Supports the body
Nervous tissue	Carries messages
Muscle tissue	Allows movement
Epithelial tissue	

The table lists the functions of the four different types of human tissues. Which choice correctly fills in the missing information in the table?

A   Removes wastes from the body

B   Controls other tissue types

C   Performs the function of sight

D   Makes up body coverings

46 Muscles move bones by

A   bending.

B   relaxing.

C   contracting.

D   lengthening.

47 What keeps blood flowing in only one direction through the circulatory system?

A   blood pressure

B   heart contractions

C   valves

D   ventricles

48 Which three body systems work together to transport wastes from cells and remove them from the body?

A   circulatory, respiratory, excretory

B   circulatory, respiratory, digestive

C   digestive, circulatory, excretory

D   nervous, digestive, excretory

49 The body system that exchanges oxygen and carbon dioxide between the atmosphere and the blood is the

A   digestive system.

B   respiratory system.

C   excretory system.

D   circulatory system.

Biology/Life Sciences Standards: Practice Test

50 The digestive system breaks down food into smaller, simpler molecules that cells can use. These molecules are made available to body cells by the

A digestive system.

B excretory system.

C nervous system.

D circulatory system.

51 The central processing unit of a computer receives and processes information from the computer's peripheral devices such as the keyboard and mouse. It also sends messages to peripheral devices such as the monitor and printer, telling them how to respond. If a computer models the human nervous system, which part of the nervous system would be modeled by the central processing unit?

A nervous impulses

B peripheral nerves

C central nervous system

D sense organs

52 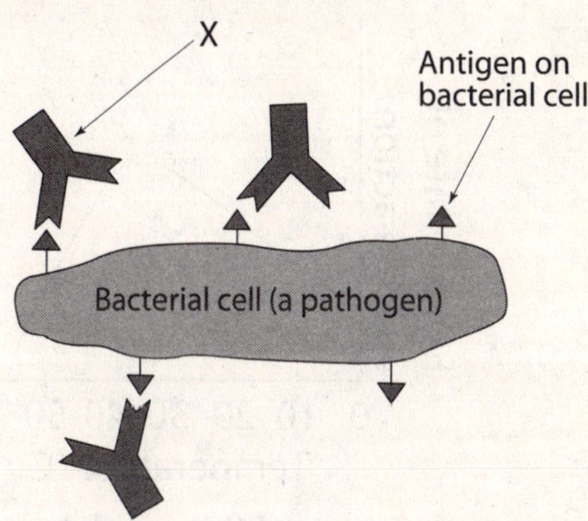

The diagram shows one way that the immune system fights pathogens. What is the structure labeled X?

A an antibody

B a white blood cell

C a virus

D a foreign protein

53 A vaccination can protect you against a pathogen because it

A destroys toxins from the pathogen before they can make you sick.

B stimulates your immune system to respond to the pathogen.

C finds and kills all the pathogenic organisms in your body.

D makes the pathogen less harmful so it does not make you sick.

54 Which statement is true about bacteria?

A Most of them are harmful to humans.

B They do not have cell membranes.

C They invade and destroy cells.

D They are living organisms.

Biology/Life Sciences Standards: Practice Test

55

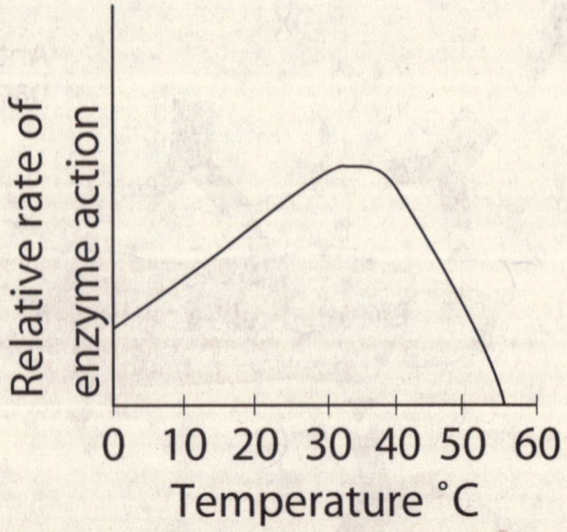

A student used this graph to show the results of an investigation on the effect of temperature on the relative rate of enzyme action. Why is a line graph the best choice for showing these data?

A   The data show how a responding variable changes when the manipulated variable is changed.

B   The data are divided into categories that do not overlap.

C   The data show percentages of an entire group.

D   The data show that there was no manipulated variable in the investigation.

56   **Water Flea Heart Rate**

Water Temperature (°C)	Average Water Flea Heart Rate (beats/minute)
5	40
15	119
25	205
35	280

A student measured the effect of temperature on the heart rate of water fleas. He recorded his data in this table. These data best support which conclusion?

A   The heart rate of all aquatic insects changes when water temperature changes.

B   As water temperature increases from 5°C to 35°C, water flea heart rate increases.

C   Water fleas live only in ecosystems with water that is between 15°C to 35°C.

D   Water fleas cannot survive in water with a temperature greater than 35°C.

Biology/Life Sciences Standards: Practice Test

57

Measurement #	Mass (g)
1	15.5
2	15.4
3	15.8
4	15.6

A student measured the mass of a single soil sample four times and recorded his measurements in the table. The actual mass of the soil sample is 18.5 grams. What is the best description of the student's data?

A both accurate and precise

B precise but not accurate

C accurate but not precise

D nether accurate nor precise

58 A student was interested in learning how soil composition and amount of rainfall affected the plants in a particular ecosystem. She grew plants in three different types of soil. The plants all received different quantities of water. After a week, the student measured the amount each plant had grown. Why can't this student draw a valid conclusion using her data?

A The student did not have any variables in the investigation.

B The student should not have measured the plants' growth.

C The student's question cannot be answered through investigation.

D The student changed more than one variable at a time.

59 During succession, a series of predictable changes occurs in an ecosystem. What change in abiotic conditions is *most directly* connected to the change in the biotic components of the ecosystem during the process of primary succession?

A accumulation of water

B formation of soil

C stabilization of temperature

D development of minerals

60 A student used three beakers of water for an experiment. He measured the temperature of the water in each beaker four times. Then he calculated the average deviation of the four sets of measurements. He can be sure that the set of data with the greatest average deviation

A is the most accurate.

B has the least precision.

C has the smallest range.

D has the least median.

Biology Standards: Practice Test

1 **How does a large sample size help to ensure that experimental results are reliable?**

  A by eliminating measurement errors during the experiment

  B by ensuring that only one variable is changed

  C by ensuring that differences in individuals do not impact results

  D by eliminating the possibility of human error occurring

2 **A student investigating the effect of water temperature on the growth of water plants grew three different varieties of plants, each at a different water temperature. She found that her results were not consistent with the results of others in the class. What is one way that this student could obtain more consistent results?**

  A by using only one kind of plant

  B by using more temperatures of water

  C by using a different set of data for comparison

  D by using a greater variety of plants

3

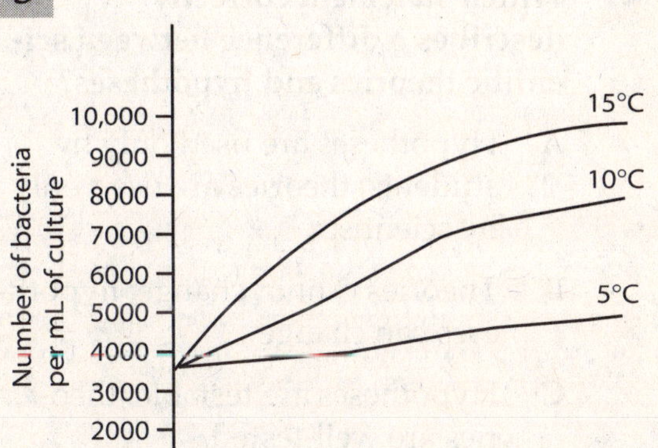

This graph shows the results of an investigation of the growth of a particular type of bacteria at different temperatures. What is a logical statement that can be made using this evidence?

  A This type of bacteria cannot grow at 5°C.

  B Temperature does not affect the reproductive rate of this type of bacteria.

  C Refrigeration will most likely slow the growth of this type of bacteria.

  D At 20°C, this type of bacteria does not reproduce.

4 **The pH scale is a logarithmic scale used to measure the concentration of H^+ ions in a solution. Stomach acid has a pH of 1.5. Lemon juice has a pH of 2.5. How does the concentration of H^+ ions differ between stomach acid and lemon juice?**

  A by a factor of 0.1

  B by a factor of 1

  C by a factor of 10

  D by a factor of 100

Biology Standards: Practice Test

5 Which statement correctly describes a difference between scientific theories and hypotheses?

A   Hypotheses are used only by students; theories are used only by scientists.

B   Theories cannot change; hypotheses can change.

C   Hypotheses are testable; theories are well-tested.

D   Theories are always correct; hypotheses are rarely correct.

6

Data Set	Mean Value	Range
A	25	12
B	25	2
C	25	16
D	25	6

Compare the four data sets shown in the table. Which statement about these data sets is correct?

A   All of these data sets have the same amount of variability.

B   Data Set C has the greatest variability.

C   These data sets must contain the same values.

D   Data Set B has the greatest average deviation.

7 One solute can easily diffuse across a cell membrane. A different solute must have help from a protein to diffuse across the membrane. This occurs because the cell membrane is

A   ionic.

B   nucleic.

C   permeable.

D   semipermeable.

8

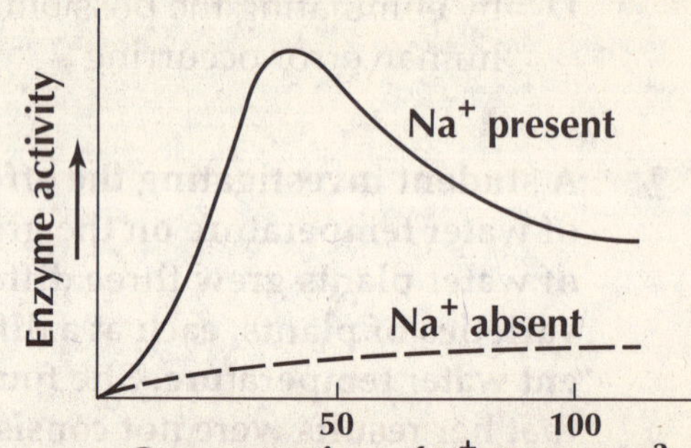

The graph shows the rate of activity of an enzyme at different concentrations of potassium ions (K+), both with and without sodium ions (Na+) also being present. What can you conclude from the graph?

A   Both sodium and potassium ions are required for maximum enzyme activity.

B   Enzyme activity depends only on the concentration of sodium ions.

C   The presence of sodium ions has little effect on enzyme activity.

D   Enzyme activity increases at first and then gradually decreases in the absence of sodium ions.

Biology Standards: Practice Test

9 **Which statement about eukaryotic cells is true?**

   A They do not have a cell membrane.

   B They have a protein coat.

   C They contain few internal structures.

   D They have a nucleus.

10 **Which of the following shows the correct sequence of molecules involved in the synthesis of proteins?**

   A mRNA → DNA → tRNA → polypeptide

   B DNA → mRNA → tRNA → polypeptide

   C tRNA → DNA → mRNA → polypeptide

   D DNA → mRNA → polypeptide → tRNA

11 **What occurs on a ribosome during protein synthesis?**

   A Amino acids are added to a growing polypeptide chain.

   B Messenger RNA translates a strand of DNA.

   C Messenger RNA carries amino acids to the ribosome.

   D A polynucleotide is formed from messenger RNA.

12 **A function of the endoplasmic reticulum is**

   A transporting proteins to ribosomes.

   B helping proteins cross cell membranes.

   C producing proteins for secretion.

   D making ribosomes for protein synthesis.

13

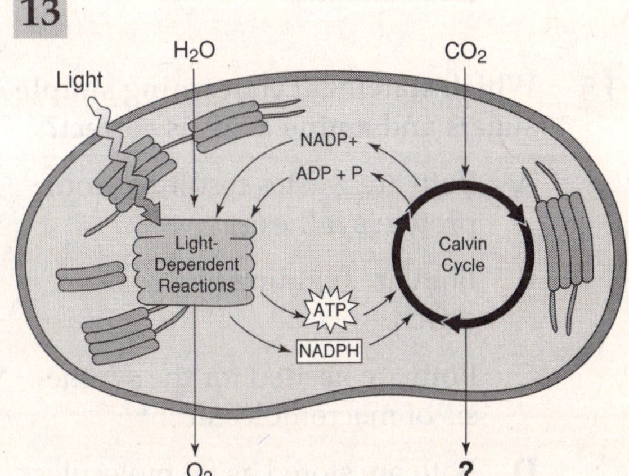

The diagram shows the process of photosynthesis. Which choice is represented in the diagram with a question mark?

   A glucose

   B oxygen

   C water

   D energy

Biology Standards: Practice Test

14 The first stage of cellular respiration is called glycolysis. What happens during this stage?

A Electrons are carried in $FADH_2$ and $NADP^+$.

B Glucose is broken down into pyruvic acid.

C Electrons from the Krebs cycle are used to produce ATP.

D Glucose is produced from water and sunlight.

15 Which statement concerning simple sugars and amino acids is correct?

A Both are wastes resulting from protein synthesis.

B Both are building blocks of starch.

C Both are needed for the synthesis of macromolecules.

D Both are stored as fat molecules in the liver.

16 Meiosis results in four daughter cells that have half as many chromosomes as the original cell. Meiosis has this outcome because it involves a

A haploid cell dividing once.

B diploid cell dividing twice.

C haploid cell dividing twice.

D diploid cell dividing once.

17 Which cells in the body divide by meiosis?

A all body cells

B certain cells in reproductive organs

C sperm cells

D gametes

18 When gametes form, homologous chromosomes

A always go to the same gametes.

B always go to different gametes.

C sometimes go to the same gametes.

D never go to different gametes.

19 How does fertilization increase genetic variation?

A by leading to natural selection

B by causing new mutations to occur

C by creating new allele combinations

D by allowing crossing-over to occur

20 The number of chromosomes in each body cell of a sexually reproducing species remains the same from one generation to the next as a direct result of

A meiosis and fertilization.

B mitosis and genetic equilibrium.

C mutation and natural selection.

D homeostasis and mutation.

Biology Standards: Practice Test

21 A human offspring inherits an X chromosome from the mother. What does this tell you about the sex of the offspring?

   A The offspring is definitely female.

   B The offspring must be male.

   C The offspring could be female.

   D The offspring could not be male.

22 A certain trait in guinea pigs is controlled by a gene with two alleles, represented by the letters *T* and *t*. What possible genotypes could there be in the offspring of two heterozygous guinea pigs?

   A *TT*, *Tt*, and *tt*

   B *TT* and *tt*

   C *Tt* and *tt*

   D only *Tt*

23 Color blindness in humans is a recessive X-linked trait. What percentage of sons of a color-blind father are likely to be color-blind if the mother has two normal alleles for color vision?

   A 0 percent

   B 25 percent

   C 50 percent

   D 100 percent

24 A female frog has the genotype *RRSs* for two genes on nonhomologous chromosomes. Each egg produced by this frog will have one of two different allele combinations:

   A *RR* or *Ss*.

   B *RS* or *Rs*.

   C *RS* or *rs*.

   D *Rs* or *rS*.

25

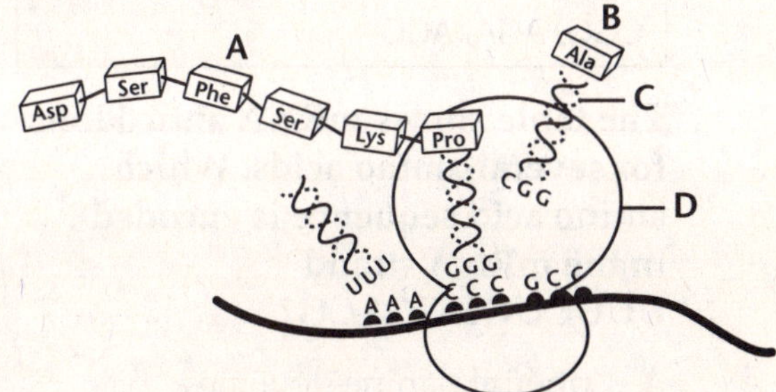

The diagram shows the translation stage of protein synthesis. Which type of molecule is C?

   A tRNA

   B mRNA

   C rRNA

   D amino acid

Biology Standards: Practice Test

26

Anticodons	Amino Acid
UUU, UUC	Phenylalanine
CUU, CUC, CUA, CUG, UUA, UUG	Leucine
GUU, GUC, GUA, GUG	Valine
GGU, GGC, GGA, GGG	Glycine
ACU, ACC, ACA, ACG	Threonine
CGU, CGC, CGA, CGG, AGA, AGG	Argenine

The table shows mRNA anticodons for several amino acids. Which amino acid sequence is encoded in the mRNA strand UUUCUGGGCACG?

A phenylalanine–leucine–glycine–argenine

B leucine–argenine–glycine–threonine

C phenylalanine–leucine–valine–threonine

D phenylalanine–leucine–glycine–threonine

27

First Base	Second Base				Third Base
	T	**C**	**A**	**G**	
T	Phe	Ser	Tyr	Cys	T
	Phe	Ser	Tyr	Cys	C
	Leu	Ser			A
	Leu	Ser		Trp	G
C	Leu	Pro	His	Arg	T
	Leu	Pro	His	Arg	C
	Leu	Pro	Gln	Arg	A
	Leu	Pro	Gln	Arg	G
A	Ile	Thr	Asn	Ser	T
	Ile	Thr	Asn	Ser	C
	Ile	Thr	Lys	Arg	A
	Met	Thr	Lys	Arg	G
G	Val	Ala	Asp	Gly	T
	Val	Ala	Asp	Gly	C
	Val	Ala	Glu	Gly	A
	Val	Ala	Glu	Gly	G

The table shows the genetic code for DNA. Assume a mutation occurred in the DNA strand ACTGGGCTCTTT. The mutation did not cause a change in the amino acid sequence of the encoded protein. Which of the following mutations might have occurred?

A ACTGGGCTCGTT

B ACCGGGCTCTTT

C ACTGGGGTCTTT

D ACTGGGTTCTTT

Biology Standards: Practice Test

28

Inherited Gene	Environmental Condition	Plant Color
A	Light	Green
B	Light	White
A	Dark	White
B	Dark	White

The table shows relationships between genes, the environment, and color in tomato plants. Which statement best explains the relationships in the table?

A The expression of gene A is not affected by light.

B The expression of gene B varies with the presence of light.

C The expression of gene A varies with the environment.

D Gene B is expressed only in darkness.

29

Influences → Protein shape → Determines → Protein function

A →

The diagram explains how proteins can differ from one another. Which phrase is represented by A?

A Number and sequence of simple sugars

B Number and sequence of starch molecules

C Number and sequence of amino acids

D Number and sequence of ATP molecules

30 Which of the following molecules is found in DNA but not in RNA?

A uracil

B ribose

C deoxyribose

D adenine

31 Proteins form bones and muscles, transport substances across cell membranes, help fight disease, and

A store genetic information in the nucleus.

B speed up chemical reactions in living cells.

C provide energy for chemical reactions.

D transmit impulses through the nervous system.

32 What sequence of mRNA bases translates the following strand of DNA bases: TACTGCA?

A ATCACGT

B CGACAGC

C AUGACGU

D UTGUCGT

33 A gene that codes for resistance to glyphosate, a chemical used to kill weeds, has been inserted into certain corn plants. As a result, these corn plants will be more likely to

A produce chemicals that kill weeds.

B die when exposed to glyphosate.

C convert glyphosate into fertilizer.

D survive when glyphosate is applied.

Biology Standards: Practice Test

34 Which best describes the changes that occur when a meadow eco-system is altered to become a farm field?

   A Biodiversity and stability increase.

   B Biodiversity increases and stability decreases.

   C Biodiversity decreases and stability increases.

   D Biodiversity and stability both decrease.

35

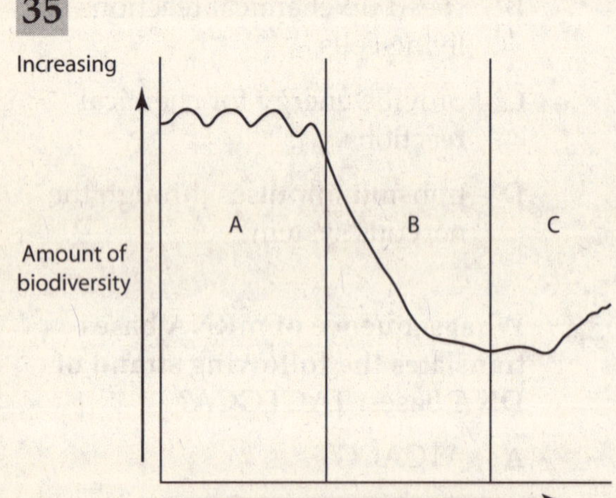

Which of the following is *most likely* to have caused the change in biodiversity shown from Point A to Point B on the graph?

   A stable climatic conditions

   B plentiful supplies of resources

   C increased human activity in the area

   D lack of human activity in the area

36

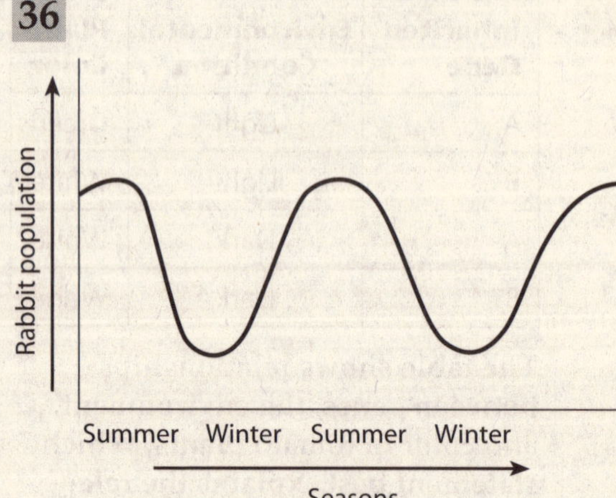

The seasonal changes in the size of a rabbit population are shown on the graph. Which of the following could cause the change in the rabbit population that occurs from summer to winter?

   A an increasing birth rate

   B an increasing death rate

   C a decrease in emigration

   D an increase in immigration

37 Population size is limited by the available resources in an area. When a population gets so large that there are not enough resources for each individual, which of these is *most likely* to occur?

   A an increasing birth rate

   B a decreasing death rate

   C an increase in emigration

   D an increase in immigration

Biology Standards: Practice Test

38 The nitrogen cycle includes processes that move nitrogen between the living and nonliving parts of the environment. Which of these processes is *most directly* involved in the movement of nitrogen from the atmosphere to the bodies of living things?

A denitrification

B decomposition

C nitrogen fixation

D evaporation

39 A sudden decrease in the population of decomposers in an ecosystem would have the *most immediate* impact on

A the transfer of energy from herbivores to carnivores.

B the input of the sun's energy into the ecosystem.

C the amount of energy available at each tropic level.

D the recycling of matter in wastes and dead organisms.

40 Which statement concerning the energy in an ecosystem is correct?

A Energy given off as heat at one level is available to the next tropic level.

B Consumers contain more energy than producers.

C Available energy decreases as it is passed from one tropic level to the next.

D Decomposers are the source of energy in most ecosystems.

41 The process of natural selection is based on the assumption that

A environmental changes will cause changes in body structure in individuals.

B all changes in a gene pool are the result of neutral mutations.

C the gene pool of a population always remains the same.

D inherited traits cause differences in fitness among individuals.

42 A recessive genetic disorder in moles causes death before the animals are old enough to reproduce. How is the allele for the disorder passed from generation to generation?

A Moles that are heterozygotes for the recessive allele pass it on.

B Moles with the disorder pass the recessive allele to their offspring.

C Moles with the disorder have new mutations that cause the disorder.

D Moles that are homozygotes for the disorder pass on the recessive allele.

43 Mutations can become part of the gene pool if they occur in

A body cells.

B nerve cells.

C gametes.

D proteins.

Biology Standards: Practice Test

44 Which two factors would increase the chance that at least some members of a species would survive a change in environment?

A many mutations and asexual reproduction

B few mutations and sexual reproduction

C many mutations and sexual reproduction

D few mutations and asexual reproduction

45 A population of mosquitoes was sprayed with a new pesticide. Most of the mosquitoes died, but a few resisted the pesticide and survived. The next generation of mosquitoes was sprayed with the same pesticide. This time, even more mosquitoes survived. What explains these results?

A The insecticide caused a mutation in the mosquitoes.

B The mosquitoes learned how to avoid the insecticide.

C Mosquitoes with resistance passed the trait to their offspring.

D The mosquitoes developed immunity to the insecticide.

46 Throughout the history of life on Earth, which factor probably has been the chief cause of extinction of species?

A human interference

B lack of adaptive variations

C warfare within species

D too many mutations

47 A very small population of rodents lives on an isolated island. Genetic drift is likely to change the gene pool of this population by

A reducing the variety of alleles.

B increasing the variation in alleles.

C causing new alleles to appear.

D increasing genetic diversity.

48 Two groups of snakes are often found in the same habitat, but they do not interbreed. What is the *most likely* reason they do not interbreed?

A The two groups are geographically isolated from one another.

B Neutral mutations occurred more often in one group than the other.

C One group has a higher rate of survival than the other.

D The two groups belong to different species.

49 The fossil record shows that

A organisms did not become diverse until mammals evolved.

B more complex organisms appeared earlier that simpler organisms.

C speciation always occurred slowly and continuously.

D mass extinctions occurred more than once.

Biology Standards: Practice Test

50 Which two major body systems are *most directly* involved in providing molecules needed for the synthesis of proteins in human cells?

A   digestive and circulatory

B   digestive and excretory

C   immune and excretory

D   immune and circulatory

51 The role of the nervous system is to

A   store genetic information.

B   circulate materials through the body.

C   extract energy from food.

D   coordinate other body systems.

52 The thyroid gland produces a hormone that regulates the rate of activities of cells throughout the body. The thyroid gland is controlled directly by the

A   pituitary gland.

B   hypothalamus.

C   cells of the body.

D   cells of the brain.

53

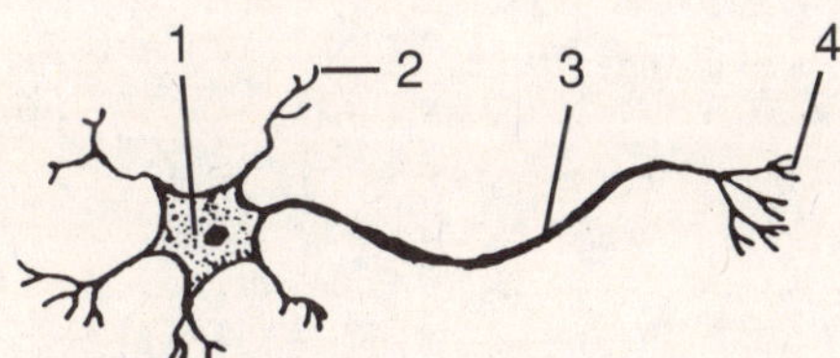

The diagram shows the structures of a typical neuron. Which structure receives incoming nerve impulses?

A   1

B   2

C   3

D   4

54 How are motor neurons and skeletal muscles related?

A   Motor neurons send impulses that stimulate skeletal muscles to contract.

B   Skeletal muscles send impulses that motor neurons carry to the brain.

C   Motor neurons help skeletal muscles synthesize proteins for muscle fibers.

D   Motor neurons stimulate skeletal muscles to send impulses to the brain.

55 Which of the following is an example of a nonspecific defense?

A   killer T cell production

B   cell-mediated immunity

C   humoral immunity

D   the skin

56

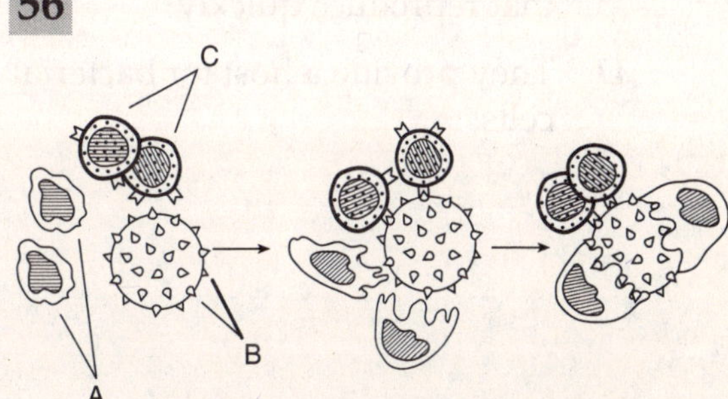

The diagram represents a humoral response by the immune system. Which structures triggered this immune response?

A   A

B   B

C   C

D   A and C

Biology Standards: Practice Test

57 **What generally happens when an individual receives a vaccine containing a weakened pathogen?**

A The ability to fight disease increases due to antibodies in the vaccine.

B The ability to fight the pathogen increases due to antigen exposure.

C The ability to produce antibodies decreases after the vaccine is injected.

D The ability to resist most types of diseases increases because of the vaccine.

58 **Why are viruses considered parasites?**

A They destroy the cells in which they multiply.

B They are tiny cells found within protists.

C They are single-celled organisms that reproduce quickly.

D They provide a host for bacterial cells.

59 **Two ways bacteria may cause disease are by using the cells of the organism they infect as food and by**

A making antibodies.

B releasing toxins.

C producing viruses.

D invading cells.

60 **Why do many people with HIV infections eventually develop opportunistic diseases?**

A Their immune system has been damaged by HIV.

B HIV causes opportunistic diseases as well as AIDS.

C Opportunistic diseases are highly contagious.

D Opportunistic diseases infect everyone who is exposed to them.

Cell Biology

1. A
2. D
3. A
4. C
5. D
6. C
7. B
8. A
9. D
10. C
11. A
12. B
13. C
14. D
15. B
16. D
17. A
18. B
19. A
20. D
21. B
22. C
23. C
24. B
25. A
26. C
27. B
28. B
29. A
30. A
31. C
32. B
33. D
34. C
35. D
36. B
37. D
38. B
39. A
40. C
41. A
42. C
43. D
44. A
45. B
46. B
47. D
48. B
49. B
50. D
51. A

Genetics

1. A
2. B
3. C
4. A
5. D
6. D
7. C
8. C
9. A
10. B
11. D
12. A
13. D
14. B
15. B
16. C
17. C
18. C
19. B
20. C
21. D
22. C
23. B
24. A
25. D
26. A
27. A
28. C
29. D
30. B
31. C
32. B
33. B
34. C
35. B
36. B
37. A
38. B
39. D
40. B
41. B
42. A
43. D
44. A
45. C
46. A
47. A
48. B
49. B
50. D
51. B
52. B
53. C
54. D
55. B
56. B
57. A
58. A
59. D
60. C

Ecology

1. A
2. A
3. D
4. D
5. D
6. A
7. C
8. B
9. A
10. A
11. B
12. B
13. C
14. A
15. D
16. A
17. A
18. A
19. C
20. D
21. B
22. B

23. D
24. A
25. D
26. B
27. D
28. C
29. B
30. A
31. C
32. D
33. B
34. A

Evolution

1. B
2. A
3. A
4. D
5. C
6. A
7. B
8. B
9. D
10. A
11. A
12. A
13. D
14. A
15. C
16. A
17. D
18. B
19. C
20. C
21. A
22. C
23. A
24. C
25. A
26. A
27. C
28. D
29. C
30. D
31. B
32. A
33. A
34. A
35. C
36. D
37. A
38. D
39. B
40. A
41. C
42. B
43. B
44. A
45. C

Physiology

1. B
2. B
3. C
4. C
5. D
6. A
7. C
8. A
9. A
10. B
11. A
12. D
13. B
14. C
15. C
16. A
17. D
18. C
19. B
20. C
21. C
22. B
23. B
24. A
25. C
26. D
27. C
28. B
29. A
30. D
31. B
32. A
33. A
34. A
35. B
36. C
37. B
38. A
39. D
40. D
41. B
42. C
43. A
44. B
45. A
46. D
47. A
48. D
49. A
50. D
51. B

Investigation and Experimentation

1. B
2. A
3. D
4. A
5. A
6. C
7. D
8. A
9. D
10. A
11. A
12. D
13. D
14. A
15. B
16. D
17. B
18. C
19. B
20. A
21. B
22. B
23. C

24. B
25. D
26. B
27. A
28. C
29. C
30. A
31. A
32. A
33. B
34. B
35. C
36. B
37. A
38. B
39. C
40. A
41. B
42. D
43. A
44. B
45. C
46. C
47. B
48. C
49. A
50. C
51. B
52. C
53. C
54. B
55. A
56. C
57. A
58. D
59. B
60. A
61. D
62. A

Biology/Life Sciences Standards: Practice Test

1. B
2. A
3. A
4. D
5. C
6. B
7. A
8. C
9. B
10. B
11. C
12. C
13. B
14. C
15. B
16. C
17. B
18. D
19. C
20. C
21. B
22. A
23. B
24. D
25. A
26. B
27. B
28. B
29. D
30. B
31. C
32. B
33. A
34. D
35. D
36. A
37. B
38. B
39. D
40. B
41. C
42. A
43. B
44. C
45. D
46. C
47. C
48. A
49. B
50. D

51. C
52. A
53. B
54. D
55. A
56. B
57. B
58. D
59. B
60. B

Biology Standards: Practice Test

1. C
2. A
3. C
4. C
5. C
6. B
7. D
8. A
9. D
10. B
11. A
12. C
13. A
14. B
15. C
16. B
17. B
18. B
19. C
20. A
21. C
22. A
23. A
24. B
25. A
26. D
27. B
28. C
29. C
30. C
31. B
32. D
33. D

34. D
35. C
36. B
37. C
38. C
39. D
40. C
41. D
42. A
43. C
44. C
45. C
46. B
47. A
48. D
49. D
50. A
51. D
52. A
53. B
54. A
55. D
56. B
57. A
58. A
59. B
60. A